BREAKING NINETY

BREAKING NINETY

A History of the Country Club of Ithaca

1900–1989

by Julian C. Smith

The Country Club of Ithaca, Inc.
Ithaca, New York • 1990

Cover photographs:

(upper) The clubhouse in 1901. Department of Manuscripts and Archives, Cornell University.

(lower) The clubhouse in 1989. Photo by J. C. Smith.

Back Cover: Photo courtesy of the College of Engineering, Cornell University.

Book design by Julian C. Smith, with the assistance of The WORDPRO, Ithaca, NY

Typesetting by The WORDPRO

Printing by Thomson-Shore, Inc.

ISBN 0-9625479-0-5

*To all the members,
past and present, of the
Country Club of Ithaca*

CONTENTS

PREFACE

This book grew out of a series of historical notes in the Club's monthly publication *Chip Shots*. Assembling the material for these notes gave me fascinating glimpses into the early days of the Club and raised many tantalizing questions. Since the Club is nearing its ninetieth birthday it seemed appropriate to record what I have learned about its rich history, so closely tied for many years to Cornell University and to the development of Cornell Heights and the Village of Cayuga Heights.

The original constitution, by-laws and list of charter members are available, with some later material, at the DeWitt Historical Society in Ithaca. Other early sources include the 1902–1937 cash books, the 1906 and 1907 treasurer's reports, and notes and tapes of reminiscences of old-time members of the Club. Minutes of the Board of Directors' meetings, from 1921 on, are available at the clubhouse, as are all the *Chip Shots*.

The Department of Manuscripts and Archives at Cornell provided me with valuable information and photographs. Important sources, especially for the first half of the Club's existence, are the Ithaca City Directories and the microfilms of the *Ithaca Journal* in Cornell's John M. Olin Library. Records of the Club's land transactions are at the Tompkins County Courthouse in Ithaca. Air photo maps of the Ithaca area were supplied by the Tompkins County Division of Assessment.

Other sources included Morris Bishop's *A History of Cornell*; Carol Sisler's book about Ithaca, *Enterprising Families*; and her chapter on Cornell Heights in *Ithaca's Neighborhoods*. Information on the early days of golf in the United States was gathered from various histories of golf and through visits to the USGA Museum in Far Hills, New Jersey. Perhaps best of all, the members and employees of the Club, both past and present, gave me pictures and scorecards and other memorabilia, plus anecdotes in great profusion. Their memories made the dry records come alive.

The list of dues-paying members in Appendix C came from the 1902–1921 cash book. The lists in Appendix D came from cash books (1920,1925, and 1930); printed pamphlets (1936, 1950, and 1960); and computer printouts (1975, 1989). The numbers of members shown in Appendix E were taken from the cash books from 1900 to 1920, from the annual reports of the Club from 1921 to 1982, and from the Club's membership records from 1983 on.

The richness of available material inevitably led to problems of selection and emphasis. I have tried to be even handed, but my treatment undoubtedly reflects my personal biases. A non-golfer, I am sure, would have written things differently. I have also attempted to be accurate, but with no hope of perfection or omniscience; I apologize in advance for any errors or omissions. I will not take responsibility, however, for errors in the original sources.

I owe thanks to a great many people—beyond naming—for their assistance in this enterprise. Special thanks, however, must go to Carol Sisler, Ithaca historian, and Nancy Morris (formerly at Cornell and now at the Brunswick School, Greenwich, Connecticut) for their careful and through editing of the manuscript. Special thanks, also, to Pat Bucci, for sharing his memories and the pictures and memorabilia from his voluminous scrapbooks. Many other people read part or all of the manuscript and made helpful comments; they included Betty Balderston, Margaret Raynolds, Jim Clynes, Charlie Treman, Mark Davies, Bud Tisdale, Reeder Gates and Fran Benedict. Bob Farnsworth gave me a great deal of valuable information; so did Wally Rogers, Hanley Staley, and Charlie Bell.

Chet Hill provided tapes of Bob Hutchinson's reminiscences. Photos and memorabilia came from Sterling Mac Adam, Jim Rothschild, and the late John Listar. Paul McGraw and Zelda Johnston gave me interesting insights into the problems of club management. Wes White, Gary Ellis and Gordon Richardson told me of their days as Club professional; Wes also contributed many useful photographs. Others who provided assistance include Gretchen Sachse of the DeWitt Historical Society; Gould Colman, Julia Parker and Nancy Dean of Cornell's Department of Manuscripts and Archives; Marie Gast and Barbara Berthelsen of Cornell's Department of Maps, Microtexts and Newspapers; Ralph Jordan of the Tompkins Country Trust Company; Robert Dutcher of the Tompkins County Division of Assessment; and Karen Bednarski and Janet Seagle of the USGA Museum. The membership graph in Chapter 9 was prepared by Douglas Alfors.

Finally, I must acknowledge the assistance of my wife, Joan E. Smith, who put up with me and my compulsive research, gave me encouragement, proofed the manuscript, and suggested the title for this *magnum opus*.

For all the help I have received I am deeply grateful.

Ithaca, New York
October, 1989

Chapter 1

THE BEGINNINGS

The three golfers stood on the Arts Quadrangle of Cornell University on an evening in late spring. One of them took his club back, swung hard and connected well—his ball flew straight and far, then curved toward a distant building on the right.

"*Another* window!" exclaimed Wilder Bancroft. "That's the third this month. Where did you get these balls, Louis? They go too far."

"Not for me," said Louis Dennis. "But you're right—we can't go on using them here. We need a real golf course."

"There's a lot of interest in golf in Ithaca," offered Charles Hull, "especially since the Elmira course opened two years ago. Let's get some people together and see if we can start a country club with its own course."

A purely imaginary conversation, of course, but one like it, in May or June of 1899, may well have been the origin of the Country Club of Ithaca. Professors Bancroft and Dennis of Chemistry and Charles Hull of History (and probably other faculty members, as well) did play golf, after a fashion, on the Cornell quadrangle in the late 1890s. Dennis was the one who started it. He traveled almost every summer to Jena, Germany, to buy chemical glassware, and on one of these trips, probably in 1897, he was introduced to golf while visiting a friend in Paris. He took it up with characteristic enthusiasm, ordered clubs and balls from Benjamin Sanford of the Campus Store, and set out some holes on the Arts quadrangle.

The Haskell wound-rubber golf balls became available in 1899 and Louis Dennis must have been among the first to try them out. These balls flew twenty or thirty yards further than the gutta percha balls then in use; they were so lively they became known as "bounding billies." Once the Cornell players adopted them the windows near the quadrangle were no longer safe, and the golfers decided (or were told) to leave the campus and play elsewhere. They began the planning and discussions that led to the founding, in 1900, of the Country Club of Ithaca.

This is the story of the development of that club, its growth and difficulties and successes, and—most of all—of the people that have been part of it during its first ninety years.

Eighty people crowded into the Choral Club rooms in the Blood-Schuyler block on Tioga Street on March 1, 1900 to organize the Country Club of Ithaca. The discussion meetings which began in 1899 had come to an end, and now everything moved quickly. The group adopted a constitution, elected officers, established classes of membership, agreed upon dues and authorized the construction of a course and a clubhouse. The officers were:

> President: Wilder D. Bancroft (professor of chemistry)
> Vice Pres.: John H. Tanner (professor of mathematics)
> Secretary: Charles H. Blood (lawyer)
> Treasurer: Charles E. Treman (Treman, King & Co.)
> Governors: Louis M. Dennis (professor of chemistry)
> Ernest W. Huffcut (professor of law)
> Clarence F. Wyckoff (president, R. T. Booth Co.
> and C. F. Wyckoff Co.)

Most of these men are pictured in Fig. 1-1. Ernest Huffcut's picture is in Chapter 2, Fig. 2-7.

Voting membership was limited to townspeople and members of the Cornell faculty; non-resident membership was open to Cornell students. The entrance fee for regular members was $5.00; yearly dues were $15 for a family, $10 for a single man and $5 for a single lady. Student memberships cost $5.00 a semester. Ithaca residents and students who were not members could not use the club, but persons living more than ten miles from Ithaca could be introduced as guests, without charge, for a period of not more than two weeks.

The meeting must have ended with great feelings of satisfaction and accomplishment, especially for Louis Dennis. There was clearly a lot of promise for the future. The *Ithaca Daily Journal* for March 2, 1900 thought so too: "The organization is in most excellent hands and should become one of the principal clubs of the city."

A second membership meeting was held on April 17, also in the Choral Club rooms. By then the Board of Managers had leased approximately fifty acres from Franklin C. Cornell (Ezra Cornell's son) for up to ten years, but subject to possible earlier sale of the leased property. A golf architect had been hired and the construction of a nine-hole course was underway. Some members of the club had offered to

(a) Louis M. Dennis.

(b) Wilder D. Bancroft.

(c) Charles H. Blood

(d) John H. Tanner.

(e) Charles E. Treman, Sr.

(f) Clarence F. Wyckoff.
Courtesy of Betty Balderston.

Figure 1-1. Officers and board members, 1900. (For Ernest Huffcut, see Figure 2-7.)

raise a fund for building a club house; the main purpose of the April 17 meeting was to approve their proposition and give the Board of Managers authority to make the necessary contract. With the meeting notice went a provisional list of members and a bill for the entrance fee and first year's dues.

In May the club issued its first printed booklet showing a list of the 97 charter members who had paid their entrance fee and dues (Appendix A). Twelve names from the provisional list had been dropped and fourteen new ones added, to give fifty-two family memberships, fifteen single ladies and thirty single men. ("Single" was a membership category, not an indication of marital status.) The booklet also lists the officers and committee members, the constitution and by-laws, and the "etiquette of golf," as reproduced in Appendix B. The five committees were House, Grounds, Tournament, Auditing, and Entertainment, the last of which had by far the most members. The Tournament Committee included one Cornell student member. According to one by-law, membership proposals could be made to the Board of Managers by any two active members; two negative votes by Board members prevented admission. Another by-law stated, "The course and clubhouse shall be open to members and guests seven days a week, but no game shall be played on Sunday." The etiquette of golf was not widely different from what it is today, except for the arcane method of reckoning strokes.

The charter members were the prominent citizens and intellectual leaders of Ithaca at the time. Over half the members were affiliated with Cornell University in one way or another (see Appendix A), including President Schurman; the dean of the faculty; the dean of Arts and Sciences, Thomas F. "Teefy" Crane; the deans of Law, Civil Engineering and Veterinary Medicine; department heads; professors, instructors; even two students. The manager of Sage College was on the list, with other Cornell administrators. Ezra Cornell's daughters, Miss Mary E. Cornell and Mrs. Charles H. Blair, were charter members; so were Frank Boynton, superintendent of schools, and Hollis Dann, director of music for the Ithaca school system and later Professor of Music at Cornell.

Lawyers were especially well represented among the townspeople— county judge Bradford Almy; district attorney Charles Blood; Edwin Banks, Charles Bostwick, Samuel Halliday (who was also chairman of the executive committee of the Cornell Board of Trustees), Jared Newman, Samuel Turner, Mynderse Van Cleef and DeForest Van Vleet. Edwin C. Stewart was a New York State senator from the 40th district. There were two architects, Arthur Gibb and William Henry Miller, and one physician, Dr. Charles Beaman.

Bankers included George Williams, president of the First National

Bank, and his brother Roger, president of the Ithaca Savings Bank (Carol Sisler, *Enterprising Families*, p. 44). From the Tompkins County National Bank (now the Tompkins County Trust Company) came the cashier, Henry L. Hinckley, vice president John Gauntlett, and president Robert H. Treman. Ebenezer Treman was head of the Ithaca Water Works; Charles E. Treman and Leander King ran the Treman, King & Co. hardware business. Calvin Stowell was head of J. C. Stowell, Son & Co. Edward G. Wyckoff, developer of Cornell Heights and president of the Ithaca Trolley system, was a family member; his brother Clarence, president of the R.T. Booth Co. which made eucalyptus nasal inhalers (*Enterprising Families*, p. 93), had a single membership.

It was an impressive group of educators, professional people and successful business men, many of whose names are now attached to streets, buildings, schools or parks in Ithaca and the surrounding area.

In 1900 golf was a game for the elite, for people who had the money and the time for it. Especially the time. Most Americans worked long hours for six days a week and envied those who had free time under their control. A squib in the *Ithaca Daily Journal* for July 7 says, "'Law offices are closed on Saturday afternoons'—who would not be a lawyer?" Costs, at $1.25 for a golf club and 25 cents for a ball (see Fig. 1-2), would have been high for the average workingman, even assuming he were given an opportunity to play. His sport was baseball. Golf, as Gibson reports in his *Pictorial History of Golf*, was considered by the average American to be "a snobbish, panty-waist pastime indulged in only by the elderly and idle rich."*

Whatever else the charter members may have been, they weren't pantywaists and they weren't idle. On the contrary, many of them were entrepreneurs with oversize egos and colorful personalities who knew how to get things done. Louis Dennis, for example, was known as "King" Dennis from the autocratic way he ran Cornell's chemistry department. Estevan Fuertes was called "the Mogue" because he looked and acted like the Great Mogul (and smoked Mogul cigarettes). (Bishop, *A History*

---

*Golf's image changed overnight in 1913 when the young American Francis Ouimet beat Britain's giants Harry Vardon and Ted Ray to win the U.S. Open, after which even "ordinary" Americans became interested in the sport. Even now golf is considered by some as one of the upper class "small ball" sports—golf, tennis and squash—as opposed to lower class "large ball" sports: football, basketball, baseball, volleyball and bowling. (Paul Fussell, *Class*, Ballantine Books, 1983.)

GOLF GOODS.

B. G. I. Clubs, Caddy Bags,

St. Andrews Clubs (from Scotland) only $1.25,

The Celebrated Henley Balls are best, a good ball for Practice, only 25c.

Tennis Goods,
Base Ball Goods,
Pocket Cutlery and Shears,
Fine Fishing Tackle.

We will save you money on all at

HANFORD'S

BICYCLE STORE, 110-112 N. Cayuga St.

... AT ...

OSBORN'S

For the GOLF LINKS

Caddy Bags: Leather. Scotch Plaid and Canvas.

Vardon Golf Clubs.
Spalding Golf Clubs.
Morristown Golf Clubs.
Very large stock.
Silvertown Golf Balls.
Remade Golf Balls.
Vardon Flyer Golf Balls.
Spalding Golf Balls.

Japanese Lanterns.
Japanese Napkins.
Paper Plates.
Crepe Paper for Decorating.
Cornell Banners.

A Box of Candy, a Fountain Pen, a Book, or a pretty Basket make an acceptable graduating present

Ice Cream Soda, cold and refreshing, 5 cents.

OSBORN'S, Near the Post office.

Figure 1-2. Advertisements from the *Ithaca Daily Journal*, 1900.

of Cornell, p. 113.) As described in Sisler's *Enterprising Families*, Charles Blood, Jared Newman, the Tremans and the Wyckoffs were noted for their ability to take action. Quite a few of the charter members could probably be characterized using Morris Bishop's description of Cornell president Jacob Gould Schurman: "...he possessed what the Italians call *prepotenza*, ruthless self-confidence approaching arrogance and overpassing tactfulness." (Bishop, p. 307) We would probably call it *chutzpah.* At any rate, with so many strong personalities involved it's surprising that they were able to agree so readily on plans for the new club.

Eighteen of the charter members were women, three with family memberships and fifteen singles. All three family members and three of the single members were married; two of these six were widows. Emma Cornell Blair's husband was a lawyer in New York City and was away much of the time. Mrs. Schuyler's husband was a major in the United States Army, and Mrs. St. John's husband was busy with his Autophone Company and insurance business; apparently none of these husbands was interested in golf. One of the unmarried ladies was gainfully employed: Miss Louise MacBeth was assistant to the warden of Sage College at Cornell. Perhaps the most remarkable woman was the indomitable Mary Hardy Williams, widow of Josiah Butler Williams, Ithaca banker, philanthropist and one of the first three Cornell trustees (Fig. 1-3). In 1900 Mary was 76. She had had twelve children, of whom nine were still alive. Of her five daughters, Jane was married to Jared Newman and Clara to John Tanner, both charter members; three were still unmarried. Her sons George and Roger were also charter members (*Enterprising Families*, p. 39).

Figure 1-3. Mary Hardy Williams.

Cornell students were an important part of the Club in its early days, as they were until Cornell built its own golf course in 1941. Presumably some of the Cornell professors in 1900 were interested in providing golfing facilities for their students; in addition, a number of the townspeople were Cornell alumni and had a similar concern. Robert H. Treman was graduate treasurer of the Cornell Athletic Association (*Register, Cornell University*, 1899–1900). He may have been the one who made sure that students could use the new course. He probably also organized the Cornell Golf Club, which started at the same time as the Country Club of Ithaca (Hewett, *Cornell University—A History*, p. 383). According to the Country Club by-laws, proposals for student membership were made by the Membership Committee of the Cornell Golf Club. Though their names are not listed in the May 1900 booklet, there were some fifty Cornell student members of the Country Club by that time (*Ithaca Daily Journal*, June 1, 1900).

Construction of the first golf course began in early April, 1900. The architect was John Harrison, a Scotsman and sales representative of the Crawford, McGregor and Canby Company, makers of golf supplies. The Cornell Cooperative Society was their local representative. According to the *Ithaca Daily Journal*, Harrison was "an expert whose skill delighted the Ithacans." He laid out the course and supervised the start of construction, but left Ithaca on April 19. James A. Seeler of New York, another "expert," was hired to oversee completion of the course. It didn't take long to build a course in those days: less than three months after the organizational meeting the course was ready for use. Built by a local contractor and builder, S. M. Oltz, for $1,200, the clubhouse, with "piazzas, lockers, washing facilities, etc." was also completed.

Of the golf course construction the *Journal* for June 1 reported as follows:

> The fields after being cleared of stones by about 50 boys, were seeded and for two weeks the city steam roller was used to perfect the fields. The club house stands on the west end of the grounds and makes a

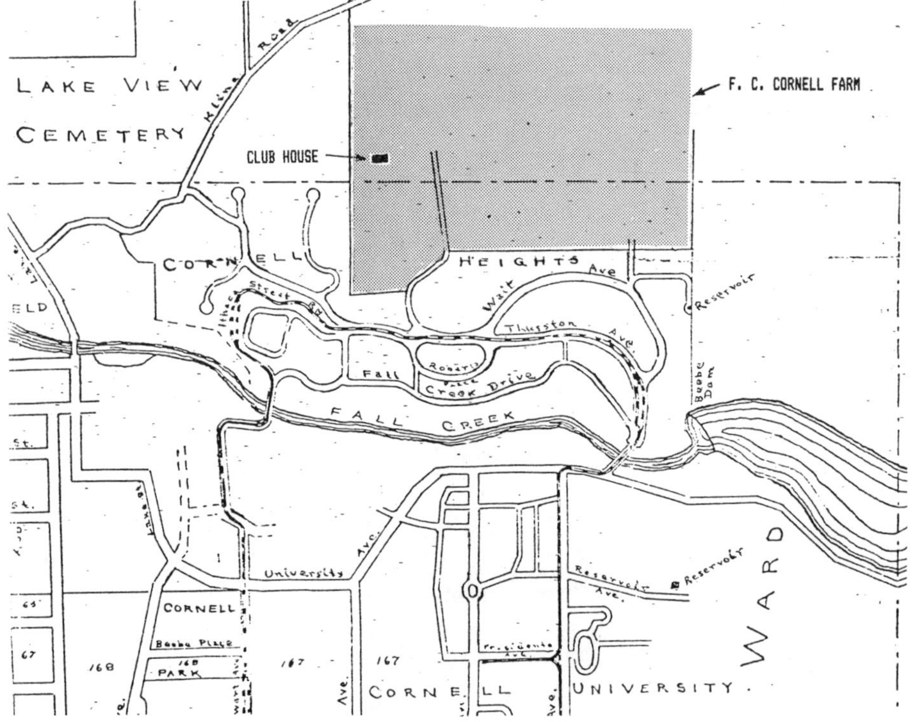

Figure 1-4. Map of Cornell Heights, 1899.

pretty and convenient resting and visiting spot with a magnificent view of the lake and valley directly below it. The fields are already quite green and pleasant to view and appear from a short distance like well kept lawns. Wednesday afternoon [May 28] the golf links were in use and many prominent Ithacans were enjoying the exercise now so popular in large towns.

The course was located on Franklin Cornell's farm of about eighty-six acres, just north of the developing Cornell Heights. Figure 1-4 is an 1899 general map of the area showing the approximate boundaries of the farm; Fig. 1-5 shows more clearly its relationship to present-day roads. In 1899 Highland Road had no name, and ended at the gully just beyond where Wyckoff Road crosses it now. Triphammer Road wasn't there at all; in fact, there were almost no roads in what was later to become Cayuga Heights. It was all open farmland, with far fewer trees

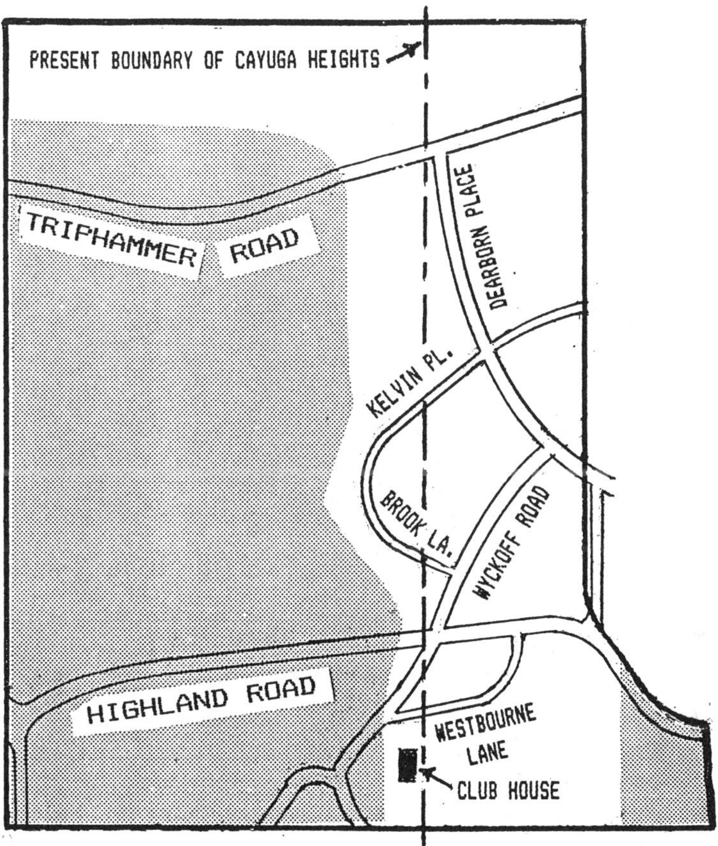

Figure 1-5. Golf course area (unshaded) and F. C. Cornell farm, in relation to present-day roads.

Figure 1-6. Cornell Heights and the golf course in 1902, looking north. The clubhouse is visible in the circle on the left.

than now. Figure 1-6 is a remarkable photograph, taken in 1902 looking north from the Cornell library tower, which illustrates how empty the area was at that time.

The Country Club had the use of the southern portion of the farm for its links, south of the gully plus part of the eastern end, as shown in Fig. 1-5. Figure 1-7 is a photograph of the clubhouse in 1901. It stood in the northwest corner of the Club's portion of the farm, about where the Westbourne Apartments are now. The clubhouse can be seen at the left edge of Fig. 1-6 at the level of the top of the large McGraw Hall tower in the foreground. The golf course extends horizontally almost all the way across the picture at the same level.

Figure 1-7. Clubhouse in 1901 (from the 1901 *Cornellian*).

There is no record of the course layout, but the scorecard* illustrated in Fig. 1-8 shows the yardages and local rules. The "road" mentioned in these rules may have been the proto-Highland Road, which ran right across the course, but more likely it was Triphammer Road which was under construction by then. There was almost no traffic on either of these roads, of course, and certainly no cars—there were only three or four automobiles in all of Ithaca in 1900. How quiet and peaceful it must have been out there in the country on a sunny summer day!

The founding of the Country Club was part of the surging growth and change in Ithaca and elsewhere in the country at that time. Locally it was closely tied to E. G. Wyckoff's development of Cornell Heights which

---

*This card, found among Allan H. Treman's papers, was sent to Robert H. Treman by C. L. Durham with a note stating that the match took place on May 30, 1902. The Treman named on the card was most probably Robert H.; Mr. Teller was presumably a guest.

ITHACA COUNTRY CLUB.

Date................................190....

Self *Treman*   Opp't *Teller*

	FIRST ROUND						SECOND ROUND			
HOLES.	YDS.	BOGEY.	SELF.	OPP'T.		HOLES.	Yds.	BOGEY.	SELF.	OPP'T.
1	288	4	6	8		1	288	4	5	5
2	264	4	6	6		2	264	4	6	6
3	476	5	7	7		3	476	5	6	8
4	130	3	3	3		4	130	3	5	4
5	270	4	6	7		5	270	4	7	6
6	371	5	8	7		6	371	5	7	9
7	400	5	6	6		7	400	5	6	6
8	410	5	9	7		8	410	5	6	7
9	183	4	4	4		9	183	4	6	4
Total	2792	39	55	55		Total	2792	39	54	55

Won o.   Lost x.   Halved —

Free lifts { From road on drive from 2d Tee. / " Brook Hazard "   "   3d Tee. / " Bunker on 2d stroke to 6lb Green.

1st Nine Holes / Gross Total, 18 Holes / Hd'k / Net

Certified to by {

Figure 1-8. Scorecard from May 30, 1902.

had begun in 1895; the officers of the Cornell Heights Land Company were all charter members of the Club. (*Enterprising Families*, p. 93) Nationally it was part of the phenomenal growth of golf in the United States which began in 1888 when John Reid built the first course in Yonkers, New York. By 1895 there were forty-one golf courses operating and forty more under construction. Then the pace quickened enormously: by 1900 there were over a thousand courses in the United States, with at least one in each state.* (N. H. Gibson, *Encyclopedia of Golf*, pp. 14–15)

Thus within one year of its origin on the Cornell quadrangle the Country Club of Ithaca was in full operation. It provided golf and other services for its members, organized social events, hired a caretaker/golf professional, and soon added many new names to the membership roll. The club flourished. All too soon, however, it faced its first serious problem: the possible loss of its leased land.

But that's for another chapter.

---

*Thus the average construction rate for the preceding five years was an astonishing 180 new courses per year. The pace slackened somewhat after that, but not a great deal. There were 12,405 golf courses in the United States in 1987, corresponding to an average construction rate of 132 new courses for every year since 1900. (*Statistical Abstracts*)

Chapter 2

THE HIGHLAND ROAD COURSE— 1903–1919

> Hanks and Binks went on the links
> To have a spell at goffing.
> Hanks took aim, and missed the same,
> And Binks near died a laffing.

Ithaca Daily Journal, May 21, 1900

Then, as now, "goff" was a frustrating game, and lessons were in great demand. From its earliest days the Country Club offered instruction to its members from the club's own golf professional and, on occasion, from outside instructors. The Club's first professional, Walter Bells, was probably hired in 1900; he was definitely on the payroll in 1902. He worked each year for the Country Club from May through October, and at Cornell University during the other months. This was an ideal arrangement for the Club, one which lasted for almost thirty years.

Walter J. Bells was born in Tobyhanna, Pa. in 1859. He worked for several years as a railroad engineer but quit about 1881 "in accordance with his mother's wishes," and came to Ithaca to manage his mother's farm. In 1896 when Cornell began to have organized winter sports on Beebe Lake, he was asked to oversee the hockey rink and toboggan slide; later, when the Johnny Parsons Club was established, he became its manager. Apparently he had little to do in the summertime and welcomed the opportunity to work for the Country Club.

Walter was one of the first Ithacans to take up golf, and became what was regarded as "a skillful player." He gave golf lessons as part of his duties at the Club, but he probably wasn't outstanding either as a player or as a teacher. His main duties were as caretaker: he oversaw and maintained the clubhouse and grounds, collected locker fees and greens fees, monitored the players, and supervised the caddies. He also sold golf clubs and balls, and, like most golf professionals of the day, made and repaired clubs. His logo, stamped into the back of the iron clubs he made, was an outline of two bells. For all this he received a salary of $35.00 per month.

To supplement Mr. Bell's somewhat limited teaching skills the Club sometimes occasionally used visiting instructors. For example, in April 1902 a postcard to the members (Fig. 2-1) announced that Mr. Venters, the professional at Lakewood and Shinnecock Hills, would give lessons at the Club for ten days in May. Mr. Venters charged $1.00 per hour.*

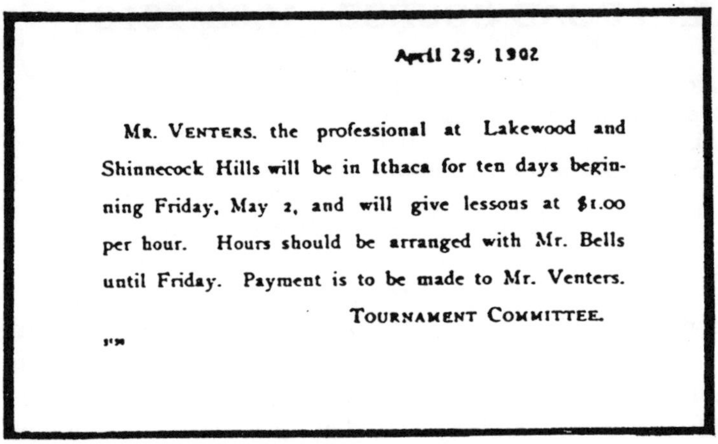

April 29, 1902

MR. VENTERS. the professional at Lakewood and Shinnecock Hills will be in Ithaca for ten days beginning Friday, May 2, and will give lessons at $1.00 per hour. Hours should be arranged with Mr. Bells until Friday. Payment is to be made to Mr. Venters.

TOURNAMENT COMMITTEE.

Figure 2-1.Postcard to Club members, 1902.

In the autumn of 1901 Franklin Cornell gave the Board of Managers the unwelcome news that he was planning to sell his farm for development. It must have sparked some emergency Board meetings and a lot of worried discussion. With the loss of the land, what would happen to the course? Was the fledgling club to fail before it had fairly begun?

Fortunately the prospective developer, the Cornell Heights Land Company, was well represented among the officers and members of the Club, and soon the following agreement was reached: the Land Company would buy the entire Cornell farm, then sell the Club a suitable portion of the land for its golf links. "Suitable," it was agreed, did not mean the land which the golf course occupied at the time; the course would have to be moved to the north, to the other side of the gully that ran east and

---

*Shinnecock Hills, Long Island, founded in 1891, was the first incorporated golf club in the country. It was the scene of the 1896 (and the 1986) United States Open.

west down the middle of the property. After that, however, the Country Club would have its own land and need no longer fear displacement.

The deed of sale from Franklin Cornell to John Tanner is dated November 1, 1901. (For a list of land transactions, see Appendix F.) Notice of the proposed sale to the Country Club appeared in the *Ithaca Daily Journal* on November 16, 1901, but the actual sale was somewhat delayed. To own land the Club had to become incorporated, which it did on December 21. The transfer of the property to the Club quickly followed: the deed from John H. Tanner and his wife Clara is dated December 30, 1901.

In neither of the deeds is there any mention of the Cornell Heights Land Company—they seem to indicate only a purchase and a sale by John Tanner and his wife. But John was vice-president of the Land Company (*Ithaca's Neighborhoods*, p. 180) and acted on its behalf; he was also vice president of the Country Club.*

The certificate of incorporation lists the same Board of Managers as the May 1900 booklet except that Ernest Huffcut has been replaced by Dr. Charles P. Beaman. The date of the annual meeting is given as the third Thursday in February.

In February 1903 the Land Company gave the Country Club $300 toward the cost of moving the clubhouse. The actual move was done by S. M. Oltz in early April, to a point on the southwest corner of the new property about 180 yards northwest of the original location (Fig. 2-2), just south of where the Congregational Church is now. Oltz charged $663.32 for the moving. Apparently he didn't set the building quite right, for in June $25 was paid to E. McGreery "for turning house."

The golf course had been under construction since the previous fall. Large quantities of seed and fertilizer had been purchased the preceding June; also a horse, for $70, in July and a wagon, for $45, in October. More grass seed was bought in March 1903, when the links were being brought into condition for use.

The new course opened in May 1903. According to the *Ithaca Daily Journal* of March 28, the club members were "enthusiastic about its situation and beauty, considering it much superior to the old grounds.

---

*The deed makes it clear that, contrary to statements in *Enterprising Families* (p.93) and *Ithaca's Neighborhoods* (p. 180), the land was not given by the Land Company to the Country Club. Also, in February 1902 the Country Club sold a small strip of land back to the Land Company for $30, in connection with the construction of Triphammer Road. This would hardly have been done if the land had been given to the Club in the first place.

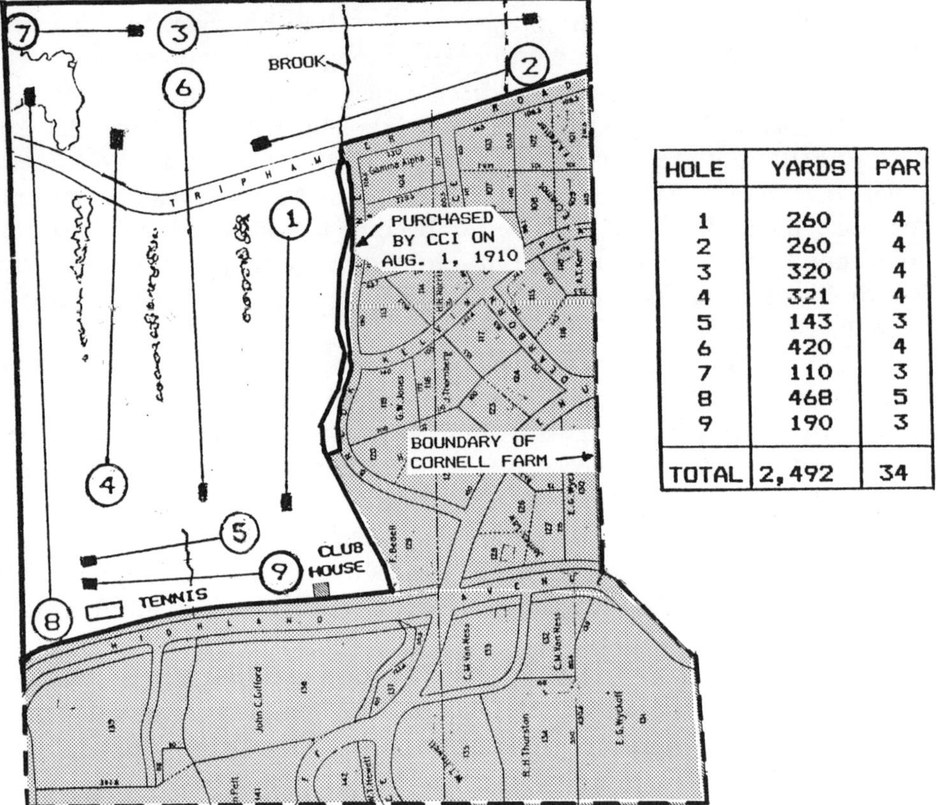

HOLE	YARDS	PAR
1	260	4
2	260	4
3	320	4
4	321	4
5	143	3
6	420	4
7	110	3
8	468	5
9	190	3
TOTAL	2,492	34

Figure 2-2. Layout of Triphammer Road course.

The road entering the old course just west of the Wyckoff property [i.e., Highland Road] is being extended some distance north...The ground is much more uneven [than the old course] and has more obstacles to overcome, which is an advantage in scientific golf playing."

The move and the course opening received little publicity, for they took place during the great typhoid epidemic in Ithaca. There were over 900 cases and 66 deaths in 1903, many of them of Cornell students. With the threat of death constantly present, the affairs of the Country Club seemed of minor importance. (See Morris Bishop, *A History of Cornell*, pp. 421–2.)

The approximate course layout shown in Fig. 2-2 is based on the recollections of Margaret Thilly Raynolds and Charles E. Treman, Jr.; from a 1983 tape of Bob Hutchinson's reminiscences; and from 1937 air photos showing the old lines of trees between fairways. The yardage is from a 1911 Club booklet. The course, about 300 yards shorter than the original one, was apparently designed by club members, for there is no mention of a course architect. Possibly the second green and third tee were the same as before; otherwise the holes were all new.

This course was probably easier to play than the earlier one, but it did have its challenges. Although the uphill first hole was short and fairly easy, the brook and trees on the right, and an old tumbledown building, seemed to attract tee shots like a magnet. Hole No. 7 was known as "the punchbowl hole," a frightening little par 3 beside the woods, with bunkers surrounding a sunken green which was cut into the foot of a hill. Beside the 8th fairway, about halfway down, were three large moundlike glacial deposits known as "chocolate drops." Both the 5th and 9th holes were par 3's that crossed a gully from an elevated tee.

Several of the fairways crossed Triphammer Road, which became much busier as Cayuga Heights developed. This kind of arrangement was common in those days: shooting across roads and mounds and other obstacles was thought to add to the excitement of playing golf, making it more "scientific."

This Highland Road course was used with only minor modifications from 1903 to 1920. The 9-hole course record of 33 was set by Robert H. Treman on July 29, 1910. If, as seems likely, the scorecard shown in

Figure 2-3. Highland Road, showing part of course— 1910.

Chapter 1 (Fig. 1-8) belonged to him, his golf had improved mightily since 1902 when he scored 55 and 54 on the original course.

For many years there was a barn on the northwest corner of the Club property (see Fig. 2-11). This barn is in the center of the 1910 photograph (Fig. 2-3) which looks southeast over the curving extension of Highland Road; the course extends up the hill, eastward, behind the barn. Figure 2-4, taken about 1905, looks south across the course, with Sibley dome and the Cornell towers in the right background. Triphammer Road is on the left. The 8th fairway was just beyond the trees and fence in the left foreground.

Figure 2-4. Looking south across the golf course— about 1905.

To raise money to buy the land and build the Highland Road course, the Club sold $100 bonds to its members through the Ithaca Trust Company. By January 1903 one hundred bonds had been sold, a number of them to John Tanner. This gave the club $10,000 in capital and an equal amount of debt, on which it annually paid $500 interest to the Trust Company. Franklin Cornell was the bank's president at the time. In 1904, after some ups and downs, the club membership numbered 103 and things looked promising. In that year new members included some well-known names: Andrew Dickson White, first president of Cornell, who was 72 when he joined; William Strunk, Jr., of Cornell's English Department (and of Strunk and White's *Elements of Style*); and Captain Frank Barton, United States Army, commandant of the Cornell cadets, for whom Barton Hall is named.

In 1906 Professor W. A. Hammond (Fig. 2-5), head of Cornell's Department of Philosophy, was elected president to succeed Wilder D. Bancroft. For some reason, probably having nothing to do with him, things began to turn sour. Many people left the Club, and few joined. In 1905, as shown in Appendix E, membership had fallen to 92; in 1906 it dropped to 87. The club's future seemed very much in doubt.

Figure 2-5. William A. Hammond, the Club's second president.

When membership falls, financial stresses rise. In 1906 the stresses were compounded by the fact that treasurer Samuel B. Turner, elected in 1905, fell ill in 1906 and failed to pay any bills after February 15, the start of the club's financial year. He died the following August. By autumn things were in bad shape: some $300 worth of unpaid bills were outstanding, and $150 of bond interest was owed to the Ithaca Trust Company. Against this the club's Trust Company account contained all of $9.18.

The United States Army came to the rescue, in the person of Captain Barton (Fig. 2-6). He was appointed treasurer in October and took hold

Figure 2-6. Frank A. Barton.

Figure 2-7. Ernest W. Huffcut.

with military efficiency. By February 1907 he could report that all bills were paid and that cash assets totalled $146. To do this he had borrowed $285 from members, collected some of the 1907 dues early, and sold $183 worth of wood from the eastern end of the Club property. Several members made special gifts to the Club of $10 or so to help cover the deficit. These numbers seem trivial now, but at a time when the daily wage of Ithaca's street sweepers was $1.25 and tuition at Cornell was $100 a year, they were far from insignificant. The Club's total income in 1906 was $958.43.

The next year the membership increased to over one hundred and all debts were paid; in addition the Club was able to add new lockers, a clock golf green (with twelve "tees" around a single hole) and a tennis court. Things were once more on an even keel.

An unusually large number of charter members died in 1907, including Herman V. Bostwick, Francis M. Finch, Samuel D. Halliday and George R. Williams. Especially saddening was the news that Professor Ernest Huffcut (Fig. 2-7), a member of the first Board of Managers, had committed suicide. He had become dean of Cornell's Law School in 1903, the same year he resigned from the Country Club; he gave up the deanship a few years later and became legal adviser to New

York's Governor Higgins in 1905 and to Governor Hughes in 1906. Everything seemed to be going well, but in May 1907 he bought a one-way ticket on the Hudson River steamer from Albany, went out on the upper deck some time after midnight, and shot himself. He left a letter to his sister which said, "I am going down the river enjoying the prospect of going out to sea...I was never so glad to rest in my life. After all, in the end one must have his own way of escape." He quoted the lines,

> "Sweet after toil is sleep.
>   Then wherefore sorrow for him who sleeps,
>   Who will not wake tomorrow?"

In August 1910 the Club bought a strip of land from the Cornell Heights Land Company just south of the first hole, as shown in Fig. 2-2. It also bought another horse, for $135. In 1911 a booklet was issued to celebrate the Club's first ten years, listing the officers and members, the yardage of the golf holes, and the current bylaws. These were essentially unchanged from 1900, except that the voting membership (families and singles) was now limited to a total of 150. Sunday games were still prohibited.

Professor W. A. Hammond was elected in 1912 to his seventh year as president of the Club. (*Ithaca Daily Journal*, Feb. 23, 1912, p. 3.) His officers and Board of Managers were much like the earlier ones, still dominated by Cornell faculty members, yet something had changed. It was almost a new era for the club. The limitation on total membership was disregarded: a vigorous campaign for new members, especially among the townspeople, raised the membership to 167. The membership base was greatly broadened. The first Jewish members, Jacob Rothschild and his son Leon, department store owners, and Isaac K. Bernstein, tailor (later in real estate) joined at this time.

Also in 1912 the Club took out it first mortgage from the Ithaca Trust Company, for $4,000, which was paid to A. H. Landon to build a new men's locker room adjacent to the clubhouse. (See Fig. 2-8.) New electric wiring, water pipes and a cesspool were added and, probably, the tennis courts at the northwest corner of the Club's lands (Fig. 2-2). The barn was moved to the southern part of the property. The total project cost $6,250.

Charles E. Treman, a banker, became the Club's third president in 1913. (*Ithaca Daily Journal*, February 22, 1913, p. 7.) Membership continued to rise, passing 200 in 1914. Growth brought a lot more money, but also problems. The club was no longer the same small group of friends and relatives that had started things back in "the old days." New faces were everywhere. The golf course and tennis courts became crowded. The proportion of Cornell-affiliated members diminished. "All those townspeople!" says Maggie Raynolds. "They cluttered up *our* course." A dues increase of 33 per cent, to $20 per year for a family membership and other dues in proportion, did reduce the number of members by about ten per cent in 1915, but the club's net income still increased considerably. Talk began about building a new course, preferably with 18 holes.

In 1916 Charles Treman was re-elected president.* Despite a small further drop in membership, the Board approved plans to enlarge the main room of the clubhouse and employ an expert to survey the course and improve the system of hazards. The "expert" actually hired was the noted golf architect, A. W. Tillinghast, who was paid $350 for his advice. (There's more about Tillinghast in the next chapter.) It's clear what he must have said about the course: "You can't do anything with this small area. Build a new course. Buy more land."

And they did. The Board of Managers and the members approved the purchase of the McKinney farm east of the existing golf course—forty acres for $12,000—plus a small triangular piece of the adjacent Kline farm. At the same time the Club sold about 1 1/2 acres of the southeast corner of the its property to Professor Ernest Merritt for $2,000, and George Coleman agreed to pay the Club $9,000 for some of its land west of Triphammer Road. The Merritt and Coleman contracts were used as collateral for a demand note to the Ithaca Trust Company to raise funds to pay for the McKinney farm. (Professor Merritt eventually paid the promised $2,000; the Coleman deal fell through.) A special fund was established "for the new course."

But World War I postponed the realization of all of these dreams.

From 1914 through 1916 the distant war in Europe had little effect on the Club, or on Ithaca or Cornell, for that matter. Professors Othon Guerlac and Georges Mauxion, both club members, were called to the

---

*He apparently served as president during the war and on through 1920. The formerly "accepted" roster of presidents, based on someone's memory (probably Bob Hutchinson's), lists Louis Dennis as president in 1918–19 and Charles Durham in 1920, but there is no published evidence of this. The roster is clearly wrong for the 1912–1917 period and seems to be wrong here also. Charles Treman appears to have served for eight successive years. In 1921 the bylaws were revised to set the president's term at one year with a maximum of five consecutive terms, probably to prevent this from happening again.

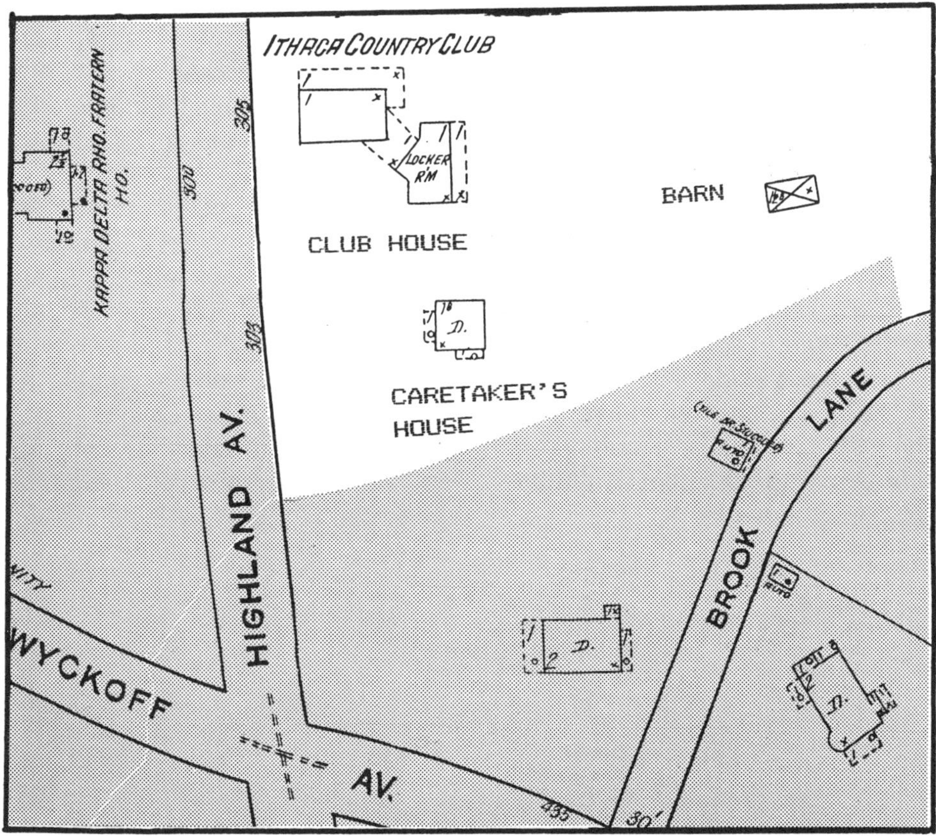

Figure 2-8. Detail of 1919 Sanborn map, showing clubhouse.

French colors in September 1914. (Bishop, p. 425) Professor Mauxion was killed in April 1917, leading a charge from the trenches; Professor Guerlac kept up his club membership while he was away and returned safely after the war. Most Ithacans, however, opposed any intervention in what seemed to be someone else's conflict. As far as possible they went on with business as usual.

Things changed overnight after the United States entered the war in 1917. Cornell became a largely military operation with endless cadet drills, bayonet practice, artillery practice. The national mood was serious and dedicated. Social clubs largely disappeared and the few that remained were hard put to keep going. Membership in the Country Club dropped to 157 in 1917 and to 135 in 1918, for most of the younger members were in the armed services. Social events and golf tournaments were sharply curtailed, although some public dances were held in the clubhouse to raise money for the war effort.

Income in 1917 failed to match expenses, but not by much—the overdraft was only $98. In 1918 Frank Barton, now a colonel, took over as treasurer from F. L. Morse and, despite the reduced income from dues, was able to pay off the overdraft and show a net gain of $70 for the year.

In 1918 many young women served as "farmerettes" to replace farmers and hired hands who were off to war. Figure 2-9 shows Margaret Thilly and Hester Bancroft on a farm in Mount Kisco, New York, in the summer of 1918. Margaret later became Mrs. Harold Raynolds; Hester, one of Wilder Bancroft's daughters, married Romeyn Berry.

Cornell's Andrew D. White died in November 1918 on his eighty-fifth birthday. For the last thirteen years of his life he had been a member of the Country Club. Presumably he played golf; he did have a locker for a number of those years. His funeral was held on November 7, the day of the "false armistice."

Figure 2-9. Margaret Thilly and Hester Bancroft as "farmerettes," 1918.

After the real armistice on November 11, in the exuberant certainty that the world had been made forever safe for democracy, social activities quickly resumed their importance. Membership rose to 172 in 1919 (see Appendix E); the number of "single lady" members almost doubled. The Club prospered, and treasurer Barton had more money to work with. The Club's income was $6,476 in 1918 and $7,862 in 1919. Planning for the new course was resumed, to be implemented as described in Chapter 3.

Some social habits were changed permanently by the war. Sunday golf, permitted in 1917–18 for the diversion of the soldier-heroes in the area, was continued indefinitely for all. For many years afterwards, however, it was limited at the Country Club to Sunday afternoons. Alcoholic liquor, in theory at least, disappeared when Ithaca went dry on October 1, 1918, by vote of local option, well before Prohibition became law in January 1920. But the Country Club had never had a bar. Public drinking (by the men only) was pretty much confined to the local saloons. That's not to say that liquor bottles were unknown in the men's locker room at the club—surely a triumphant or calamitous round of golf was appropriately celebrated—but the advent of Prohibition probably had little immediate effect on either the club or the locker room activities.

Social events, before and after the war, centered on the weekly teas. Every Wednesday and Saturday during the season Clementia Bells, the professional's wife, would fill a punchbowl with the special tea that only she could make. Some of the senior ladies—Mrs. Treman and Mrs. Wyckoff, perhaps—would pour. The ladies would talk; the children would play quietly and eat the cookies. Men never came.

The records are full of payments to Mrs. Bells for preparing these teas and for keeping the clubhouse clean. By this time she and her husband Walter and son Truman were living in a small house on the Club property at what is now 305 Highland Avenue. Today this house, much modified and added to, is one of the units of the Brookside Apartments.

Throughout the years tennis was enjoyed by the members, especially the younger ones. The original court, probably the one built in 1907, was behind the club house. The newer courts and the tees for the fifth and ninth holes were so close together, according to Maggie Raynolds, that from the fifth tee you could chat with your friends who were playing tennis or waiting to play the ninth hole.

Golf, of course, was the principal activity, the *raison d'être*, of the club. Avid golfers were found among the women as well as among men. But the course was small and narrow, and after 1914 there must have been considerable danger of injury from errant shots. Tournaments were fairly frequent, including interclub matches, but no official individual club champions were reported until 1921. Bob Hutchinson, in his reminiscences, said that he, Charlie Newman and Henry Hinckley shared the 9-hole course record of 31.

A story from these days involves Robert E. Treman, one of the Club's better golfers. One day in 1916 or 1917, according to his cousin Charlie Treman, Bob hit a great drive on the par 5 eighth hole, almost down to the chocolate drops. Bob took out his brassie and sank his second shot for a double eagle 2. "That's it!" he said. "I'll never do better than that." He picked up his ball and walked to the clubhouse, not even finishing the round, put his clubs away, and said he never play again. According to cousin Charlie, he never did. (He did keep up his membership, however— he even changed from a single to a family membership in 1919, after he married the dancer Irene Castle.)

Today there's not much left of the old Highland Road course. The clubhouse area is now occupied by the Congregational Church, and nearly all the holes west of Triphammer Road are covered with houses and fraternities and apartments. The upper part of the first fairway is still visible: it is shown in Fig. 2-10, looking east toward Triphammer Road. The building in the background is Cornell's Africana Center, which is just about on the site of the original first green.

The list of the 565 people who paid dues to the Country Club between 1900 and 1919 (Appendix C) provides a lot of information about the club. Many individuals, of course, joined for a few years only, then died or moved away or lost interest. Martha Van Rensselaer and Flora Rose, for example, codirectors of what was then Cornell's Department of Home Economics (now the College of Human Ecology), were members in 1912 and 1913, but not after that. Other single ladies married and changed their names. Louise MacBeth and Charles Blood, both charter members, were married in 1905. Alice King married Georgio de Grassi in 1910, continued her single membership the next year, then persuaded her husband to take out a family membership. Undoubtedly there were others.

Twenty-four of the ninety-seven charter members were still paying dues in 1919, including six of the seven members of the first Board of Managers. Sixteen of the twenty-four, among them Miss Bertha Wilder who worked in the Cornell Library, Ithaca Mayor Edwin Stewart and Cornell's President Schurman, had a perfect dues-paying record. Some professors missed a year or two on occasion, probably because they were on leave— in those days the club permitted members who were away

Figure 2-10. Upper part of original first fairway, in 1987.

from Ithaca for a year or more to retain their membership "with dues remitted."

Although not listed in Appendix C, student members were an important part of the Club, contributing ten to twenty per cent of its annual income. Typically forty to eighty Cornell students joined for one term or more each year. A well-known name appears in the list of student members for 1902: Henry Schoellkopf, for whom Cornell's football field house is named. Some other students—Lawrence Pumpelly, for example—later joined the Club as regular members. Local people, in the very early days, could join for the summer only, as temporary members, for a $5 fee. The "non-resident" membership category, for persons who lived more than ten miles from Ithaca, was apparently used exclusively by students until 1919 when W. W. Taylor joined as a non-resident regular member.

By 1919 the pressures on the Country Club to expand its golf course and to sell some of its land for development were too great to ignore. The days of the Highland Road course were coming to an end. It was a time of general optimism; nonetheless, the war had destroyed America's innocent belief in the inevitability of peaceful progress toward a better world. Prohibition had arrived; social attitudes had changed, and more change was imminent as the 1920s began. The Club, as we will see, changed too.

Figure 2-11. Golf course in 1908 from McGraw Tower, Cornell. Barn and clubhouse are circled.

Chapter 3

THE TILLINGHAST COURSES
AND THE ROARING TWENTIES

Under construction since the fall of 1919, the new 9-hole course was formally opened on Saturday, May 8, 1920. An afternoon tea was followed by dancing in the evening. According to the *Ithaca Journal-News* the clubhouse was decorated with large branches of shadbush and hemlock, and with daffodils and English primroses. Those who poured were Mrs. F. A. Barton, Mrs. C. D. Bostwick, Mrs. F. C. Prescott and Mrs. W. D. Carver. It must have been a quite an event.

The course layout in Fig. 3-1 is based on the recollections of Charles Treman, Jr. From newspaper articles we know the lengths of some of the holes, but no scorecard from this period has come to light and the yardages of Holes 1, 6, 7 and 9 are therefore estimates. The first hole of the old course, leading up the hill from the clubhouse, was lengthened so that it crossed Triphammer Road; the former 6th hole, lengthened and turned end for end, became the 9th. All the other holes of the original course were abandoned, and seven new holes were built through and around McKinney's woods.

George Boyer and Albert Collins, workmen, were hired within a few days of each other in 1919. They both later became head greenskeeper. In 1956, in an interview for the *Ithaca Journal*, Albert recalled how it took three to four weeks to build a single green when he first started to work for the Club. In those days the greens were mowed with hand-powered mowers without grass catchers and were weeded by hand. The putting surface was ordinary lawn grass. Greens averaged 2000 square feet in size, compared with about 5000 square feet in 1956. Before World War I the fairways were mowed with horse-drawn mowers, but by 1919 Fordson tractors pulling three mowers had largely replaced the horse-drawn machines.

The new layout must have been quite a shock to the average golfing member. As originally planned, it was almost six hundred yards longer

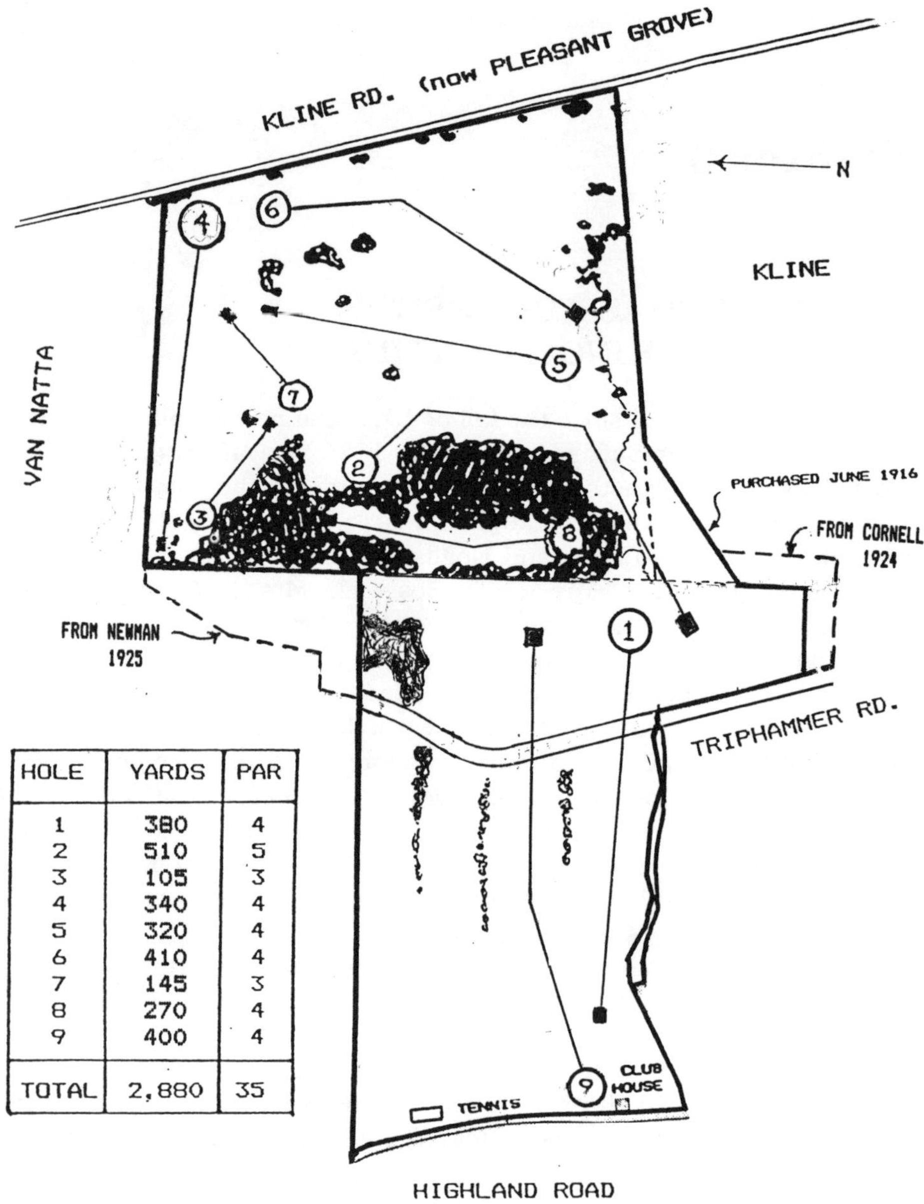

HOLE	YARDS	PAR
1	380	4
2	510	5
3	105	3
4	340	4
5	320	4
6	410	4
7	145	3
8	270	4
9	400	4
TOTAL	2,880	35

Figure 3-1. Layout of the 1920 Tillinghast course.

than the old course, with a par of 38. Fairways were narrow and trees and hills were cleverly used to increase the difficulties. Number 2, a sharply angled dog's-leg par 5, was especially formidable. Number 8 was a short but narrow par 4 cut through the forest, with an elevated tee and a brook guarding the green. Frustration and disappointments must have escalated as scores climbed five or ten or more strokes for each 9-hole round.

But challenging layouts were typical of the course architect, A. W. Tillinghast (Fig. 3-2). He was the designer of many of today's famous courses, among them the courses at Winged Foot, in Mamaroneck, New York; Baltusrol, in Springfield, New Jersey, and fifteen other courses now used for national and international golf tournaments. His 1921 course at Brook Hollow in Dallas was the first to have a complete irrigation system. Locally he designed two courses for the Country Club of Ithaca and reconstructed and extended the Elmira Country Club course.

Figure 3-2. Golf architect A. W. Tillinghast. Courtesy of USGA Museum.

An article* by Frank Hannigan of *GOLF Magazine* describes Tillinghast as a "superb golf architect, whose courses improve with age," and also as "one of the wildest and most outlandish figures in golf history." In the early 1900s he was one of America's top amateur golfers, and helped found the PGA in 1916. He was a golf writer, editor and historian, and a top-quality golf photographer. With a group of friends,

---

*"Golf's Forgotten Genius," *The Golf Journal,* May 1974, pp. 14–28.

he invented the term "birdie" in Atlantic City in 1903. On the negative side, according to Hannigan, he was a drinker on a heroic scale; in addition,

> he was prone to occasional rages, made bizarre because of his penchant for waving around a pistol. And there were the classic benders,which occurred two, three, four times a year and lasted as long as a month. He would simply takeoff, disappear—in better times with a limousine and chauffeur, in not-so-good times with his wife's jewelry and furs. Eventually he would come home.

He apparently had never known discipline of any kind, and boasted that he never finished any school he attended. As Hannigan says, he could be outrageous. Once, when a medical school student came to ask formally for the hand of his younger daughter, he sat for a while twiddling his spiky waxed moustaches, then finally announced: "Young man, I want to know only one thing about you, and that is the result of your Wasserman test."

Membership in the Country Club of Ithaca, after the wartime low of 137 in 1918, quickly recovered and rose to new heights (see Appendix E). This was in spite of a dues increase in 1921 to $30 per year, up from $20, for a family membership. Single men now paid $25, single women $12.50 and non-residents $15. In 1923 a new category was added: minor members— defined as daughters of family or single members, fourteen years of age or older, and sons fourteen to eighteen. (A few years later the lower age limit was reduced to twelve.) For each minor member the parent paid $5 per year. Associate members were redefined as men over eighteen and less than thirty and all women not otherwise classified. Non-residents, minor members and associate members had no vote in the affairs of the Club. Student members continued to be a major source of income for the club, and in 1924 this category was expanded to include students at the Ithaca Conservatory of Music (later Ithaca College).

New members in 1920–21 included Livingston Farrand, Cornell's new president; Gilmour Dobie, the new football coach; and Fred H. "Dusty" Rhodes, who was later to found the School of Chemical Engineering at Cornell. Jim Van Natta, whose farm adjoined the new fourth hole, was given a free family membership in compensation for the inevitable trespassing by Club members on his property to retrieve wandering golf balls. Membership peaked at 296 in 1923, including 12 non-residents. As many older members resigned, it declined to 274 in 1925, with 19 non-residents and 19 minor members.

In December 1921 the Board of Managers was authorized to proceed with plans and construction of an 18-hole course. This had been a goal ever since 1916 when the Club bought land east of Triphammer Road. Tillinghast had probably designed both the 9-hole and 18-hole courses before the war; in late 1922 he was paid $424 for "services," presumably to complete his design. In 1923 a committee was set up to oversee construction of the new course: Louis Dennis (who had been on the Board of Managers continuously since the Club was founded); Cedric Guise, a Cornell professor of forestry; Charles Treman; and L. C. Urquhart, professor of bridge engineering, chairman.

A little more land was needed. From Cornell University in 1924 the Club repurchased part of the land it had once sold to Professor Merritt in 1916, plus a small plot on Kline Road*, at a cost of $5,000. In 1925 Jared T. Newman sold a plot of land to the Club, also for $5,000, just east of Triphammer Road and north of the Club's property. In 1926 Cornell agreed to lease to the Country Club some 38 acres of the former Kline farm, rent-free, "until needed by the University," but for a minimum of ten years.

Meanwhile the Board had been busy selling the Club's twenty-five acres west of Triphammer Road. In 1923 the whole parcel was offered to George Coleman, S. L. Howell and R. W. Sailor for $47,500, but the offer was rejected. Subsequent negotiations were prolonged. Not until July 1925 could President Charles Treman (who had been "resurrected as president", as he said, to see the new course completed) report that about twenty acres had been sold to the Acacia, Eleusis and Kappa Delta Rho fraternities, and to Franklin C. Cornell Jr., who thus bought back about one-eighth of his father's farm. He paid $2,000 an acre, ten times what his father had received for the same land in 1903. The remaining 5 1/2 acres of the Club's "western lands" were bought in 1926 by Professor Paul Lincoln and architect J. Lakin Baldridge. The total amount realized by the Club was $50,096.

Most of the members, of course, knew or cared little about the land transactions. They were more interested in golf. A formal competition for the Club championship was instituted in 1921, won the first year by Ralph Jones and in 1922 by John Quine (see Appendix H). New interclub matches were held with neighboring clubs, with Ithaca usually winning. The Finger Lakes Tournament began in 1922 as a result of a

---

*Renamed Pleasant Grove Road in 1954.

suggestion by Bob Hutchinson; it was approved by the Board of Managers "provided the cost to the Club does not exceed $50.00." S. G. Harding of Binghamton won the individual Finger Lakes championship in 1922; the next year Ralph Jones won it for Ithaca. In 1924 the Club joined the United States Golf Association (USGA).

In June 1921 the managers voted to extend the privileges of the Club to the country clubs in Auburn, Cortland, Elmira, Geneva, Owego and Waverly. Apparently these reciprocal arrangements were somewhat haphazard and not renewed every year. The minutes for 1925 record a lack of interest in extending privileges to other clubs "unless at least five or six other clubs are favorably inclined."

In the early 1920s there was an unusual kind of mixed doubles tournament, in which the winning couple had to defend the title against any other couple that challenged them. One year Margaret Thilly (Raynolds) and John Bancroft teamed up to win the championship, only to lose it to challengers Dorothy Smith and Bob Hutchinson.

Club members must have rebelled against the length and difficulty of Tillinghast's design, because by August 1923, when Gene Sarazen played an exhibition match at the Country Club, the course had been shortened and par reduced to 35. This was the first of Sarazen's several appearances in Ithaca. He had won the U.S. Open the year before at the age of twenty. His partner was to be Bobby Cruikshank, runner-up to Bobby Jones in the 1923 U.S. Open, but Cruikshank fell sick and Sarazen played instead with Abe Chandler, "a local professional." (This must have been J. Halsey Chandler, of whom more later.) They beat two other professionals, Alan Townes of Cortland and Tom Bonner of Elmira, 3 up. Sarazen set an 18-hole course record of 72. Both he and Bonner tied the 9-hole record of 35 held by Bob Hutchinson.

By 1925 the first hole had again been lengthened to a par 5 and par for the nine holes was 36. In June of that year Clarence Elmer set a new 9-hole record of 34 and equalled Sarazen's record of 72 for the eighteen.

J. Halsey "Chan" Chandler, who was to become the Club's second golf professional, joined as a single member for the 1923 season. Before the war he had been a professional at various midwest golf clubs, then had returned to Ithaca to live with relatives. He must have impressed everyone with his golfing skills, particularly in teaching. In 1924 he was authorized to give lessons on the Club grounds "subject to the approval of the Greens Committee." This proved to be a good move for the Club, because Walter Bells was fully occupied in overseeing the clubhouse and grounds and no longer played golf. In 1925 their duties were spelled out in detail: Bells was to maintain the grounds around the clubhouse, the road, the putting and practice greens, and the tennis courts; collect fees, monitor players and have the sole privilege of selling balls and selling and repairing clubs. George Raymond, the greenskeeper, was to maintain all the other greens and all fairways, traps and rough. Chandler was to give instruction to members and students on Club property, with no sales of balls or clubs, and instruct in the rules and etiquette of golf. He could teach anyone, club members or not, but was not to play with non-members on the regular course.

The winter of 1926 was stormy and bitter cold. By February the new 18-hole course, under construction since 1922, lay almost completed under the snow. The last of the Club property west of Triphammer Road had been sold. The sales agreement stipulated that the clubhouse be removed from the "western land" before March 1—yet on February 15 it still hadn't been moved, although a contract to do the work had been signed with C. D. Clark.

Heavy snows fell during the last two weeks of February, but sometime during that period the clubhouse was skidded from Highland Road up the hill to Triphammer Road, to a point just south of the intersection with the present Jessup Road. About the move itself Bob Hutchinson wrote: "This was a precarious undertaking and there were times when it seemed the flimsy structure would never survive its ride across the snowy, rolling fairways to its new home." But it did. Repairs and refurbishing began immediately: roof shingles, new linoleum in the kitchen, new china, rugs, and kitchenware. The general contractors were Wilson Barger and J. Dall, Jr., Inc.

The new course was supposed to have opened in 1925, but when architect Tillinghast visited in May of that year he found that some Club members had made well-intentioned but unacceptable changes to his plan. He insisted his original plan be used. This necessitated building four new greens and delayed the opening for over a year.

April 1926 was especially wet and rainy, and during May and June the golfers played a temporary 9-hole arrangement since work was still in progress on the clubhouse and the course. At last everything was ready and the long-awaited 18-hole course was formally opened on Saturday, July 3, 1926, with a tea from 4 to 6 p.m. Mrs. A. C. Phelps was chairman; Mrs. Walter Willcox, Mrs. Frank Thilly, Mrs. Ralph Tarr and Mrs. Fred Albree poured.

The total cost of moving and repairing the clubhouse was $10,456, of which the movers received $4,704. The cost of building the new course itself, spread over four years, was about $25,000, not counting the cost of the land. In earlier years there had been much talk of building a new clubhouse, but it was considered too expensive, and even with the cost-cutting approach that was actually taken the additional costs of an 18-hole course necessitated raising the dues. In March 1929 they were increased by $7.50—to $37.50 per year for a family membership. Single men paid $30 and single women $25—no longer half the men's dues, but more nearly the same. For the first time all dues were subject to 10 per cent Federal tax.

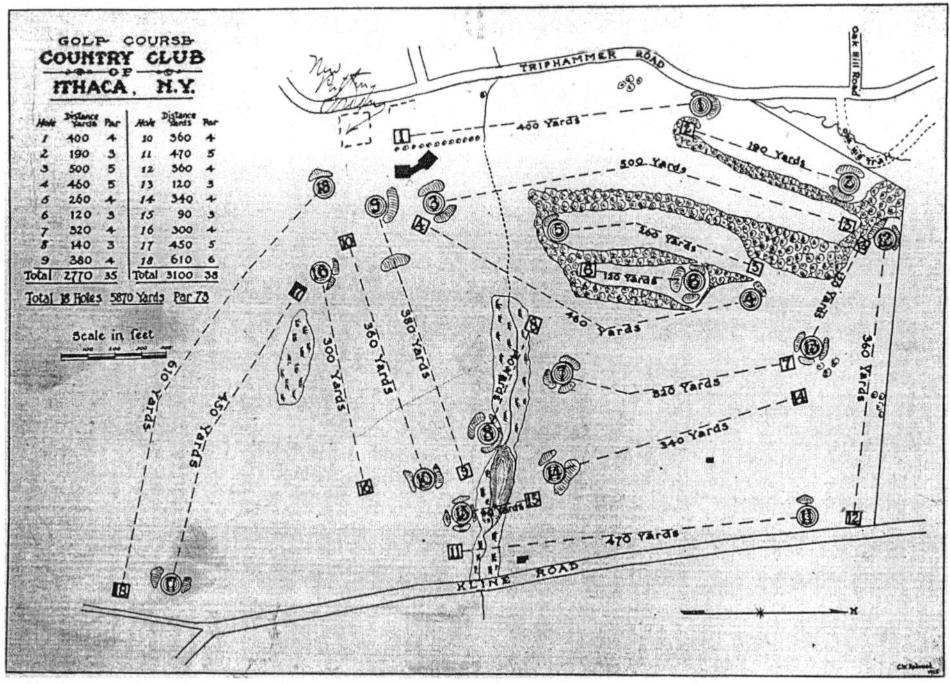

Figure 3-3. Architect's 1925 drawing of the proposed eighteen-hole course.

An architect's drawing of the proposed course layout is shown in Fig. 3-3. (This is upside down compared with the other course layouts, and the order of the holes is not the same as the way they were actually used (see Fig 4-4).) Only nine holes were entirely on Club property; the other nine were partly or completely on land leased from Cornell University. Almost all the holes were new: only No. 5 was used unchanged from the 1920 course, although No. 4 was much the same as the old No. 2, with a new green and the tee moved a hundred yards to the southeast. The twelfth hole was the old fourth hole turned end for end. The course length, as proposed by Tillinghast, was to be 5870 yards, par 73. It's clear the members thought that his monster 18th hole—610 yards, par 6—was too long; by 1927 it had been shortened to 480 yards, par 5. Two brooks ran through the course, originally open ditches but later tiled over. For years a dam just west of No. 15 created a pond in the bottom of the deep gully, adding to the worries of anyone playing this tricky little par 3.

Within two weeks of the opening of the new course 17-year-old Charles Treman, Jr., known as "Carl" in those days, defeated Bob Hutchinson to win his first Club championship. The next week he won the Finger Lakes Tournament in Elmira. The following year, 1927, in the semifinals of the club championship, Charles set a course record of 68 while defeating former club champion Ralph Jones. (See scorecard, Fig. 3-4.) Jones was a very serious golfer who didn't like to be beaten, especially by an 18-year-old Cornell student— hence his comment on the card. Charles went on to beat Bob Hutchinson again in the finals for his second consecutive championship.

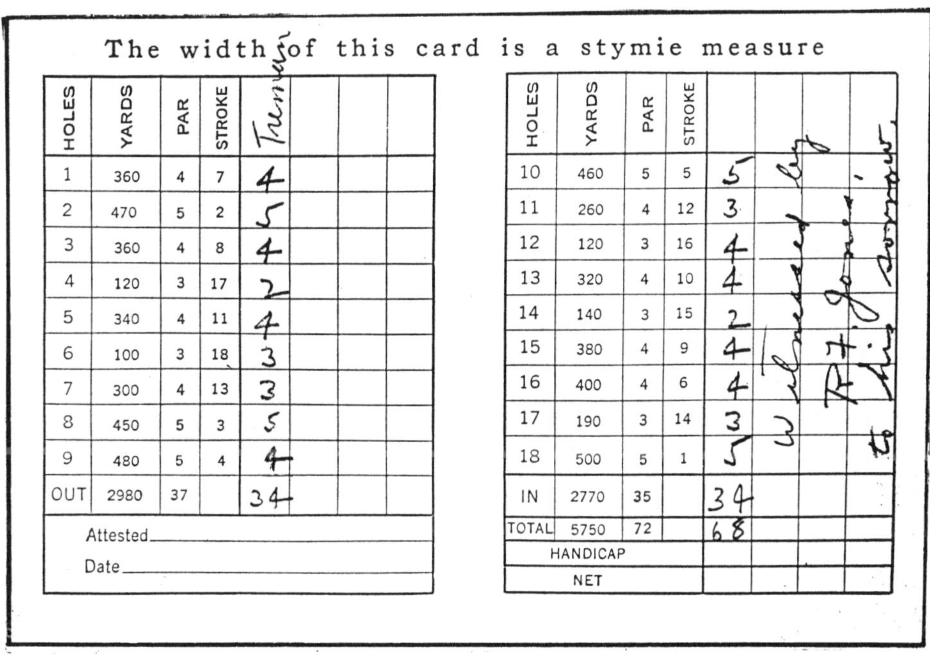

The width of this card is a stymie measure

HOLES	YARDS	PAR	STROKE				
1	360	4	7	4			
2	470	5	2	5			
3	360	4	8	4			
4	120	3	17	2			
5	340	4	11	4			
6	100	3	18	3			
7	300	4	13	3			
8	450	5	3	5			
9	480	5	4	4			
OUT	2980	37		34			

Attested_______

Date_______

HOLES	YARDS	PAR	STROKE				
10	460	5	5	5			
11	260	4	12	3			
12	120	3	16	4			
13	320	4	10	4			
14	140	3	15	2			
15	380	4	9	4			
16	400	4	6	4			
17	190	3	14	3			
18	500	5	1	5			
IN	2770	35		34			
TOTAL	5750	72		68			
HANDICAP							
NET							

Figure 3-4. Scorecard of course record, August 1, 1927. Courtesy of Charles E. Treman, Jr.

At last the Country Club of Ithaca had facilities it could be proud of. At the annual meeting in December 1926 President McDaniels summarized the Club's financial progress, saying:

> We began twenty-six years ago last spring with practically nothing but
> plenty of nerve. Today we own about 70 acres of land and a house worth
> over $20,000, the whole mortgaged for $15,000. We have thirty or forty
> acres of land under lease from the university *for nothing* until they need
> it, which will probably be [in] fifteen or twenty years. We have a first-
> class 18-hole course and the only improvements necessary are such that
> they can be gradually added. We owe a note of $700, and that is all.

The "improvements" referred to were additional traps recommended by Tillinghast to be built around six of the new greens. Tillinghast favored large grass traps, but when these hazards were eventually built they were made smaller and filled with sand.

Golf at the Club was immediately and greatly stimulated by the expanded facilities. In 1928 there were fourteen local tournaments, ten interclub matches, the Governor's Cup tournament and the Club championship. In both 1928 and 1929 the men's champion was Lieut. A. K. Hammond and the women's champion was Mrs. G. M. (Ann) Weeks. Frequent items in the *Ithaca Journal* chronicled the heightened activity—two or three notices appeared every week during the golfing season. Before 1920 the Club was mentioned in the paper at most two or three times a year, recording elections or real estate transactions, not golfing events.

In 1927 a new practice putting green was built in front of the clubhouse. Professor R. W. Curtis of Ornamental Floriculture at Cornell had become interested in studying grasses under various conditions, and began a cooperative research project with the Country Club. As part of this study he gave the Club enough creeping bent stolons from the Arlington Turf Gardens in Washington, D. C., for the practice green and a turf garden. Most of the Club's greens were eventually resodded with this new turf.

The chairman of the Greens and Grounds Committee at the time was Cedric H. Guise, Professor of Forestry at Cornell, whose lengthy annual reports on the greens contain much informative detail. Ced became president of the Club in 1933–34. His nearly sixty years of membership ended in November 1982 when he was killed in a car accident at the age of 92.

Tennis had ended at the Club in 1926 when the old courts near Highland Road were abandoned. Construction of new courts near Triphammer Road began in 1927 but was completed only in 1929. The ground under the courts proved unstable and the playing surfaces constantly cracked and needed repair.

There were also, of course, the perennial problems that plague all golf clubs. At the annual meetings the Greens and Grounds Committee

Figure 3-5. Walter Bells, the Club's first professional. (From the *Ithaca Journal,* April 10, 1931)

complained that members didn't replace divots; dogs and children wandered about the course; student members didn't observe the proprieties of golf; non-members sneaked on to the course in the evening and played some of the outlying holes. And the caddies—they lounged about the clubhouse porch, even after a small caddy house was provided for them, joking and making noise. Pat Bucci, who was a caddy in those days, recalls that the professional Walter Bells once caught him high in a tree carving his initials in the bark, and promptly fired him. Pat went home, saying nothing, and reappeared for caddy duty two days later. Mr. Bells said nothing either—apparently the firing had been forgotten.

Walter Bells (Fig. 3-5) is remembered by older Club members as a courtly old gentleman with a large, pleasant wife. He would send her out each morning to collect lost golf balls. One morning, says Pat Bucci, her basket was only half full and he angrily sent her out again. The most vivid memories, however, are of their son Truman, who was big, brash, obnoxious and wild. "He was the type," said Charlie Treman, "who would cross Triphammer Bridge walking on the railing and go down the Beebe Lake toboggan slide on ice skates."*

---

*Morris Bishop in *A History of Cornell,* p. 361, confirms such an exploit on the toboggan slide; the boy, though knocked unconscious, survived. Probably this was Truman Bells. Bishop joined the Club in 1928 and may well have met Truman; he certainly would have heard a lot about him.

Truman was also sent out to hunt lost golf balls. According to Paul O'Leary, Truman once said to him, "My father tells me to walk through the rough and to always turn my feet out and scuff my way along. 'With feet the size of yours,' he says, 'you'll be surprised how many balls will pop up!'"In later years there was a darker side to Truman's activities; in Pat Bucci's words:

> He was a wild Indian. He attacked a girl one night—tried to throw a potato sack over her head, but he got scared off for some reason or other. He was always driving new balls out toward the pond—to hit them into the pond—they were his dad's golf balls which were sold in the pro's shop. That was one of his tricks.He just didn't show anything toward his dad or his mother. He was kind of a wild kid—and a *big* man, a big guy—he was smoking cigars all the time. I don't know what became of him.

Truman was not popular among the members of the Club.

By the late 1920s golf was no longer a sport only for the elite. Those were the days of Walter Hagen, Gene Sarazen, Bobby Jones and Glenna Collett Vare, legendary figures whose exploits were followed by an ever-increasing number of devotees. The public's adulation of the leading professionals was deplored by most sportswriters, who pointed out that "in Britain golf professionals are automatically placed in a social class below the amateur." The growing popularity of golf itself also received harsh words: in June 1925 Robert T. Small, special correspondent to the *Ithaca Journal-News*, wrote about "this pesky game of golf—the same golf that is winning business men away from business and professional men away from their professions and youths away from school and tennis players away from the courts, yachtsmen away from their yachts...The utter depravity of golf knows no depth."

Small also reported that the president of the National Association of Credit Men, after careful study, had concluded that golf was a distinct liability to U.S. business. "Exercise for bankers and business men should not take so much time," he had said. "Golf may make for health and long life, but it is doubtful if it makes for prosperity." Another writer noted that some churches had opened their doors to men and women in golfing attire. "This must be going too far," he concluded. "Some day golfers may wake up to find the game strictly regulated or prohibited as a pernicious influence in American life." The game did have its defenders, however. One said, "Golf has made more gentlemen in manners than almost any other influence. There are very few criminals among golf players. The 'crook' hasn't time to play golf, and the degenerate has no interest in it."

For The Golfer

We have an interesting assortment of Rubberized Ginghams and Cretonnes that make chic rain costumes for the Fair Way when the weather is dubious. We would be pleased to have you come in and see them.

Treasure House

220 N. Tioga St.

Muriel J. Denniston   Jane K. DuLavan

Decorative Furnishers

Figure 3-6. Advertisement for women golfer's rain costumes. (*Ithaca Journal*, July 2, 1926)

Society and social attitudes had changed enormously during the ten years following World War I. Sunday golf, for example, which after 1917 was permitted in the afternoon, could be played at the Club after 1926 on Sunday mornings as well. Weekly teas for ladies continued every Saturday during the season, but in 1929 the Tuesday afternoon teas were replaced, with great success, by lunches and bridge.

Clandestine drinking was a growing problem. Pat Bucci recalls that in the late 1920s several professors and doctors each had two lockers, one for golf clothes and one for gin. Pat helped Chan Chandler serve "set-ups" (glasses of ice) to the drinking members for 5 cents each, and small bottles of Lime and Lithia, a soft drink, for 10 cents. By 1929 Prohibition had led nationwide to speakeasies and gangster wars and a general lowering of respect for the law. Even such staunch advocates of the Volstead Act as Robert H. Treman, who spoke strongly in its favor at Ithaca churches and civic organizations, began to see that it wasn't working as expected. Reasoned voices in favor of repeal were beginning to be heard.

Figure 3-6 is a 1926 Ithaca advertisement for women's "rain costumes for the Fair Way..." Women's golf clothes had become looser, shorter and more functional. While they would hardly be considered revealing by today's standards (if today has any standards), the designs contrasted sharply with the description in the 1915 *Ithaca Journal* of appropriate golfing apparel for women:

> For spring tennis and golf there have been provided pleated and gored skirts of serge, of gabardine and of linen, very short as to length and wide as to hem. They find their complement in the tailored shirtwaists of silk or linen, completed by a Windsor tie of some brightly figured silk.

Membership increased dramatically in 1926 from 274 to 362 and reached a new high of 380 in 1929. This was another period of great optimism: the Club was in good financial shape, with a fine course and active programs, and the stock market had carried everyone to new dreams of riches. The future seemed inescapably rosy. Then came October 1929, and Wall Street laid its egg. The euphoric twenties came to an abrupt end and the thirties arrived, bringing a heavy load of unexpected troubles.

Chapter 4

THE TROUBLED THIRTIES

"Why do they always call me at dinnertime?" thought Wilder Bancroft as he made his way to the telephone.

"Professor Bancroft?" said the voice. "This is Chandler. Thought you ought to know—the clubhouse is on fire...No, I don't know how it started. The firemen think they've got it under control, but half of the clubhouse is gone."

It was Saturday, January 11, 1930. Wilder D. Bancroft, founder and first president of the Country Club, had been reelected president just a month before. He had seen the clubhouse built, added to, and twice moved to a new location. And now this...*

The fire had started about 5.30 p.m. in a woodpile beside the northwest section of the clubhouse. It eventually destroyed the women's locker room and the main hall—the original part of the building, constructed in 1900. As the firemen concentrated on saving the rest of the rambling structure, the lighting system failed. In great confusion, members searched the men's locker room in the smoke and the dark for their belongings, hauling out some lockers and smashing open others when they couldn't find the right key. Lockers and their contents were taken to the new toboggan house on Beebe Lake, and all day Sunday the golfers searched for their own effects. The men's golf equipment was saved, but many women lost all of theirs. By 8.30 p.m. the fire was out. According to the *Ithaca Journal*, it was believed that boys sometimes went to the woodpile to smoke, but the cause of the fire was officially listed as unknown.

What to do? Should the 30-year old building be repaired, or replaced with a new one at a cost of some $50,000? A new clubhouse would mean

---

*Did it really happen this way? Probably not. But President Bancroft must have heard the disturbing news from someone, and it could well have been from Chandler.

a dues increase to $60 per year. Repair costs were estimated at $10,000, largely covered by insurance, with no dues increase needed. The matter was submitted to the membership* for a vote, and despite some enthusiastic promotion of the idea of a new clubhouse, the motion was lost, 51 to 129. So the old clubhouse was rebuilt at a total cost of $13,280, of which insurance paid $9,078. J. Lakin Baldridge was the architect; the general contractor was J. Dall, Jr., Inc. By the end of the year the Board of Managers concluded that the fire actually benefited the Club: the women had gained a new locker room, with showers (at long last); the men's locker room got a new and much more sanitary floor. A hundred new lockers had been installed. The one major loss not covered by insurance was a painting that had been donated to the Club by member-artist Louis Agassiz Fuertes.

Another troubling situation developed later that winter when 71-year-old Walter Bells fell while working at Beebe Lake, and broke his arm. It was all downhill for him after that, and fifteen months later, on April 9, 1931, he died at his home on the Brooktondale Road, ending thirty years of service. The Club, which had been giving him $50 a month during his final illness, sent his widow condolences and a check for $100.

And Walter's son Truman? He was no longer around. In 1927 the Ithaca City Directory indicates that he was married by then, and lists him as "golf pro" though he certainly never held that position at the Country Club. Within the next year or so he and his wife Elizabeth must have left the Ithaca area, for there is no mention of him in the 1929 City Directory. By 1931, according to his father's obituary, Truman had two children of his own.

In April 1930 J. Halsey "Chan" Chandler was appointed professional in Walter Bells' place, at a salary of $100 per month. Chandler, the Club's second golf professional, was born in Mecklenburg on September 27, 1877. He grew up in Interlaken; played baseball at Ithaca High School; entered Cornell in architecture in 1897 but left after a year or so. He worked briefly for the Chicago Telephone Company as a draftsman and found office work most confining. He took up golf in 1899, discovered he was good at it, and soon left the Telephone Company to become a golf pro. A friend and professional, Chick Evans, got him a job in Kansas City at the Milburn Golf Club; from there he went to the Windsor Golf Club in Chicago where he was pro until 1919. By 1921 he

---

*At membership meetings prior to 1963, the husband and wife in a family membership each had a vote.

was back in Ithaca and began his association with the Country Club three years later.

As a young man Chan was a very good golfer. He shot a 68 on a championship course, a remarkable feat in those days. He once had eight consecutive 3's, a record later equalled by Bobby Jones. Of golf in 1899 he once said, "There were very few golfers back then—if you walked down the street with golf clubs you had a crowd following you. They thought there was something wrong with you... We played with solid gutta percha golf balls. A man was very good if he could hit a ball 200 yards." (*Ithaca Journal*, Oct. 2, 1945)

Chandler's real strength was in teaching, which he loved. His most successful pupil, from the years before he came to Ithaca, was Miriam Burns of Kansas City who won the national women's amateur championship in 1927.

In 1931 the country was in the depths of the Great Depression, but there were no signs of it at the Country Club of Ithaca. Membership increased to 388 in 1930 and to a record 412 in 1931. Since 1921 Benjamin Sanford had been paid $100 a year as the secretary-treasurer of the Club; in 1931 he was given a raise to $150. The talk was of expansion, not contraction. "The growth of golf in this area," said President Minor McDaniels, "will soon justify our having at least 27 holes." Recognizing that the lease arrangement with Cornell University would run out in a very few years, the Board of Managers made plans to buy land—a lot more land. The Club may not have felt the Depression's pinch, but other Ithacans, especially farmers, did. Soon the Club was able to buy two plots adjacent to the Club's property at very modest prices. The purchases were unanimously approved at a special membership meeting on April 23, 1931, and by June 28 the Club had taken title to the 50-acre Asai farm for $15,000 and the 90-acre Hanford farm for $8,000. The Club's land holdings (the most it ever owned) are shown in Fig. 4-1. A new mortgage of $24,000 was arranged with the Ithaca Trust Company.

Also in June 1931 the Club retained the Buffalo firm of Thompson and Jones* to plan a 27-hole layout, with the understanding that if the plans were accepted, the firm would be paid $2,250 for the final design. A set of plans was prepared and delivered and the Club paid the firm $1,000. For the next several years Thompson and Jones billed the Club for the remaining $1,250, and each year the Club replied that the

---

*Jones' given names were Robert Trent; this was at the very beginning of his distinguished career as golf architect. He had attended the two-year ("short-horn") special agriculture program at Cornell in 1928–1930.

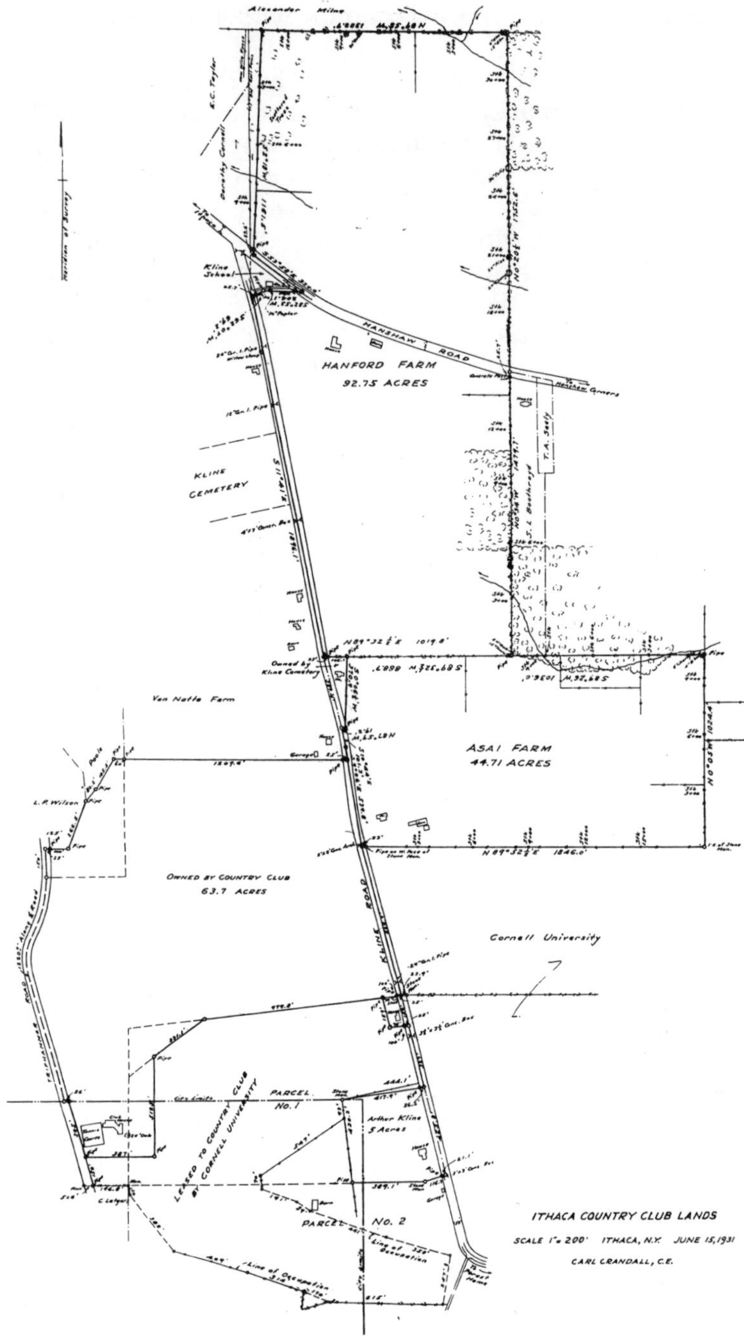

Figure 4-1. Map of Club property, 1931.

$1,000 already paid was plenty for the amount of work the firm had done, and that the matter was closed. The controversy was not resolved until 1939.

The expansive mood continued through the first half of the following year, 1932. In March the membership approved, by a mail vote of 138 to 95, increases in the dues and entrance fees according to the following schedule:

	Entrance Fees			Yearly Dues	
	1931	1932		1931	1932
Regular	$25.00	$50.00	Family	$37.50	$45.00
Associate	10.00	25.00	Single—men	30.00	40.00
			Single—women	20.00	30.00
			Social—women	—	20.00

The new category of "social membership" for non-golfing members was restricted to women.

Then the Club began to feel the impact of the great Depression. Almost as soon as the dues increase was announced, resignations started to come in. By the end of 1932 the number of members had dropped to 356, and this included 54 who were given special leaves of absence "so as not to force resignations." No one had money to spend. The Club's income for the year was $5,100 below the budgeted amount. Dues income plummeted, especially student dues, which were $2,000 less than expected. Greens fees brought in $1,000 less than in 1931. The Club had to borrow $3,500 from the Ithaca Trust Company just to pay current bills. Membership continued to fall for the next two years as shown by these discouraging figures:

Year	Members in Good Standing	Delinquent Members
1931	412	—
1932	356	—
1933	240	81
1934	188	96

Cost cutting and economy became the watchwords. Salaries were cut in 1933—Chandler's to $85 a month and greenskeeper Boyer's to $125 (from $150). Laborers' wages were lowered to 40 cents per hour. Insurance coverage on the clubhouse was reduced from $21,000 to $17,000. Payments to the City of Ithaca for the recent paving of Triphammer Road were spread out over ten years instead of five. Committee budgets were cut drastically and all tournaments were required to be self-supporting. But some things survived the cost-cutting fever: the salary of the secretary-treasurer, now Bob Hutchinson, remained at $150 per year, with dues remitted. The Club even hired a woman to look after the ladies' locker room for $20 per month, and Chandler was relieved of that responsibility.

Leaves of absence were now granted even to members who remained in Ithaca. For a $10 annual fee they could use the golf course during the year by paying the regular greens fees. Greens fees were reduced to $1.50 on weekdays and $2.50 (later $2.00) other days; for guests playing with their sponsoring members they were $1.00 and $1.50. To attract new members, entrance fees were deferred for a year and could then be paid in two annual installments. Student dues were lowered to $15 per term. Tennis memberships for Ithaca residents, at $30 a year, had been instituted in 1931; the dues were now cut to $15. Elsie Matson was allowed to use the clubhouse for Wednesday night bridge sessions, with half the profits to go to the Club. Anything to make a dollar! Unfortunately the bridge sessions brought in only $8.49 during their first month and were quietly discontinued.

In early 1933 the sale of 3.2% beer was made legal and by April arrangements were made with J. H. Chandler to oversee the beer sales at the Club. After much discussion, the beer bar was set up in the former student locker room. The Twenty-first Amendment repealing Prohibition was ratified in late 1933; the Cornell *Alumni News* for December 14 commented: "Almost immediately drinks became smaller, poorer, more expensive and harder to get. Cocktails ran from 40 to 50 cents each..."At the 1935 annual meeting Lew Durland proposed that whiskey and other liquors be sold at the Club, but the motion was defeated. It wasn't until 1937 that the Club had its first liquor bar and first bartender.

All the scrimping and saving paid off. The Club not only survived but managed to keep all its regular employees on the payroll. In spite of the drop in membership, the deficit in 1933 was only $443. In 1934, with even fewer members, the Club showed a profit of $1,307. In 1935 the membership rose to 258 and in 1936 to 267, with not one in poor standing. The Depression's storm had ended.

In 1936 leaves of absence, with dues remitted, were once again restricted to members who actually left the Ithaca area for the year. These members paid no fee at all.

Despite the fire, despite the Depression, golf flourished at the Club during the 1930s as never before. Holiday tournaments, handicap tournaments, interclub tournaments, mixed doubles tournaments, women's tournaments, student tournaments, junior tournaments, even caddy tournaments...and the Club championships, too, of course. Newspaper coverage was excellent. Some item about the Club appeared in the *Ithaca Journal* almost every day from May through September. This largely resulted from the arrangement under which, in return for publicity, a sports writer from the *Journal* was given Club membership for half the regular dues (and the *Journal* paid that half). In the late 1920s and early 30s the designated writer was Bill Waters; in later years it was Bernard M. "Buck" Clarey.

In 1930 Rodney Bliss, a Cornell freshman, set a new course record of 66. During the 1920s a great many Cornell students had played at the Country Club course, but about 1923 the University golf team had been disbanded. In 1931 the Cornell team was reestablished, with Bliss as its captain. According to Charlie Treman, Bliss was the best golfer the Club ever had. In 1932 he was the Nebraska State amateur champion. He later won the Trans-Mississippi championship and did well in the United States Amateur.

Charlie Treman also told this story about himself:

> In 1932 I played in the Finger Lakes Tournament at Ithaca, but lost in the semifinals. The consolation match was with Amory Houghton (later United States Ambassador) and others from Corning. We were scheduled to play early Sunday morning, but they talked to the Tournament Committee and got an afternoon starting time so they wouldn't have to come over early. They did come over for lunch, however. Arthur L. 'Dutch' Hoffman of Elmira said, 'I'll be referee.'

> It was a very good lunch. To save time we decided, when tee-off time came, to go off together. Dutch would count 'One—two—three!' and we'd all hit at the same time. I was at a disadvantage because I had a slower swing than the others—so on my downswing I would hear 'Click-click-click!' We hit some surprisingly good shots, and attracted a crowd. By the end we had a bigger gallery than the finalists.

Gene Sarazen, the 1932 U.S. and British Open champion, returned to Ithaca on July 25, 1933. With trick-shot artist Joe Kirkwood he played Bob Hutchinson and Chan Chandler in an exhibition match. The visitors won easily, 7 and 5. Sarazen tied the course record of 66 held by Rodney Bliss; Kirkwood shot a 70. Hutchinson had 75 and Chandler 83.

In August 1935 Sam Parks, Jr., the U.S. Open champion, and Tom Newlove of the Syracuse Yacht and Country Club gave an exhibition at the Club; their fee was $150 plus 50% of gate receipts over that amount. They shot 71 and 70 and beat Hutchinson and Martin (Dodie) Speno in match play 3 and 1. Pat Bucci, by this time Assistant Pro under Chandler, caddied for Parks; his brother Adam caddied for Newlove.

Caddy fees were set in 1936 at 80 cents for 18 holes for an "A" caddy and 65 cents for a "B." Chandler and Bucci were authorized to classify the caddies and collect 5 cents from them for each round for "shop fees." The club minutes also state: "If a strike like that on the day of the women's invitational is tried by the caddies at the Left Handers State tournament here on July 30, the committee [Chandler and Bucci] is given the right to handle the situation drastically...and employ outside caddies."

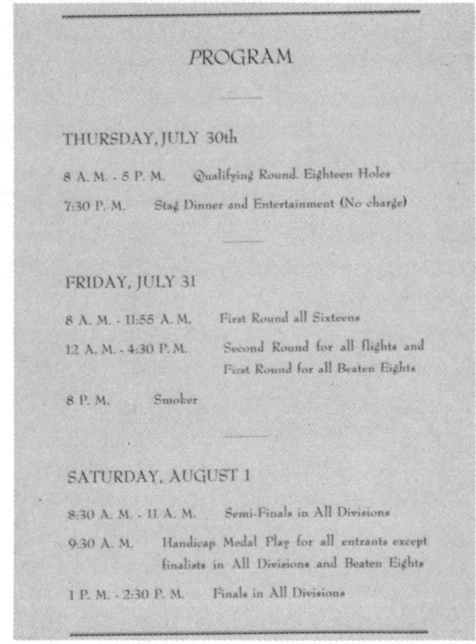

PROGRAM

THURSDAY, JULY 30th

8 A. M. - 5 P. M.   Qualifying Round. Eighteen Holes

7:30 P. M.   Stag Dinner and Entertainment (No charge)

FRIDAY, JULY 31

8 A. M. - 11:55 A. M.   First Round all Sixteens

12 A. M. - 4:30 P. M.   Second Round for all flights and First Round for all Beaten Eights

8 P. M.   Smoker

SATURDAY, AUGUST 1

8:30 A. M. - 11 A. M.   Semi-Finals in All Divisions

9:30 A. M.   Handicap Medal Play for all entrants except finalists in All Divisions and Beaten Eights

1 P. M. - 2:30 P. M.   Finals in All Divisions

Figure 4-2. Program, 1936 NYS Left Handers Tournament.

Bob Hutchinson was club champion four times in a row from 1932 through 1935. Dodie Speno won in 1936 and 1937 (Fig. 4-3).

Figure 4-3. Martin (Dodie) Speno, John Carver and caddy Clarence Cleveland in 1937.

In 1938, after a nine-year lapse, Charlie Treman re-established himself as club champion, beating Dodie Speno in the finals. He won again in 1939, beating out John Carver. The Robbs dominated the women's play: Beulah Robb was club champion in 1931, 1933, 1934 and 1936; her daughter Betty won her first championship in 1939 at the age of fifteen.

In June 1939 Craig Wood and Joe Kirkwood played an exhibition match against Jack Gordon and Russell Gowland, a pro and an amateur from Buffalo. The week before Wood had lost a 36-hole playoff to Byron Nelson* for the U. S. Open title. He shot 70 at the Country Club and did one thing no one had done before— he reached the green on the 570-yard 9th hole in two. Joe Kirkwood had a 74; Gordon had 75 and Gowland 78. The match was followed by an exhibition of trick shots by Kirkwood and a stag dinner at the clubhouse. Golfers from the downtown Newman course made up much of the gallery; afterwards they were invited to join the members of the Country Club at the dinner. It was a good day.

In those years the tennis courts saw a lot of use, although the number of tennis memberships never approached the Board-imposed limit of twenty. In 1934 the Ithaca city tennis championship was played on the Country Club courts. From 1935 on the Ithaca High School tennis team could use the Club courts after school on weekdays and on Saturday mornings, for $5.00 per term per player— in advance. Tennis memberships were discontinued in 1938, reinstated in 1939, and abolished in 1940.

During the early 1930s piecemeal changes were made in the layout of the golf course. Between 1932 and 1936 four holes (1, 7, 9 and 12) were lengthened substantially by moving the tees. Number 9 was stretched to 570 yards; 8 was shortened by ten yards and converted from an easy par 5 to a hard uphill par 4. Number 7, a 300-yard downhill hole, was lengthened first to 365 yards, then 420 yards. This required putting the tee on Arthur Kline's property, to which— according to the Club minutes— he had no objection.

An old barn once stood just east of No. 8 fairway, as shown in Fig. 4-4; it was torn down in late 1932. Originally the 9th fairway was narrow, with out of bounds on both sides; in 1934 the 8th fairway was moved east into an apple orchard, and the 9th was widened and the right-hand out-of-bounds stakes removed. Figure 4-5 shows the order of the holes and the location of the tees in 1927 and 1938. The total yardage in 1938 was 6,160, versus 5790 in 1927; par was 71 against the earlier 72.

---

*Byron Nelson made $1,000 by winning the 1939 U. S. Open. That same year George Jacobus, president of the PGA, pleaded for lower costs, saying "There is no reason why a first-class golf ball should cost more than fifty cents or the finest club more than $5.00." (*Ithaca Journal*, May 8, 1939, p. 9)

Figure 4-4. Players and gallery at the 9th green, probably 1932.

Hole 14, a par 3, crossed a deep gully which came to be known as "Snavely's Gulch." It seems that Carl Snavely, football coach at Cornell, was a very good golfer with one outstanding characteristic: he never lost a ball. If he hit a ball into the bushes or the brook he would look until he found it. He wouldn't let anyone play through, either, so sometimes play on the entire course would grind to a halt. And the cry would go up, "Snavely's in the gulch again!"

The air photos in Figs. 4-6 and 4-7 show the course in 1933 and 1938. They also show how little building there had been on the former Club property west of Triphammer Road—so little, in fact, that the Club was able to use the former No. 1 fairway as a practice range. George

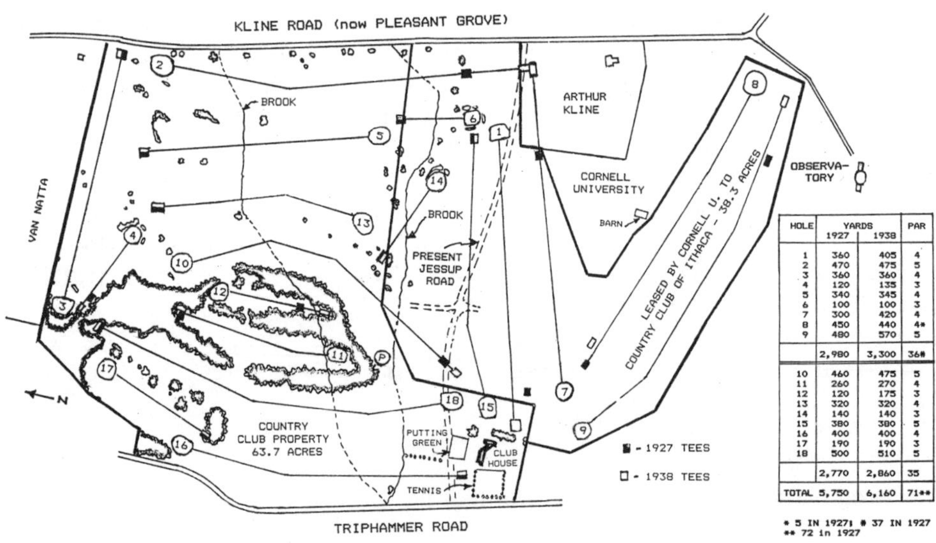

HOLE	YARDS		PAR
	1927	1938	
1	360	405	4
2	470	475	5
3	360	360	4
4	120	135	3
5	340	345	4
6	100	100	3
7	300	420	4
8	450	440	4*
9	480	570	5
	2,980	3,300	36#
10	460	475	5
11	260	270	4
12	120	175	3
13	320	320	4
14	140	140	3
15	380	380	5
16	400	400	4
17	190	190	3
18	500	510	5
	2,770	2,860	35
TOTAL	5,750	6,160	71**

* 5 IN 1927; # 37 IN 1927
** 72 in 1927

Figure 4-5. Layout of the 1926–1940 Tillinghast course.

Figure 4-6. Air photo looking north, about 1933.

Hall, the new Cornell golf coach, was allowed to use this range, and also part of the former Asai farm, for teaching students.

Named for Jared T. Newman, city mayor and developer of Cayuga Heights*, Ithaca's municipal golf course at Stewart Park opened in May 1935 with Lewis Adesso as professional. (Lew has been giving golf lessons at the Country Club during 1988 and 1989, some fifty-three years later.) The new course closed again in July because of the flood. "There were carp all over the course," said Lew. It reopened briefly in September, but the mosquitoes were so bad that playing was no fun at all.

By 1935 the Country Club's dream of 27 holes had faded away. Seeking funds, the Club sold its forty acres of land north of Hanshaw Road to Stanley Warren, assistant professor of farm management at Cornell, for $5,000. The Club received $4,500 and the real estate agent $500. Stan Warren still lives on part of this tract.

---

*Also a member of the Country Club of Ithaca from 1900 to 1932.

Figure 4-7. Air photo map, June 20, 1938. (Tompkins County Division of Assessment)

In 1937 Edmund Ezra Day, a keen golfer, became president of Cornell, and encouraged the University to develop its own golf course. In 1938 Cornell hired alumnus Robert Trent Jones (Fig. 4-8) to design and build nine holes between Kline (now Pleasant Grove) and Warren Roads, adjacent to the University poultry farm. The next year Cornell reclaimed the Country Club's 8th and 9th holes as a site for Clara Dickson Hall. The Club also offered Cornell the 7th hole, and quickly hired R. T. Jones,

Figure 4-8. Golf architect Robert Trent Jones. Courtesy of Robert Trent Jones, Inc.

who was coming to Ithaca anyway, to plan three new holes on Club property east of Kline Road. It worked out well. Jones submitted plans in July, got the Club's approval in August, and had the new holes completed by the end of October. He charged $7,248. He also agreed to consider the 1931 Thompson and Jones bill for $1,250 paid in full.

With Jones' approval the Club sold a strip of land, 175 feet wide, along the south side of Hanshaw Road to James Krizek, a local contractor. Sale price for the 5 1/2 acres, plus the former Hanford farm house and barns: $3,000. Also in 1939, on Jones' recommendation, the Club purchased Frank Tyler's 14-acre plot in the angle of the former Hanford and Asai properties for $1,800. Figure 5-1 in the next chapter shows the Krisek and Tyler plots and the location of the three new holes.

Rebuilt after the 1930 fire, the clubhouse received minimal attention during the Depression-clouded years. Optimism and some extra dollars reappeared in 1935—and in 1936, during David Robb's presidency, it received a coat of paint, a new furnace, new plumbing, eaves troughs, more parking area and some outside lighting. A basement was built by J. L. Rohrer under the main part of the clubhouse for $2,511, providing space for a new men's locker room. A grill room was installed, with a cash register, refrigerator and beer bar.

In 1937 the new liquor bar was located in the basement, out of sight; it was moved to the upstairs grill room two years later. One of the concerns voiced during the 1939 discussions of possibly moving the clubhouse was that it be kept in the City of Ithaca—the Town of Ithaca was dry. (Perhaps this new facility had some influence on social behavior at the Club. One night in May 1939 Professor Urquhart drove his car over much of the 10th fairway and was charged $25 for the damage. In November Charles Barker and Dr. Dillenbeck appeared before the Board of Managers in connection with a report of their gambling at the Club. Dr. Dillenbeck was censured, not so much for gambling but for hiring a lawyer to press his claim against Barker.)

Dining facilities were expanded and improved over the years. In 1932–33 Mrs. Galbraith acted as stewardess and cook and also cleaned the clubhouse. Mrs. Payne had the position in 1934. By 1936 Mrs. Grace Trice, helped by her husband Monroe, was serving a hundred meals a week. For the first time the clubhouse was open all winter. From March to June 1939 Mrs. Jillson served as "hostess", but in July she was fired and club member Olive Stephenson took over the kitchen, while member George Cross oversaw the grill. Mrs. Stephenson supervised a staff of five: a cook, an assistant and three waitresses. (The cook made $15 a week, the assistant $10, and the waitresses $4 each.) The Club also had a bartender, Charles Culligan, and a lockerboy.

THE COUNTRY CLUB
OF ITHACA

OPENING TEA

Will be held at the Clubhouse Saturday, June 1, 1935, from 4 until 6:30 p. m.

For the remainder of the season informal teas will be held each Wednesday and Saturday afternoon.

Ladies' weekly luncheons will be held each Tuesday at 1 p. m. beginning June 11.

A special event will open the men's golf tournament schedule Thursday afternoon, May 30, Memorial Day.

Regular dining service will begin Memorial Day. Special luncheon and dinner parties may be arranged by communicating with Mrs. Grace Thrice, Club Stewardess.

Figure 4-9. Notice of opening tea, 1935.

At the 1939 annual meeting there was heated discussion about the growing complexity of the Club and its operation. President Ralph Mungle emphasized that more facilities for recreation and comfort were needed if the Club was to compete with Cornell's new golf course and the downtown course. The Board proposed to hire a full-time club manager for 1940 and to cut Chandler's salary to $50 per month, but after a lot of argument the proposal was tabled.

After the surge in Club membership in 1935 and 1936 the numbers declined slowly during the three ensuing years (Appendix E). In 1936 the Associated Gas & Electric Company moved its main office from Ithaca to Wilmington, Delaware, taking away 25 Club members. This loss was somewhat offset by new members from the Grange League Federation (G.L.F.), which came to Ithaca from Buffalo the same year. In 1936 seven of the Club's charter members were still on the membership rolls, including three (Bancroft, Blood and Dennis) of the original Board of Managers. Founder Louis Dennis died in December 1936. In 1939 Wilder Bancroft, now 72, submitted his resignation, but the Board refused to accept it. Instead they made him the Club's first honorary life member by granting him and his wife the privileges of the Club, with dues remitted, "indefinitely." (He died in 1952 at age 85.)

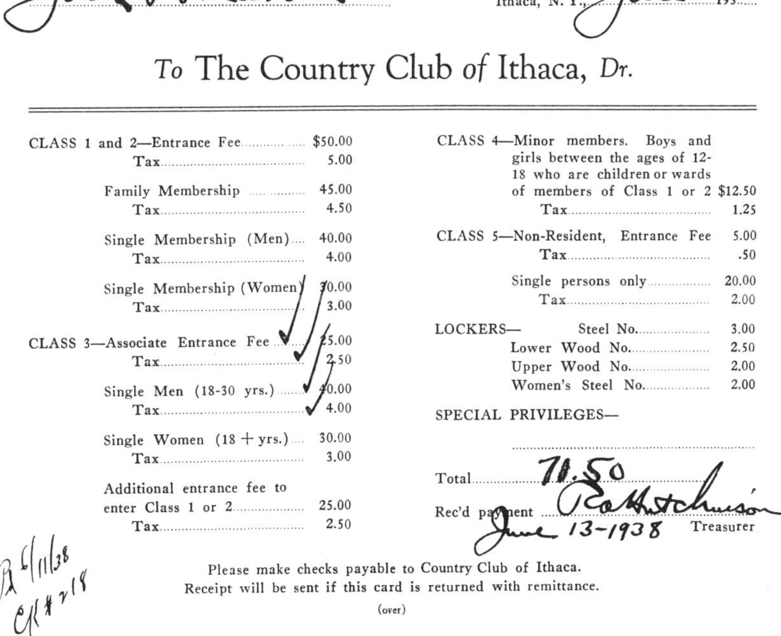

Figure 4-10. Dues notice, 1938. Courtesy of James Rothschild.

On September 1, 1939, three days after the finals of the Club championship, Hitler's troops invaded Poland and World War II began. The world changed, again.

Figure 4-11. Caddies— 1936.

Chapter 5

WAR AND PEACE—THE 1940s

The world was at war even though the United States, officially, was not. The "phony war" of early 1940 was quickly followed by the German conquest of Denmark and Norway, the invasion of Belgium and Holland, the evacuation from Dunkerque, the battle of Britain, the fall of France. But the Country Club was occupied with much more immediate matters: the new golf holes, rules for women's golf, the dining room, student memberships, the controversy over financial records.

The dry winter of 1940 was hard on greens, especially the three new ones east of Kline Road. They had to be reseeded and partially rebuilt; in consequence these holes weren't used until 1941. Their location is shown in Fig. 5-1. The new holes replaced the former Nos. 7, 8 and 9; the other holes, renumbered, were unchanged. Three greens, two tees and much of six fairways remained on Cornell property. The total length of 6,070 yards was 90 yards shorter than the previous layout. Par was 72 against the former 71.

In 1940 Martin "Dodie" Speno again won the club championship, beating Bob Hutchinson. The winner received $16 credit at a local store, the runner-up $12 credit. Dodie also received a trophy. That year Mrs. Lucius Waldo had given the Club a trophy to commemorate her late husband's great interest in golf, and it was decided to award it annually to the men's club champion. In 1941 Bob Hutchinson (Fig. 5-2) bested Charlie Treman to become the second winner of the Waldo Cup. The women's champion and winner of the Ann Weeks trophy for 1940 and '41 (and '42, '43, '45 and '46) was Doris Van Natta. (Janet Thompson recalls that her former father-in-law Bert Patten used to engrave the Club's trophies without charge.)

In an exhibition match in August 1940, on the old layout, Gene Sarazen and Ed "Porky" Oliver played the 1939 club championship finalists Charlie Treman and John Carver (Fig. 5-3). Two months earlier Gene and Porky had tied Lawson Little for first place in the U.S. Open,

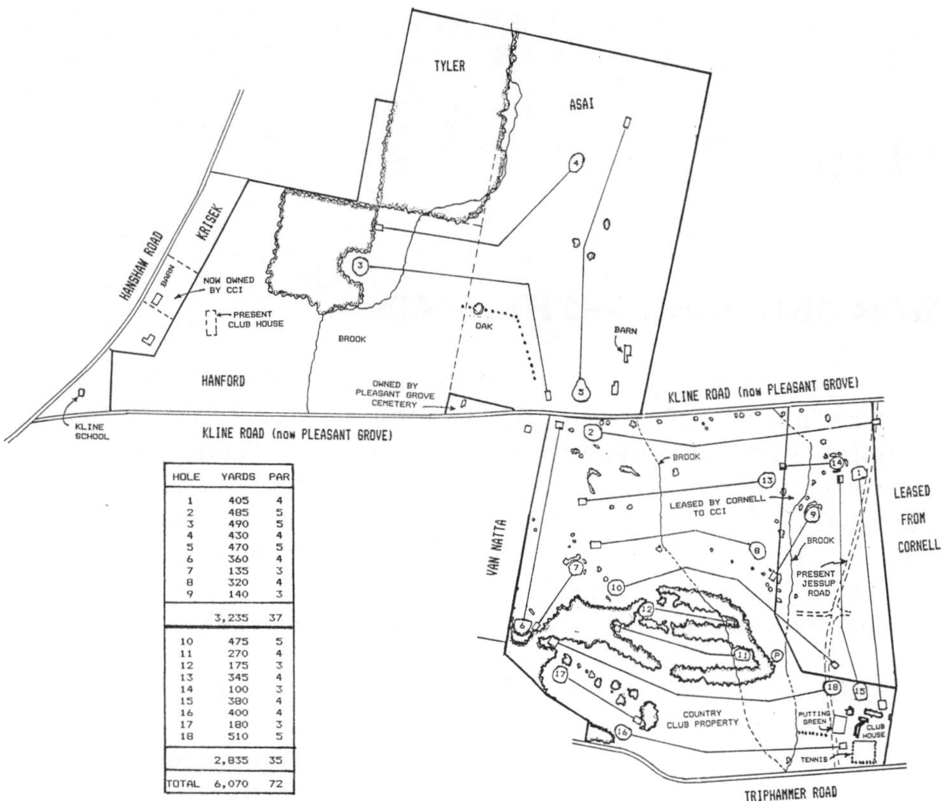

HOLE	YARDS	PAR
1	405	4
2	485	5
3	490	5
4	430	4
5	470	5
6	360	4
7	135	3
8	320	4
9	140	3
	3,235	37
10	475	5
11	270	4
12	175	3
13	345	4
14	100	3
15	380	4
16	400	4
17	180	3
18	510	5
	2,835	35
TOTAL	6,070	72

Figure 5-1. Course layout, 1941–1949.

with 287 apiece, but Sarazen lost the 36-hole playoff and Oliver was disqualified for starting ahead of schedule. Treman and Carver thought they would have a good chance against the pro's if they could shoot a best ball of 66—which they did. But Sarazen had 65 on his own ball,

Figure 5-2. Bob Hutchinson (1960 photo).

Figure 5-3. John Carver, Bob Hutchinson and Gene Sarazen, August 14, 1940.

almost tying the course record of 64 held by Dodie Speno. Oliver had 69 for a best ball of 61. After the match Oliver gave a driving exhibition, offering a dozen golf balls to anyone who could outdrive him. No one did, although Assistant Pro Pat Bucci came within two yards of Oliver's best effort, a 300-yard poke. That evening Gene and his charming wife were entertained at Charlie Treman's new house on Highland Road, where Sarazen gave about $1,000 worth of free lessons to Charlie's wife Margo. Gene had her hit over a hundred balls down the slope in their back lot. "I was still finding balls down there twenty years later," said Charlie.

In January 1940 the Board of Managers passed a rule restricting women's golf on weekends to after 3 p.m. on Saturdays and after noon on Sundays. It didn't stick. A petition signed by many members, both women and men, led to a heated discussion at a special membership meeting on April 12. Dr. Denniston was of the opinion that the congestion was caused by men, not women; he said he would rather play behind women than men in any case, especially if the men were playing for 5 or 10 cents a hole. A motion to rescind the Board's action was carried 61 to 15. Later the Club secretary wrote the women golfers, politely asking them to limit their play on Saturdays, if convenient, to after 1 p.m.

For several years the dining room and grill had been supervised by Club members on a volunteer basis. Talk of a club manager had come to nothing. In 1940 member Bob Causer, manager of the Ithaca Hotel, offered to take over the dining room and bar for an annual fee of $500, which seemed reasonable to the Board of Managers. In 1941 Bob put Joe Lisseck, chef, in charge of the kitchen and a Mr. Hopper at the bar. Joe stayed for a number of years and became something of an institution at the Club, but Hopper was soon replaced by Ray Trask.

Meanwhile J. H. Chandler continued as professional in spite of complaints about his performance (he was blamed for a caddy strike in 1941, for example). Pat Bucci was his assistant. For $65 a month Pat was supposed to act as caddy master and deputy sheriff, supervise starting times, and clean the men's locker room. Albert Collins, who had replaced George Boyer as greenskeeper in 1935, was paid $35 a week.

Membership continued its slow rise to a post-Depression high of 264 in 1941. The Van Nattas were again given free memberships "for the time spent by club members on their property, hunting for golf balls." Charter member Professor F. C. Prescott, who had resigned in 1937, was made Honorary Life Member. A number of Cornell faculty and staff members joined in 1940 and 1941, but Club President Knudson expressed concern about the noticeable dropoff of interest in the Country Club among the faculty of Cornell, and predicted that the 1941 opening of the new University course would lead further in this direction. Certainly student interest had fallen: income from student dues, $1,570 in 1939, was down to $855 in 1941.

Construction of the new holes had strained the Club's resources, and finances were again a problem. Two captious board members, Harold Reed and M. E. "Scotty" Campbell, complained that the treasurer failed to give comprehensive reports of the true financial condition of the Club, and requested (demanded, really) a study of all aspects of the Club's income, expenses, assets and liabilities. Bob Hutchinson, secretary-treasurer since 1933, was understandably upset, especially on January 29, 1940 when by a vote of 4 to 2 he was not reappointed. The minutes of the rest of that meeting are wryly amusing:

> "Mr. Campbell then moved that the Board elect a separate secretary and separate treasurer and nominated Mr. Rowe for treasurer and Mr. Treman for secretary. Mr. Treman declined the nomination. Mr. Rowe nominated Mr. Hutchinson as secretary. Mr. Hutchinson declined the nomination. Mr. Reed nominated Mr. Campbell for secretary. Mr. Campbell declined the nomination. Mr. Treman then consented to accept the nomination for secretary....Mr. Reed filed his resignation from the Board to take effect immediately. Mr. Hutchinson moved that such resignation be accepted. The motion was lost."

Figure 5-4. Charles E. Treman, Jr. Photo by Fabian Bachrach; courtesy of Tompkins County Trust Company.

In February both Reed and Hutchinson did resign from the Board. From then on neither the secretary nor the treasurer received any compensation from the Club. Instead a clerk was appointed, initially at $300 per year, to assist the treasurer. This position was filled by Norman Bakko from 1940 to 1943 and by C. L. "Dick" Dunbar from 1944 through 1961.

The 1941 annual meeting was held on December 8, the day after Pearl Harbor was bombed by the Japanese. The mood was somber, a mixture of apprehension about the future and relief, even some exhilaration, that America's course of action was clear at last. About twenty-five of the members had belonged to the Club in 1917 and 1918 and remembered the effects of World War I—the drop in membership, the shortages, the loss of income. This war promised to be worse.

The active membership shrank, as expected, from 264 in 1941 to 206 in 1942 (Appendix E.) Members were departing for service in the armed forces or for war-related work in Washington, D.C. and elsewhere. Some stayed in Ithaca but were too busy to play golf. Dues income fell, especially student income, which plummeted to $276 in 1942 and $44 in 1943. The Club tried several expedients to offset the loss of income: greens fee booklets for sale to members' friends and acquaintances; leaves of absence for a $10 annual fee, even for members who remained in Ithaca; special memberships for service men and women who were stationed in the area. The opening teas were cancelled, saving $55. Even so, in 1942 the Club had to assess its family members $10 and single members $5.

These measures all helped, but not enough, and reluctantly the Club turned to another source of income, one used by a number of other social and fraternal organizations in the area: slot machines. They had been considered and rejected in 1941; by 1942 they were seen as the only solution to the income problem. A special membership meeting was convened on May 28, 1942 to vote on the proposal. Several speakers pointed out that slot machines were illegal and that the Club would be in danger of losing its bar license; nonetheless the members voted 36 to 31 to have them installed. Professor Lewis Knudson immediately resigned the presidency, saying that he did not feel it was fair to Cornell University for him to remain as president of a club which maintained illegal slot machines. Carl Snavely, the Cornell varsity football coach, took over as president. Professor Knudson accepted a continuing position on the Board of Managers.

In the rest of the Club's minutes for 1942 there is no mention of slot machines. At the annual meeting in December, however, the treasurer reported $4,856 of unbudgeted income from a new account called a "Maintenance Fund." The machines paid well. They were owned by Joseph Riley, who assumed all liabilities in connection with them and received 50 per cent of the net income. (It is said that he also owned a number of other machines in the area.) Joe joined the Country Club in March 1943. During the rest of the war years the machines brought the Club $8,000 to $9,000 annually, more than offsetting the loss of other kinds of income.

In 1943 gasoline rationing began. The New York State speed limit was reduced to 40 mph, but it hardly mattered because driving for pleasure was banned. New cars and tires were no longer available to civilians. Food began to be rationed, first sugar, then butter and other items. Restaurants found it increasingly hard to supply meals at a reasonable price— say $1.50 for a full-course dinner— and soon good restaurant meals could scarcely be had at any price.

Joe Lisseck kept things going in the Club's dining room as best he could, which was pretty well under the circumstances, but the number of meals he could serve was strictly limited. Food privileges were restricted to members and a small number of guests— three local guests per year was suggested. In May 1943 the Kappa Alpha Theta sorority asked to be allowed to eat dinner at the clubhouse weekday evenings and Sunday noon. This was granted by giving the girls the privilege of becoming social members. (The slot machines had been moved from the dining room to the basement the month before.) By August the women's

Tuesday luncheons had to be discontinued. Help in the kitchen and dining room became scarce. Meals continued to be served, however, throughout the wartime, although a fuel emergency closed the clubhouse from January 28 to February 16, 1945.

Golf also continued to be played during the war, but under difficulties. The manufacture of golf clubs and balls ended in 1942. Most golfers could manage without new clubs, but balls were another matter. In those days golf balls didn't last anywhere near as long as they do today; tough Surlyn covers didn't exist, and one poorly hit shot with a 9-iron could open a "smile" that made the ball useless. Reprocessed balls were the answer. The A. G. Spalding Company would take old balls, put on new covers, and return them to the Club for resale. In 1943 the Old Ball Committee collected 1,600 balls for reprocessing, and continued its good work for the next two years under the more elegant name of "Golf Ball Salvage Committee." Even so, the ball situation remained critical.

Local tournaments, including the club championships, continued; interclub matches did not. Between 1942 and 1945 Lou Barnard was men's champion three times and Carl Snavely once. Doris Van Natta won the women's championship three times and Betty Robb once. The Women's Invitational Tournament scheduled for August 23, 1944 had to be called off because of a polio epidemic.

The Club's land east of Kline Road, not being used for golf, was put to wartime use. Some of it was farmed by Albert Collins and his grounds crew; some was made available to Club members for Victory Gardens. One plot was leased to Cornell's Nutrition Department for $25 a year. A larger one, 5 acres in all, was rented to Cornell for experiments in growing plants to produce rubber.

On May 23, 1943 Clarence Newhart was caddying at the Country Club when he was hit by a golf ball. He was taken to the hospital and

Figure 5-5. Greenskeeper Albert Collins.

treated by Drs. French, Sutton, Alderman and Thorslund for a fractured skull. He must have spent many days in the hospital—the bill was $214.50. He recovered fully but was out of school until January 1944. The Club paid $400 toward his expenses and tried to get the New York State Department of Labor to award workmen's compensation to Newhart on the grounds that he was an employee of the Club at the time of the accident, but the claim was disallowed in March 1944; appealed; and disallowed once more in March 1945.

Overall the Club came through the war years in remarkably good shape. True, the clubhouse suffered from lack of maintenance and more than once had to be treated for cockroaches. But meals were served and golf was played and applications for membership kept being received, especially in 1944 and 1945. Membership rose steadily, largely because of the increased number of social members and special service members. The drop in family memberships was relatively small. Even the nonresident memberships, only seven in 1943, increased again almost to prewar levels by 1945. Many members, of course, were on leave from the Club, most of them in the armed forces.

Finances were not the problem they had been in 1917–18. The "maintenance fund" saw to that. The Club was able to pay $3,000 against the mortgage in 1943, then buy $3,500 worth of War Bonds. These were cashed in and applied against the mortgage in 1945.

On December 1, 1945, after the war had ended, J. Halsey Chandler retired at the age of 68. He had grown heavier as he grew older—"portly" was the word used—and except at putting his golfing skills had diminished. He didn't care. His strength was in teaching, which he loved. When he retired he estimated he had given 8,500 lessons. Locally his best pupils were Martin Speno, Charlie Treman, Dick Neish, Doris Van Natta and Betty Robb.

Chan was also outstanding at pool and billiards—the "peer of local players." He once had a billiards run of 400. He had many other interests as well: he was a Mason and an Elk; he hunted and fished. His landscapes in pen and ink, water color and crayon were much prized, and in his later years there were exhibitions of his art in downtown Ithaca.

At the end of each golfing season at the Club, a "Chandler Day" clambake was held in honor of his birthday. (The picture in Fig. 5-6 was taken at the 1941 clambake.) Actually no one knew the date of his birth, so whatever day the event was held on became Chan's birthday. No one knew how old he was either, until he finally admitted in 1942 to being 65.

In June 1942 he had quietly married Miss Clara Apgar, teacher of

Figure 5-6. J. Halsey Chandler at his 1941 "birthday" clambake.

Latin at the Ithaca High School and and member of the Country Club since 1920. Clara was given a complimentary membership in the Club. On Chan's retirement in 1945 he and his wife were made honorary life members.

The postwar years, 1946 to 1949, were among the best the Club had known. Absent members returned and new ones joined. Most wartime shortages quickly disappeared. The world at peace was full of exciting technological possibilities— atomic energy, television, penicillin, DDT, 2-4D. More important, new golf balls and golf equipment were available again. The Club was even able to buy a new tractor and 3-gang mower in 1946 for $1,755.

With the ban on pleasure driving lifted, interclub matches were resumed, although the first one was a fiasco. In August 1946 twelve Elmira players showed up unannounced for what they thought was a scheduled match; it was hard to convince them there wasn't one. Some Club members gave them a game and took them to dinner, then billed the Club $45 for expenses. That same month Joe Kirkwood gave an exhibition of trick shots and played a match with Wes White against Lew Adesso and Aldor Jones of the Cortland Country Club. Jones and Adesso won with two 74s to Kirkwood's 72 and White's 77.

Wester A. White (Fig. 5-7) was the Club's new professional, appointed when J. H. Chandler retired. He was born on July 9, 1909 in Westhampton Beach, Long Island, where his father ran a fish market. He

Figure 5-7. Wes White in 1949.

entered Syracuse University in 1927 as a fine arts major, but two years later, after the stock market crash, he changed to something with more job potential and graduated in physical education in 1932. One of two men in his class to have a job on graduation, he came to Ithaca and started teaching at Boynton Junior High School.

His golfing career began when he was a caddy on Long Island. The "entrance requirement" in those days was to fight somebody for a spot in the caddy pen—which Wes couldn't do until 1921, when he was twelve. He caddied for five years and later worked in the pro's shop learning to repair clubs. He played a little golf with other caddies, and soon could beat most of them.

Al Meyn, industrial arts teacher and golf coach at the Ithaca High School, invited Wes to play at the Country Club. Since Wes returned to Long Island each summer, he could get a spring "student" membership for $18. In 1933 he joined the Club, paid his money to Chan Chandler, and had all of $2 left. As he walked out of the shop with his bag slung over his shoulder, he heard a huge roar: "LOOKING FOR A GAME?" It was Horace Whiteside, professor of law. "Sure," said Wes. "Okay," said Horace, "we'll play dollar-dollar-dollar." Horace was a big man, a former football All-American, who could hit the ball 300 yards. After a few holes he had Wes three down, and Wes was scared. He couldn't cover his bet. He kept talking to himself, however, and finally got back on the track and won the match. Years later Wes was talking to Dick Dunbar in the clubhouse when he felt two huge hands around his 28-inch waist and his head hitting the ceiling. "HAW-HAW-HAW!" laughed Horace. "You little S.O.B., I remember when you took $3 from me!" Horace never knew how desperate Wes had been during their first encounter.

During his years at Ithaca High School Wes played very good golf with his short flat swing, never shooting above 71 during one two-week span. "I was a hitter, not a swinger," he said. School budget problems in 1933–34 forced him to be dropped from the teaching staff, but the following year he was back on a half-time basis. Realizing he wasn't meant to be a school teacher, he became a golf pro in 1937 at the old Glen Springs Hotel course in Watkins Glen. Later that season one of the assistant pros at Westhampton offered to rebuild his compact swing into one that was fuller and more upright, in the Bobby Jones style of that era. They worked on the practice tee the entire winter. And what happened? "I lost about 20 yards on my drives," said Wes. "I never hit the ball well again."

During World War II Wes became physical education director at the Central High School in Warsaw, N.Y. In the summers he served as pro at the Newman Municipal Course in Ithaca while Lew Adesso was away at war. Just as he was about to leave for the Service the atom bomb fell on Hiroshima, so he never had to go to war himself.

In an arrangement with the Country Club in 1946 he invested $2,500, based on materials at cost and his own labor at $1 per hour, to turn the old Asai farmhouse into a home for himself and his family. He had to install electricity, plumbing and an indoor toilet. The Club still owned the building. Wes was credited with $40 per month rent until the $2,500 was paid back.

In August 1946 (an eventful month) Cornell University gave notice that in three years it would reclaim its leased land. Immediately the Club began planning for six new holes to replace the ones that would be lost. Robert Trent Jones had left sketches, though not detailed designs, for three possible 9-hole layouts east of Kline Road. The Greens Committee and Board of Managers chose one of them, checked it with Jones, and authorized construction to begin in July 1947. The estimated cost was $25,000, including $500 to purchase from S. L. Boothroyd a small piece of land adjacent to the then 4th hole. Wes White and Albert Collins and his men did the building. Working long hours, they had everything finished by the first of December. Wes especially relished the work as a change from running the pro's shop, though he tried to do that too. His artistic talents in evidence, he made clay models of the new holes, then supervised their construction. "Like sculpting with dirt," he said with great satisfaction.

Thanks to the slot machines, the Club's finances were in excellent shape. In late 1946 the final balance of $4,962 on the mortgage was paid and for the first time in its history the Club was out of debt. A mortgage-burning party was held on November 23, but the celebration was tempered by the belief that the Club would soon have to borrow $25,000 to pay for building the six new holes. As it turned out, it wasn't necessary. Dues were raised 10 per cent in January 1947. The "maintenance fund" brought in over $10,000 in 1946, $13,700 in 1947 and $18,500 in 1948. With the addition of the annual profit from the bar, the Club had more than enough money to cover its operating expenses as well as the cost of the new holes.

Beulah Robb, among others, had a strong penchant for playing the slot machines, but the most avid player, by far, was Horace Whiteside. He would break open rolls of quarters on the surface of the bar, leaving marks that were visible for years afterward. Coin after coin disappeared into the slots. Often Horace would play both quarter machines at once; on one occasion he had Pat Bucci and his wife play the two dime machines and the nickel machine for him at the same time. "His dream," said Hanley Staley, "was to hit all five machines at once." According to Dave Cynoske, Horace once broke a roll of quarters over Fred Rowe's head, which made Fred, a longtime martini drinker, turn to Imperial whisky "to ease the pain."

Memberships increased so rapidly after the war that for a time in 1946 no new applications for social membership could be accepted. The Club's facilities, especially the dining room, were taxed to the limit. Many young professionals—business men, lawyers, doctors, dentists and professors—joined at this time, among them a considerable number who are active (though older) Club members today. Total membership rose to 386 in 1948. Former assistant professional Pat Bucci, who had regained his amateur status, joined the Club as a family member in August 1949. Surprisingly, student memberships increased substantially after the war, yielding about $800 a year in dues, and in 1948 the course became so crowded that a curb on student memberships was considered, but proved unnecessary.

Serious thought was given in 1948 to a new clubhouse, to be sited near the 13th tee. Carl Tallman made sketches and a preliminary cost estimate of $210,000. This was considered prohibitively high, even though the Club was in good financial shape, and the Board of Managers decided to refurbish the existing clubhouse once again. "We'll probably be here for ten more years," said one Board member with great foresight. (He was exactly right.) So in 1949–1950 the old clubhouse had its final facelift—outside painting; reinforced floors; a new roof; a new forced hot water heating plant; and excavation to enlarge the men's locker room. The cost was $29,000, of which $10,000 was borrowed on a short-term note.

Chef Joe Lisseck continued to run the kitchen and dining room until May 1948 when he fell ill and resigned. A month earlier, Wes White had been appointed golf professional *and* club manager—the Club's first—at a salary of $2,500. Wes tried valiantly to find a reliable chef and dining room supervisor, but without success. A series of incompetent employees provided mostly unsatisfactory service and soon few members cared to eat at the Club. By year's end the dining room deficit was over $7,500. Even without these problems, Wes' role would have been difficult; with them it was impossible. He resigned as Club manager as of October 1948, saying "I have lost all desire to eat, and I am unable to sleep." For a short time in early 1949 Peter Atsedes was manager of the dining room, but it didn't work out. To everyone's relief, Joe Lisseck was persuaded to return. Wes White was rehired as golf professional in 1949 for $1,800.

The bar, meanwhile, was netting about $7,500 annually. In 1949 the Club hired two full-time bartenders plus a third one for the summer months. But there were problems. Back in 1946 the Board had discussed the "foul language and loud, ungentlemanly talk" becoming common in the bar room, and agreed that Board members would talk individually with the offenders. Signs had to be posted at various times saying that no chits or tickets would be accepted for the sale of drinks or borrowing money at the bar, and that loaning liquor from the bar would not be allowed. In 1948 Horace Whiteside scrawled a blunt note to the Board of Managers: "If you don't keep the kids out of the bar room and away from from slot machines, I will report it to the D.A." (His demands were met.)

That same year a Club member—call him Harry W (not his name)—was reprimanded and told that the bar attendants had been instructed to refuse him service "if in their opinion you are in such condition as to be objectionable to the members present at the time." This led to a delicate situation which was well handled by a large genial

Figure 5-8. Views from the clubhouse, about 1949.
        (a) Looking east, 15th green.
        (b) Looking north, 10th tee.

bartender named Duffy. Bob Farnsworth relates how one night Harry had had a bit too much to drink and when he went to the bar to order another, Duffy refused to serve him. "Gimme another drink!" said Harry. "Sorry, sir," repeated Duffy, "I can't serve you." "You won't give me another drink?" "No, sir." "Then I resign from this club—right now!" shouted Harry, pounding the top of the bar. He then wavered down the stairs to the locker room. After a while he came back up, swayed over to the bar, and said, "Give me another drink." "I'm sorry, sir," said Duffy, "We can't serve nonmembers!"

Tennis memberships were discontinued in 1940. The courts were not maintained and soon became unplayable. After the war proposals to rehabilitate them were made and rejected. Subsequent proposals recommended turning them into a parking area or a children's playground, but in spite of much talk nothing was done.

Golf, on the other hand, flourished, with innumerable tournaments and interclub matches. The women ran weekly 9-hole tournaments; in two of them in 1947 the players wore masquerade costumes. A pro-am tournament with twenty area professionals and sixty Club members was held that same year. At the hole-in-one contest on July 4, 1947 Jack Humphreys actually scored an ace. Lou Barnard won his fourth and fifth club championships in 1947 and 1949; Flo Rowe was women's champion in 1948 and 1949. But the Club minutes record numerous frustrations and complaints— slow play; cross-country runners damaging the greens; dogs on the course (and in the clubhouse); incompetent caddies; uneven greens and unfair hazards. Beginning in 1947, rounds by guests who were Ithaca residents were once again limited to three per year. The professional was instructed to enforce this rule, but it proved very hard to do— as it has ever since.

One afternoon during the late 1940s, Cornell football coach Lefty James was playing the 13th hole, a short par 4. Everything went wrong: it took him 9 strokes to get the ball in the cup. "Double par plus one," he said. "That's a *fleagle!*"

Publicity in the *Ithaca Journal* of the Club's activities, especially golf, continued to be excellent, even though the half-fee *Journal* membership had been discontinued in 1945. In April 1946 President Causer began writing a monthly newsletter to the club members, a practice continued by his successors Fred Rowe and Bob Hutchinson.

Chan Chandler had only a short time to enjoy his retirement. In early 1948 he developed cancer of the intestine and on June 15, 1949, after much suffering, he died. According to his obituary he was survived by his wife and a daughter, Elizabeth Chandler, of McKean, Pennsylvania.*

A few months before, Barney Pelotte (the 1946 club champion) and Redner Van Arsdale had organized a men's "after work" golf league; it was now named the "Chandler League" in Chan's honor. Over a hundred

---

*A puzzle, for Chan never said he had been married twice. For many years after he came to Ithaca in 1924 he boarded at 214 S. Albany St., the same place as Elizabeth A. Chandler, clerk, and Orsemus Chandler, painter, both of whom lived there from 1907 until the late 1930s. They were probably Chan's close relatives. Possibly Elizabeth was his sister and he named his daughter after her.

members participated in the weekly matches. Wally Rogers, the league's first president, captained a team called the Fleagles, the members of which wore T-shirts decorated with a weeping eagle on crutches. However, the Wiffers (Howie Williams, Jack Humphreys, Jim Simpson and Mal Mattice) won the series. The League also sponsored a golf exhibition on June 29 for the benefit of Chan's widow Clara. Cary Middlecoff, the U.S. Open champion, and Skip Alexander, 1948 PGA medalist, beat Wes White and Aldor Jones 4 and 3 in a best ball match. Alexander had a good chance of breaking the course record of 66 until he lost a ball on No. 11 (Fig. 5-9) and picked up. Middlecoff and Jones both picked up on the dogleg 4th hole. Middlecoff tried four times to cut the corner on his drive; four times his ball ended in the trees. The gallery, at a dollar a head, was the largest Ithaca had ever seen. Of the $750 collected, $200 went to the visiting professionals.

Clara Chandler continued as an honorary member of the Club until her death in 1956.

Figure 5-9. Hole No. 11, Triphammer Road course. (This was Hole No. 8 in 1920–25; No. 11, 1926–50; No. 3, 1951–58.)

Chapter 6

INTO THE DEEP ROUGH

By the end of 1950, its Golden Anniversary year, the Country Club of Ithaca seemed the picture of health. Membership had soared to 415, a record high. The Club owned 170 acres of land, 21 golf holes, and a recently refurbished clubhouse (including a juke box and a television set). A full-time club manager, Clarence Gravelding, had been on duty since June. There was no mortgage; the Club's only debt was a $20,000 short-term note to the Tompkins County Trust Company. Income from the slot machines, though a little less than expected, was still over $13,000. The Chandler League and the new women's twilight golf league had had an excellent season (Fig. 6-1). In July Gene Sarazen had played his fourth exhibition match at the Club, almost equalling the course record with a 67. He and Fargo Balliett beat Lew Adesso and Lou Barnard 2 and 1.

But even as someone may appear to be in perfect health yet have a serious or even fatal illness, the Club's actual condition was far from good. Three of the golf holes were on land owned by Cornell University, and several others were not being properly maintained. The dining room was losing money; members were not using the club for meals, even after Gravelding replaced chef Joe Lisseck with Nilo Ballardini, who for many years had been the chef at the Ithaca Hotel. The loss from the dining room was over $4,300 for the year, and other operating losses had reduced the net income to $6,400. It was clear that the Club was being supported by the "maintenance fund," a source of income with a very limited future.

The "fund" disappeared the next year. Though technically illegal, the operation of slot machines had been widely tolerated in many fraternal and social organizations in the area, but by 1951 most nearby golf clubs had lost their machines, removed by local law-enforcement officers. The Country Club's machines operated through March, 1951; then, the story goes, a member ran out of cash one night and wanted some more to buy

CHANDLER LEAGUE

SCHEDULE

1951

COUNTRY CLUB of ITHACA

President HOWIE WILLIAMS   Sec. PHIL KREBS

V. P., LYNN WAGNER   Treas. JIM McKINNEY

THURSDAY NIGHTS   STARTING 4:00 - 5:30

May 24	1- 2	3-15	4-14	5-13	6-12	7-11	8-10	9-16
May 31	1- 4	2- 3	5-15	6-14	7-13	8-12	9-11	10-16
June 7	1- 5	2- 4	3-16	6-15	7-14	8-13	9-12	10-11
June 14	1- 6	2- 5	3- 4	7-15	8-14	9-13	10-12	11-16
June 21	1- 7	2- 6	3- 5	4-16	8-15	9-14	10-13	11-12
June 28	1- 8	2- 7	3- 6	4- 5	9-15	10-14	11-13	12-16
July 5	1- 9	2- 8	3- 7	4- 6	5-16	10-15	11-14	12-13
July 12	1-10	2- 9	3- 8	4- 7	5- 6	11-15	12-14	13-16
July 19	1-11	2-10	3- 9	4- 8	5- 7	6-16	12-15	13-14
July 26	1-12	2-11	3-10	4- 9	5- 8	6- 7	13-15	14-16
Aug. 2	1-13	2-12	3-11	4-10	5- 9	6- 8	7-16	14-15
Aug. 9	1-14	2-13	3-12	4-11	5-10	6- 9	7- 8	15-16
Aug. 16	1-15	2-14	3-13	4-12	5-11	6-10	7- 9	8-16
Aug. 23	1-16	2-15	3-14	4-13	5-12	6-11	7-10	8- 9
Aug. 30	1- 3	2-16	4-15	5-14	6-13	7-12	8-11	9-10

Team No.	*Captain*	*Phone*	*Team No.*	*Captain*	*Phone*
1. Bowlers	V. Ruegsegger—	2672	9. Pipers	G. Ginnetti—	6370
2. Jr. Leaguers	J. Roberts—	4-0483	10. Cyclones	D. Cynoske—	3-2265
3. Saw Bones	Dr. Rachun—	4-2558	11. Small Fry	G. Fry—	2718
4. Cuppers	E. Dahmen—	5316	12. Double Crossers	G. Cross—	2722
5. Bombers	A. Anderson—	8425	13. 19th Holers	J. McKinney—	2950
6. Cast-Offs	J. Moynihan—	3-1493	14. High Arcs	J. McConnell—	7949
7. Double Bogies	A. Blomquist—	9273	15. Hairless Wonders	J. Simpson—	4-1321
8. Hackers	B. Clarey—	6727	16. Pill Peddlers	Dr. Wallace—	2140

Figure 6-1. Chandler League schedule, 1951. Courtesy of John Listar.

a drink— so he went to the slot machines, took out a pistol, and tried to shoot the lock off the cash box. A neighbor heard the shots; the police were called; the district attorney's office was notified. On April 2 the Club received a letter from the D. A. saying that "gambling is illegal under New York State Penal Law. The police, sheriff's office and New York State Police have been requested to periodically check your premises for the purpose of determining whether or not gambling is permitted thereon. Violations of this law will be prosecuted..."

The slot machines were locked away. Early one morning near the end of the year the police appeared unexpectedly and carted them off. Income from the "maintenance fund" for 1951, budgeted at $8,000, was $844.95. Soon after that, the Trust Company required the Club to pay off its short-term note and replace it with a long-term mortgage.

The Club's difficulties in 1951 were exacerbated by changes in leadership. This was the "year of the three presidents." Malcolm Mattice was the elected president, winning a close election over Scotty Campbell, but in February Mal was called to active duty in Korea. Charlie Fagan took over as acting president; in early November, however, he moved to Syracuse and left the Club. Dave Cynoske, acting vice president, became acting president for the rest of the year. At the 1952 annual meeting, Scotty Campbell was duly elected president; Dave Cynoske was nominated from the floor for the position, but declined to run.

The number of members fell by fifty-two in 1951. The remaining members were assessed $15 to $30 each, depending on their classification; even so, the operating deficit for the year was over $2,000. Stringent economies were imposed on the manager and the various committees. A vigorous membership campaign was begun, including advertisements in the Cornell Daily Sun to attract student members (Fig. 6-2). Dues for 1952

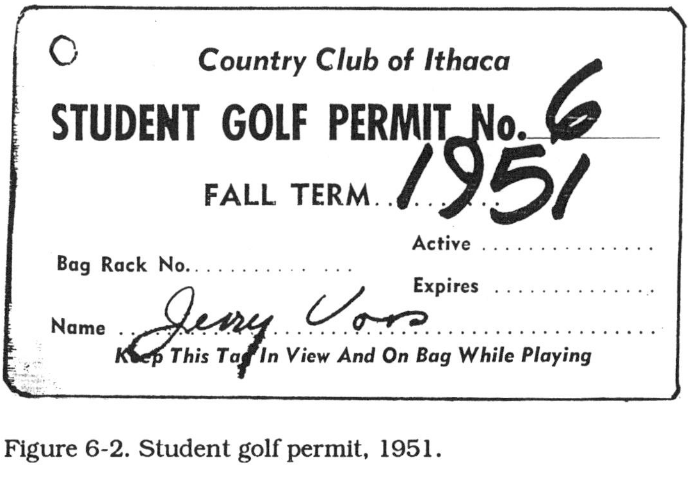

Country Club of Ithaca

STUDENT GOLF PERMIT No. 6

FALL TERM 1951

Active ....

Bag Rack No. ....

Expires ....

Name Jerry Voss

Keep This Tag In View And On Bag While Playing

Figure 6-2. Student golf permit, 1951.

were raised to $85 for families, $65 for single men and $50 for single women. "Family social" members now paid $50 a year; other social members $35. As a result, the operating deficit for 1952 was only $28, but in 1953 the deficit rose again to $2,800 and membership continued to fall. The Club was in a period of prolonged and potentially fatal decline. The reduced income led to fewer amenities; fewer amenities, in turn, meant more resignations and even less income. By 1955 the membership was only 235 and still going down.

Clarence Gravelding resigned in May 1951 and Joe Walters was appointed manager for the balance of the year. In 1952, as recommended by the Cost Cutting Committee, the position of club manager was abolished. Joe was made head bartender, and the House Committee began managing the Club once again. The change was less significant than might appear, for the Board of Managers had given the club manager little authority except in the enforcement of house rules. He had no financial authority whatever: all bills had to be individually approved by the Board of Managers at their monthly meetings.

In 1954 Pat Bucci became chairman of the House Committee and made a concerted effort to reduce costs, especially in the bar. He fired several of the bartenders who were suspected of pilfering cash or liquor,

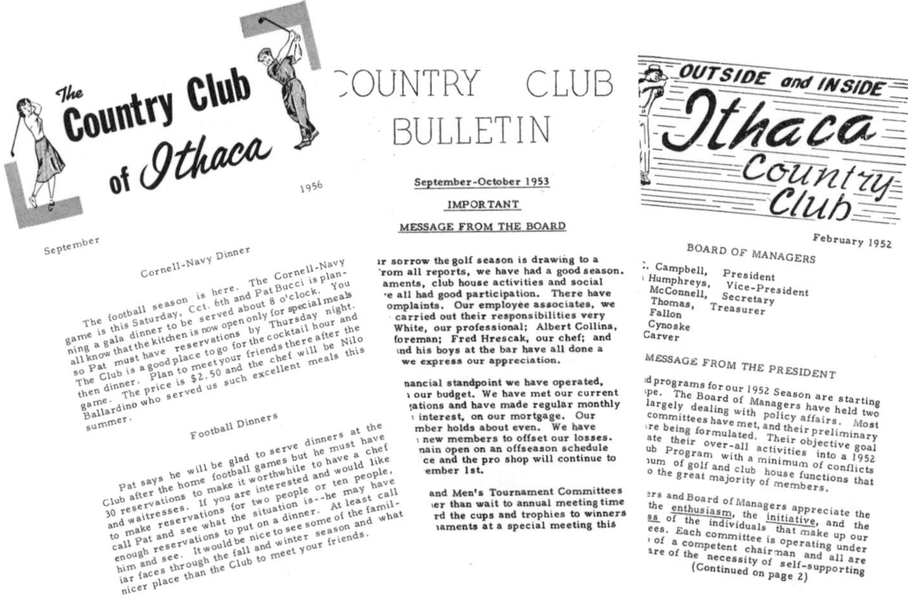

Figure 6-3. Club bulletins, 1952–56 (predecessors of *Chip Shots*).

or both, and did such a good job that the Club's net income was in the black for the first time in four years. He continued his good work in 1955. In September he was hired as "working manager" for $75 per week, to operate the clubhouse and look after repairs, supplies, and towel service. He was given $300 as a steward's fund to operate the kitchen, and a free family membership "for the period of his managership." Fred Hrescak had been the Club's chef since 1952, succeeding Nilo Ballardini, but in 1956 Fred left Ithaca and Pat asked Nilo to return. About the same time Pat hired a young waitress named Zelda Johnston.

The golf course layout posed endless problems. Even with 21 holes there seemed to be no way to arrange them so that both nines ended near the clubhouse. The nines used by the Chandler League did this, but one was par 33 and the other par 38; furthermore, they used the three holes which were on Cornell property. Each year the Greens Committee proposed a new layout, but none were really satisfactory.

Figure 6-4. Course from near 13th tee (7th tee in Fig. 6-5), looking southwest, July 1950. Photo by Curt Foerster.

The new holes east of Kline Road, used briefly in September 1949, were not maintained in 1950. In 1951 new tees were constructed and a layout adopted with par 36 for each nine, using the new holes but with the ninth hole about as far from the clubhouse as it could be. (This hole later became No. 10.) The old No. 11, now No. 3, was lengthened to 355 yards by moving the elevated tee back into the woods.*

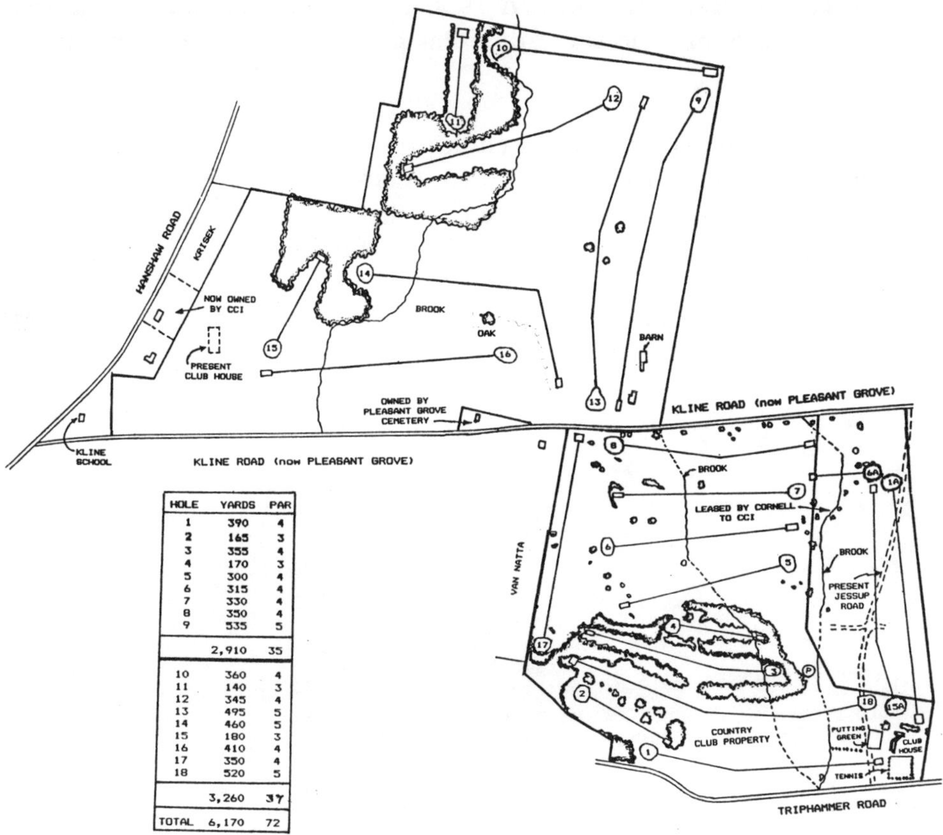

HOLE	YARDS	PAR
1	390	4
2	165	3
3	355	4
4	170	3
5	300	4
6	315	4
7	330	4
8	350	4
9	535	5
	2,910	35
10	360	4
11	140	3
12	345	4
13	495	5
14	460	5
15	180	3
16	410	4
17	350	4
18	520	5
	3,260	37
TOTAL	6,170	72

Figure 6-5. Layout of Triphammer Road course, 1954–57.

In 1952 the layout shown in Fig. 6-5 was adopted, except that the fifth hole was the old No. 8 shown in Fig. 5-1, and the sixth, with a new

---

*An unusual local rule for the original 270-yard hole permitted a free lift from the brook guarding the green, if the ball went in there on the first shot. If the second or later shots found the brook, the normal penalty for a water hazard applied.

tee, was the second half of the old No. 10. This resulted in long walks between the 4th green and the 5th tee and between the 6th green and the 7th tee; to shorten the walks Wes White proposed two new tees and a new green to give the arrangement shown in Fig. 6-5. They were built in late 1953. The new sixth green was at the top of a very steep rise.

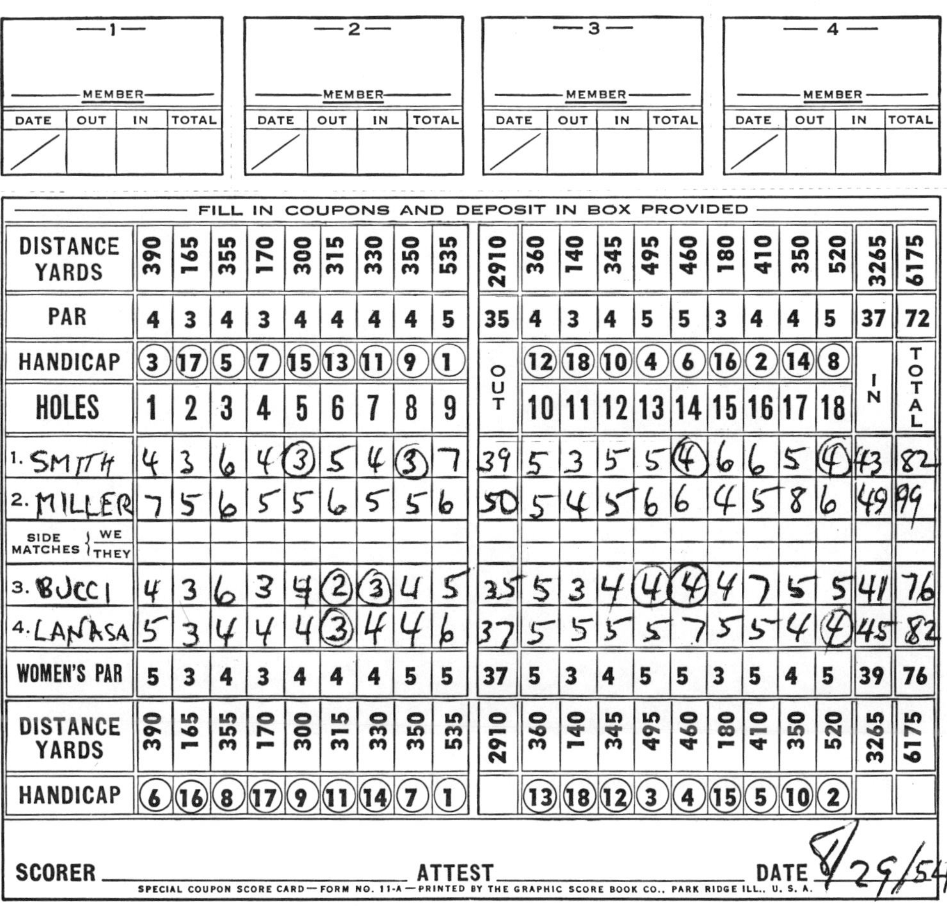

	1	2	3	4	5	6	7	8	9	OUT	10	11	12	13	14	15	16	17	18	IN	TOTAL
DISTANCE YARDS	390	165	355	170	300	315	330	350	535	2910	360	140	345	495	460	180	410	350	520	3265	6175
PAR	4	3	4	3	4	4	4	4	5	35	4	3	4	5	5	3	4	4	5	37	72
HANDICAP	(3)	(17)	(5)	(7)	(15)	(13)	(11)	(9)	(1)		(12)	(18)	(10)	(4)	(6)	(16)	(2)	(14)	(8)		
HOLES	1	2	3	4	5	6	7	8	9		10	11	12	13	14	15	16	17	18		
1. SMITH	4	3	6	4	(3)	5	4	(3)	7	39	5	3	5	5	(4)	6	6	5	(4)	43	82
2. MILLER	7	5	6	5	5	6	5	5	6	50	5	4	5	6	6	4	5	8	6	49	99
SIDE MATCHES WE / THEY																					
3. BUCCI	4	3	6	3	4	(2)	(3)	4	5	35	5	3	4	(4)	(4)	4	7	5	5	41	76
4. LANASA	5	3	4	4	4	(3)	4	4	6	37	5	5	5	5	7	5	5	4	(4)	45	82
WOMEN'S PAR	5	3	4	3	4	4	4	5	5	37	5	3	4	5	5	3	5	4	5	39	76
DISTANCE YARDS	390	165	355	170	300	315	330	350	535	2910	360	140	345	495	460	180	410	350	520	3265	6175
HANDICAP	(6)	(16)	(8)	(17)	(9)	(11)	(14)	(7)	(1)		(13)	(18)	(12)	(3)	(4)	(15)	(5)	(10)	(2)		

SCORER _____________ ATTEST _____________ DATE 9/29/54

Figure 6-6. Scorecard, 1954.

Abandoned in 1959, it was still clearly visible in December 1987 (Fig. 6-7).

In 1954 the Village of Cayuga Heights was expanded to include Kline Road, which was renamed "Pleasant Grove Road" to avoid confusion with another Kline Road already in the Village. East of Pleasant Grove Road the new No. 9 was much like our present 12th hole. No. 10 tee was the present 13th tee, but the hole ran due north along what was then Earl

Sharp's property line and across the brook to a green near the present 6th green. No. 11, a par 3, ran west through the woods; the green was to the left of today's 5th fairway, just before it bends to the right. The 12th hole ran southeast, back across the brook, to a green near the present 14th green. Nos. 13 and 14 were little changed from Holes 5 and 3 of the 1941–1950 layout (Fig. 5-1).

Figure 6-7. Sixth green still visible in December 1987.

No. 15 was a formidable par 3: the elevated tee was in the woods to the left of the present 9th fairway, and a shot down the hill had to miss the trees on the right, more trees and the brook on the left, and traps all around the green, which was just east of where the pond on No. 18 is now. No. 16 tee was virtually on the site of the the present 18th green and the green was a little to the right of the present 10th green. It was a rustic, hilly course. Paths through the woods were rough, steep and narrow—powered golf carts, had there been any, could never have negotiated them. In places it was hard to get through with a two-wheeled pull cart. But it was fun to play.

Figure 6-8. From 18th tee, 1954.

Between 1950 and 1955 Jean Langdon, daughter of founder Wilder Bancroft, twice won the women's club championship. So did Lois Murray. Lou Barnard won the men's championship four times and John Carver twice. Over a span of thirteen years Lou Barnard was champion nine times, a record which still stands. (According to Pat Bucci, some years Lou chose not to play, to give someone else a chance.) In 1951 the women's Tuesday night twilight league was named "Wes' T.N.T." in honor of the professional, Wes White. In 1958, when Wes became grounds superintendent and was no longer the professional, he asked that his name be removed.

Ignoring what had happened in 1940, the Board of Managers in 1954 again tried to restrict women's hours of play on weekends. This time they wrote to other golf clubs in the area—Auburn, Cortland, Corning, and Elmira. All of the clubs, they found, had rules restricting women's play. The most stringent were at Elmira where women could not play on Wednesdays between noon and 3 p.m., on Saturdays between 11 a.m. and 3 p.m., or on Sundays before noon. Armed with this information the Board drew up rules for the Country Club of Ithaca and submitted them for approval at the annual membership meeting. As in 1940, the restrictions on women's play were rejected by a large majority. Bob

Figure 6-9. Clubhouse in 1954.

Farnsworth, who had started the whole thing in July by bringing members' complaints to the attention of the Board of Managers, reported that "not one single complaint about slow play by women has been received since August 1." Ithaca, as in so many things, continued to differ in this matter from other nearby communities.

About the same time (according to Wally Rogers) the Board tried unsuccessfully to regulate women's golfing apparel. "No shorts on the course," they said. The day after the new rule was announced, Serena Engdahl showed up in the shortest shorts she could find. Old Dr. Robb took one look at her and said, "Another half inch and she'd be in trouble!"

The Board may have been insensitive to the needs of the women golfers, but it was well aware of the bleak outlook for the Club. In 1953 it formed a Long Range Planning Committee, chaired first by Charlie Treman and later by Scotty Campbell. Realistic assessments by this committee of the financial and membership trends made it obvious that the situation was bad and growing worse, and that drastic steps would have to be taken if the Country Club of Ithaca was to survive.

Figure 6-10. Harold Reed, Jack Maloney and Jim Smith. Old Clubhouse, 1958.

Figure 6-11. Seventeenth fairway from tee, taken in December 1987.

By 1955 the Club's facilities were minimal for what had once been the leading golf club in the area. Membership had fallen every year since 1950, especially in family memberships. The golf course was short and steep and hilly and no longer very good—it couldn't compare with Cornell's newly expanded 18-hole course, opened in 1954. The old clubhouse (Fig. 6-9) needed constant repair and was infested with roaches—the ABC Exterminating Company had a standing contract with the Club for periodic treatments. Rats, too, were a problem, and by 1955 they were seriously damaging the property. The locker rooms were cramped and unsightly and so damp that any golf shoes left there for a week or more had to be scraped clean of mold before use. The tennis courts had long since fallen into ruin. The bar and dining room, though pleasant enough, were unsuitable for family activities; except on league nights, the dining room was little used. The membership had become a small and diminishing group of golfing enthusiasts.

The Country Club of Ithaca was close to the brink of dissolution.

Chapter 7

A MARVELLOUS RECOVERY

One asset the old Club did have was land: it owned almost 170 acres, 64 to the west of Pleasant Grove Road and about 106 to the east. In 1954 the Club took an option on the 14 acres belonging to J. E. Van Natta on Pleasant Grove Road, but the next year the Long Range Planning Committee concluded that the Club had more than enough land already and shouldn't buy any more. In 1955 this committee recommended to the Board that an architect be hired to see whether a completely new course was a possibility.

What the Club needed was a president who could see beyond the present difficulties to a different and brighter future, and who would spend the time and energy needed to realize the vision. It found such a leader in W. Robert Farnsworth, then executive vice president (later president) of the Ithaca Savings Bank (now Citizens Savings). Bob had been a member of the Club since 1933 and had held a variety of responsible positions, including that of Secretary-Treasurer in 1954–5 (Fig. 7-1). He became president in January 1956. Convinced that time was running out, he devoted a great deal of effort to what became a long, tedious, frustrating, but ultimately successful series of negotiations with Cornell University.

Cornell's initial offer for all the land owned by the Club was $135,000. Bob and his vice president Ross H. (Jim) Smith turned it down flat. The next month the offer was raised to $250,000, which was also rejected. Fairly soon some better offers appeared: at one point Cornell proposed to trade the Savage farm across Hanshaw Road for all the Club's land and to pay for building a clubhouse and course. The Club turned down this offer also, since it contained some unacceptable conditions, and for a time considered selling its land to General Electric or other interested developers and moving elsewhere. Cornell then offered two new possibilities: payment of $350,000 for all the Club property, or $315,000 plus 180 acres of land near the airport. After due

Figure 7-1. Bob Farnsworth. Courtesy of W. Robert Farnsworth.

consideration Farnsworth rejected these proposals as well, and the negotiations continued.

The seemingly endless biweekly talks with Cornell were held mainly with John Burton, then Vice President for Business. During this period the Long Range Planning Committee looked around the nearby area at fourteen possible sites for a new golf course, without success: sites that were cheap enough were unsuitable, and the few suitable ones were too expensive. In 1957 it finally became clear that the Club had best keep its land east of Pleasant Grove Road, add to it if possible, and sell to Cornell only the 64 acres west of Pleasant Grove. A golf architect, James G. Harrison of Pittsburgh, made a preliminary study which supported this conclusion.

In March and April of 1957 the crucial decisions were made. After a series of proposals and counter-proposals, Cornell offered to buy the Club's 64 acres for $350,000—the same amount it had offered earlier for all the Club's land—and to allow the Club to use the old facilities for up to five years, provided that if the Club did not develop its land east of Pleasant Grove within five years, Cornell could buy it all for $50,000. The University retained a right of first refusal on any future sale of the Club's land east of Pleasant Grove Road: the University would match any other *bona fide* offer to the Country Club, or give up the option. Cornell also agreed to give the Club two acres just north of Cornell's 17th green and 18th tee, with the proviso that if this land was not used for golf, or was abandoned for a year or more, ownership would revert to the University. The Club accepted all these, on condition that the Club would not be subject to Federal income tax or capital gains tax as a result of the sale.

A few members felt that the Club's land, if developed for residential purposes, would be worth a lot more than Cornell's offered purchase price. Someone proposed to the Village of Cayuga Heights that the 64 acres be rezoned "residential," which would stop the sale, but the Village Board defeated this rezoning proposal. John Burton sent telegrams, 49 in all, to the Cornell trustees, who approved the purchase on April 24. On April 30 the agreement was signed by the Club and by Cornell.

At the same time an option was obtained on 18 acres of land owned by Earl and Margaret Sharp, some of it east of Warren Road, for a purchase price of $38,500. Both the options— for the sale to Cornell and the purchase of the Sharp's land— had to be extended. The ruling on the Federal tax, expected in early June, finally arrived from Washington on July 18. To everyone's relief, it was favorable.

Bob Farnsworth now called the Board of Managers to meetings every week. Architect Bob Tallman, who had presented plans for a new clubhouse in late April, was authorized to put them out for bids. After consultation with golf architect Harrison, the present location of the clubhouse was approved (earlier it had been proposed to locate it near our present 10th green). Harrison was hired for $5,000 to make a finished course layout.

In September the following bids were accepted:

General contract for clubhouse: A. Ward	-	$113,426
Plumbing: Failing Plumbing Co.	-	9,971
Heating and Ventilating: Brewer & Brown	-	15,000
Electric: Norton Electric	-	11,480
Architect: Tallman and Tallman	-	9,000
Contingencies, extras	-	7,123
Total		$166,000

Also approved was Hanley Staley's bid of $39,120 for the pool. Its construction began in October and proceeded quickly, despite some problems with quicksand. Quicksand was also found at the site of the new clubhouse, but it was not as serious as originally thought— all that was needed was to lower some foundations.

October 1957 saw the submission of two course layouts by golf architect Harrison, but neither one was satisfactory. His proposed fairways were much too narrow. He was also getting very hard to deal with. Harrison was dismissed, and Geoffrey Cornish of Fiddler's Creek, Massachusetts, was hired to make the design. Harrison had wanted $130,000 to build the course, not including sand for the bunkers; Cornish estimated it could be done for $95,000 including sand, using local labor and field supervision. Harrison later submitted a bill for the $5,000 he had been promised; the Club paid him $4,000, on the basis that his designs were unacceptable. Despite some mutterings he made about possible lawsuits, Harrison was never paid the other $1,000.

By the time of the special membership meeting on November 18, 1957 the pool was in, foundations were being poured for the clubhouse, the Sharp property had been purchased*, and the old mortgage of $21,100 had been paid off. The Club had received $35,000 from Cornell, with another $100,000 to come by February 1958. A 35 x 180 foot strip of land east of the present 8th green had been bought from Samuel Boothroyd for $100. Review of the financial picture, however, showed that the money from Cornell would not be enough—that more cash would be needed to complete the ambitious project. With surprisingly little discussion the annual dues for family memberships were more than doubled. New classifications and fees were adopted according to the following schedule:

Class		Annual dues	Entrance fee
1A.	Families (with children under 21)	$230	$150
1B.	Families (no children)	210	150
2.	Senior single	180	150
3.	Associate (age 21 to 29)	55	150
4.	Junior (under 21)	60	—
5.	Clergy	60	—
6.	Social	130	—

For the first time single men and single women paid the same amount in dues. Nonresident memberships and student memberships disappeared. A limit of 350 was placed on the total active membership. To stimulate use of the dining room a minimum food charge was

---

*The Sharp property was bought on a 10-year land contract. The Club paid off its obligation in 1968; the deed for the transaction was recorded in February 1969.

Figure 7-2. Official opening of the pool, July 27, 1958.

adopted: it was $10 per quarter. The vote on increasing the dues was 53 to 2. But the proposal to empower the Board of Managers to mortgage the Club property for up to $65,000 generated a lot of acrimonious debate. The vote, although favorable, was much closer— 44 to 21.

In December 1957 the Club bought kitchen equipment from the defunct Monarch Restaurant for $785. The Thursday Night Hi-Lo Club offered to outfit the new men's grill. By the end of 1957 the Board of Managers had met 36 times and the Long Range Planning Committee another 15 times. Membership was down 31 from the year before, to 204, but in spite of everything the Club showed a net income for the year of $3,438.

Things were busy but less hectic in 1958. Lou Barnard and Jack Maloney, with former pro Wes White, were put in charge of the course construction which began in late March. Bob Farnsworth said that he met with Jack Maloney every weekday night after that to discuss progress and approve charges.

The swimming pool was the first of the Club's new facilities to be put into use. A 35 x 75 ft Paddock pool built by Hanley Staley and his men, it was opened on July 27, 1958 (Fig. 7-2). Several work parties of volunteers had helped install the fences and other accessories earlier in the month. (Fig. 7-3 shows a "sodding bee" with members working near the new clubhouse.) The pool was a welcome addition, much used by the members right from the start. At a late-night party on July 25, before the pool had officially opened, Karl Phillips, fully dressed, was bending over the water to see how cold it was, when Norma Weatherby couldn't resist the temptation. Karl found out how cold the water was— he was in it. So was Norma, soon after, and then several others. It wasn't meant to be a swimming party, but that's the way it turned out.

Figure 7-3. "Sodding bee," August 1958.

In August the Board of Managers met for the first time in the new clubhouse, which was formally opened with a dinner dance on October 15. Earlier in the year Paul McGraw, who had been managing the Lehigh Valley House in downtown Ithaca, was hired as Club Manager at a salary of $7,000. Paul had grown up in Ithaca and attended local schools. After World War II he studied civil engineering at Cornell for a time, then— on the GI Bill— had a five-year apprenticeship in steel engraving at the Ithaca Gun Company, where his uncle was a master engraver. He also had a part-time interest in the restaurant business; with another person he opened a small place on Dryden Road. From there he went to the Lehigh Valley House.

Wes White found that he greatly enjoyed building golf courses, and told Jim Smith that he dreaded the thought of having to go back into the pro's shop. As it turned out, he didn't have to. In November 1958 Albert Collins, after 38 years of service to the Club, had been dismissed as greenskeeper with a $500 gratuity. The Board of Managers, after much discussion, appointed Wes as Grounds Superintendent and named Patrick Bucci as the Club's fourth golf professional (Fig. 7-4).

Figure 7-4. Pat Bucci, 1958.

Pat Bucci was born on December 7, 1915 in Norwich, New York, and moved with his family to Brooklyn in 1920. He came to Ithaca in 1925 and caddied at the Country Club where Walter Bells was the professional. In 1929 he started playing golf seriously, using some old hickory-shafted clubs given to him by one of the members. As a caddy he was able to play the course on Mondays and to practice on the abandoned first hole of the original course. Soon he was good enough to be on the high school team. (One of his teachers at the high school was Bob Farnsworth.) A powerful hitter even then, Pat once drove a ball right through the practice net into the wall. As already discussed, he

Figure 7-5. Course construction:
    (a) No. 18 green, July 1958.
    (b) Pond below No. 10 tee, September 1958.

Figure 7-6. Izzy Speno (left) and Millie Rocker, August 1958.

later became assistant pro under Chandler, chairman of the House Committee, and in 1955 club manager.

While the new course was being built in 1958 (Fig. 7-5), the members had to content themselves with a patched-together course made out of the thirteen old holes west of Pleasant Grove Road. It was inconvenient but accepted in good spirit. Isabelle (Izzy) Speno beat Millie Rocker for the women's championship (Fig. 7-6). C. Stewart Wallace Jr., known as "Skip," set a course record of 64. Skip had won the men's club championship in 1956 and 1957, triumphing over Lou Barnard, and had won the 1957 Finger Lakes championship at the Cortland Country Club (Fig. 7-7). As the new professional Pat Bucci stayed in the pro's shop at the old clubhouse, and at the end of the season moved all the golf equipment to the new facility. The sixty-year-old clubhouse was demolished in June 1960 to make room for a Cornell parking lot.

The new course was formally opened on May 30, 1959, with architect Geoffrey Cornish in attendance (Fig. 7-8). He donated a trophy as a prize for the Memorial Day tournament, won that first year by Herb Broadwell. In those days the order of the holes on the front nine, in terms of today's numbering, was 1, 8, 6, 7, 2, 3, 4, 5 and 9. During the year Wes White and his crew put in some new traps and made other minor changes to complete the course. Golfers were asked to pick up stones from the 3rd, 4th and 8th (now the 5th, 6th and 7th) fairways. Powered golf carts were not permitted on the course that year.

Figure 7-7. Skip Wallace (right) defeats John McCartney for the Finger Lakes title, Cortland Country club, July 21, 1957.

On July 3 Fred Luhr scored the first hole-in-one on the new course, using an 8-iron on No. 7 (now No. 4). Skip Wallace set a course record of 70 and also beat Dick Neish for his third club championship. Flo Rowe won the women's championship in 1959; Millie Rocker was the runner-

Figure 7-8. Jack Maloney (left) and Geoffrey Cornish holding the Cornish Cup, at the formal opening of the new club, May 30, 1959.

up. Hyman Karch died that year and in his memory his wife Mildred gave a trophy for the low gross score in the T.N.T. League. Flo Rowe won that too.

The new dining room under chef George Katsikis was well patronized from the start. Sunday tea dances and other parties all proved popular. A dress code for dinner was adopted, requiring men to wear jackets and ties and women to wear dresses (no shorts). Manager McGraw used to keep several ties and jackets in the cloakroom for members or guests who appeared without them. In July Zelda Johnston was named head waitress; in August chef Katsikis resigned and was replaced by E. B. Miller.

The biggest social event of 1959 was the Diamond Anniversary Dinner on November 21, celebrating (a little early) the sixtieth anniversary of the founding of the Country Club. The cost of the "sumptuous dinner" was $3.50 per person. Dick Dunbar gave a talk about the early history of the Club, basing his remarks on an interview with Benjamin Sanford who was then in his eighties and living in Etna.*

---

*Fortunately Dunbar's notes for this talk were preserved— otherwise all information about the beginnings of the Club would have been lost.

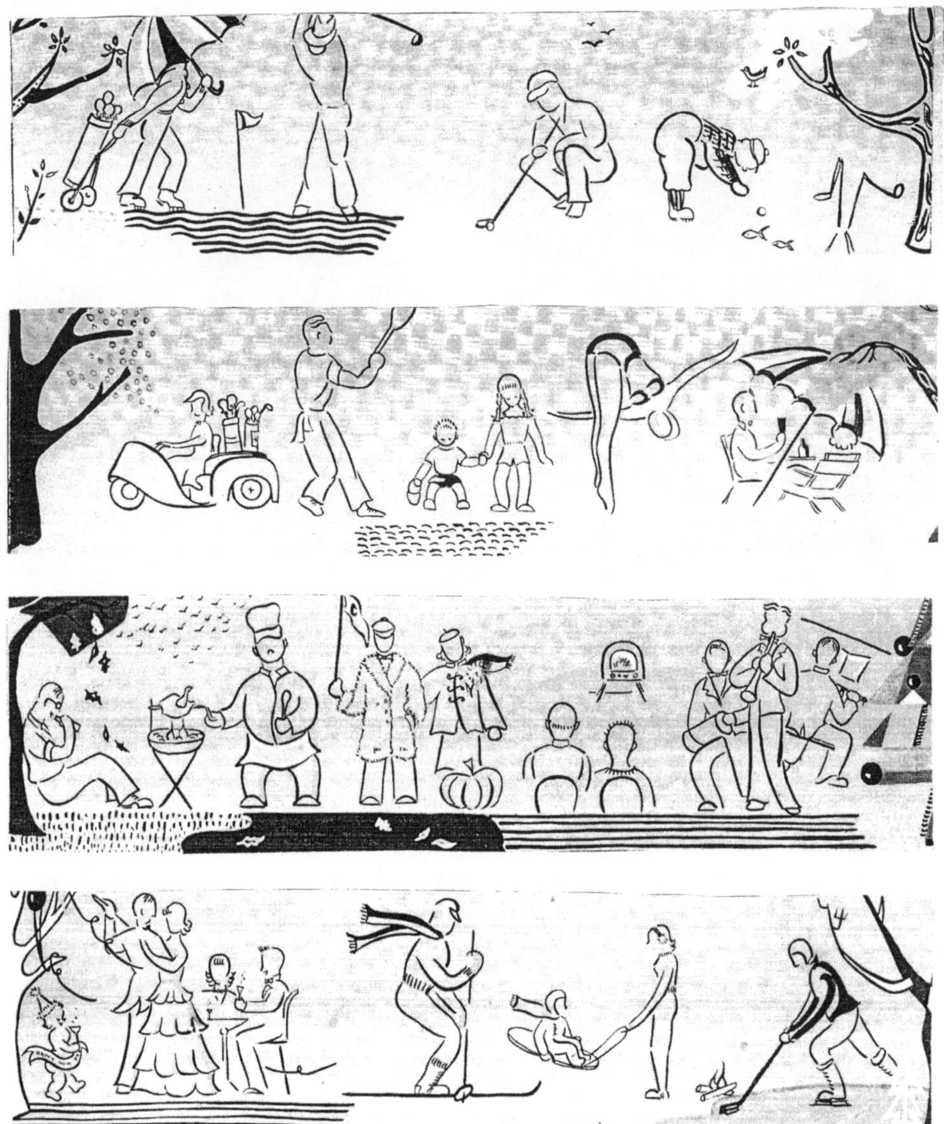

Figure 7-9. Dining room mural by June Dolph (from the 1960 Anniversary brochure).

In 1897 Ben had sold founder L. M. Dennis his first clubs and golf balls, and was later Secretary of the Club for a number of years. A short time after the dinner, Bob Earle hosted a television program on the Ithaca College station WICB-TV, in which Bob Farnsworth, Dick Dunbar and Jack Laux were interviewed about the history and activities of the Club.

Figure 7-10. Demolition of the old clubhouse, June, 1960.

Several members made substantial contributions to the new clubhouse. Furniture for the office and pool was paid for by William A. (Bud) Dillon. Henry Abt gave an 18-cup coffee maker, Harold Reed a scale for the men's locker room, and Fred Rowe a television set for the men's grill. June Dolph painted a mural on the north wall of the dining room depicting Club activities in each of the four seasons (Fig. 7-9); for this she received free membership for two and a half years.

The Publicity Committee under J. D. Laux arranged for newspaper and radio coverage of the Club's activities, especially the course opening and the anniversary dinner. It also published a souvenir booklet for the Diamond Anniversary and ten issues of the new monthly newsletter called *Chip Shots.*

The long decline in membership ended. By December 1958, even before the golf course had opened, membership had risen to 249, 45 more than in 1957; by the end of 1959 it was 295. Many old members returned and new ones joined, despite a another dues increase in November when dues for all classifications except junior and clergy were raised $30. Social memberships proved so popular that their number was limited to 150.

The old adversaries, Bob Hutchinson and Scotty Campbell, both resigned from the Club and moved to Florida. At the 1959 annual membership meeting, Bob Farnsworth was elected to his fifth consecutive term as president. Helena Kelsey was elected to the Board of Managers, the first woman to serve on that governing body.

After all the turmoil and disruption, the Country Club now had completely new facilities—clubhouse, golf course and swimming pool. It could justifiably advertise itself as a "club for the entire family." Thanks largely to Bob Farnsworth's leadership, the Club had pulled itself out of a desperate situation into one of great promise for the future. It had been a remarkable ten years, undoubtedly the most eventful decade in the history of the Club.

Chapter 8

SETTLING IN—1960–74

Settling in to new quarters can take a long time. The initial excitement quickly fades to a sense of mild satisfaction, which disappears in turn as familiarity increases. As anyone who ever bought a house knows only too well, the new place brings a multitude of unanticipated problems. Endless little things and many not-so-little ones call out for attention. And everything seems to cost more than it should.

At the Country Club, settling in took about fifteen years. The first phase, a period of warm satisfaction, lasted well into 1962. The members were enthusiastic about the course, the pool, the clubhouse and the many social programs, and membership steadily rose. In August 1960 there were so many social members that for several months no additional ones could be accepted. The Club's income more than matched expenses.

Gifts continued to enhance the new facility: an electric cash register from Karl Phillips and a coat rack from Dr. Wightman; waitress uniforms from Flo Rowe; a clock for the grill room from Pat Piacentini and rugs for the lower hall from Lou Barnard. Out of income the club installed a badly needed ventilation system in the kitchen in 1961, and an Alcor music system for "piped-in" music. A lot of furniture and equipment were added to the pool and snack shack—chaises, tables, benches, and so forth.

A major concern in 1960 was a proposed road which would run from Triphammer Road to Warren Road, in part along the edge of the Club's property. Architect Geoffrey Cornish was retained to represent the Club in the extended discussions with Cornell and the Village of Cayuga Heights—discussions which eventually came to nothing. The road was never built. The old Asai house needed renovating before it could be rented once again to university students. In 1961 the pool was found to be leaking, but this cost the Club nothing: Hanley Staley and his men repaired the leak free of charge.

The new fairways improved greatly as the golf course matured. Several traps were enlarged or moved, and new ones were added as suggested by

Geoffrey Cornish. A ridge across the 9th fairway, as originally constructed, made it impossible for players on the tee to see other players at the bend some 200 yards out. In the fall of 1960 this ridge was removed, lowering the fairway and eliminating the "blind" tee shot, making it much safer to play the hole. The bog to the left was drained and filled with the dirt obtained from removing the ridge.

After attending the turf-grass school at the University of Massachusetts in the winter of 1959–60, Greens Superintendent Wes White went on leave in 1960 and 1961, to work for Geoffrey Cornish as construction superintendent of a new 36-hole layout for the Summerlea Golf Club in Montreal. Lou Barnard acted as greens superintendent during Wes' absence. Wes enjoyed the work immensely—"I finally realized I'm an outdoor person," he said—and was offered a lucrative position at Summerlea. He turned it down, saying that he liked the Ithaca area and besides, he owed the Ithaca club something for granting him two year's leave.

In 1961 Pat Bucci attended a PGA Business School in Clearwater, Florida, to learn about bookkeeping and the general operation of a pro's shop. He returned and worked even harder than ever giving lessons, policing the course, helping with tournaments, and running a junior golf clinic. In October 1961 his wife Thelma started a women's wear department in the pro's shop.

Several members owned powered golf carts in the late 1950s, but weren't allowed to use them on the new course until 1961. The Club bought its first cart, a used one from a member, in 1961, and added two new ones in 1962. The Club still hired a few caddies, but nothing like the hundred or more it had in 1940. Caddy rates in 1961 were $3.00 for eighteen holes for a Class A caddy and $2.50 for a Class B.

In 1960 Skip Wallace set a course record of 68, which was tied by Dick Shulman in June 1961. Skip was club champion in 1960 and 1962; in 1961 Warner (Butch) Berry defeated him in a hard-fought match. In 1960 Skip also won the Eastern Intercollegiate Championship; Butch Berry won the same championship in 1961. The women's club championship was won by Isabelle (Izzy) Speno in 1960 and 1961 and by Millie Rocker in 1962. In 1962, for the first and only time, a joint Chandler-TNT League tournament was held with twenty couples participating. It was scheduled again in 1963 but cancelled for lack of interest.

In 1962 Fred Luhr donated a trophy for the Club's senior-junior membership tournament. It was first won by Lou Barnard and Harry Wasilchak. Flo Rowe, wife of T. Fred Rowe and five times women's champion, died in 1963; the next year a women's member-guest tournament was instituted in her memory.

Figure 8-1. Fred Luhr (right) and Cliff Brew, 1958.

Figure 8-2. Flo Rowe (right) and Millie Rocker, 1959.

The USGA made significant changes in the rules of golf in 1961. The penalties for out-of-bounds and lost balls were increased from "loss of distance" to "stroke and distance." On the green, cleaning the ball was henceforth permitted, as was repairing punch marks.

As the Club grew as a business enterprise its management became more formalized. At the 1960 annual meeting, Jim Clynes was appointed Legal Counsel and the past president made an *ex officio* member of the Board of Managers. Through an amendment to the constitution, club numbers and membership cards were issued to all members and dues were billed thereafter on a monthly basis instead of annually. Interest was not charged on overdue accounts, but after thirty days a member's credit was suspended, and after two months, according to the revised constitution, "the membership of such member and all his rights and equity shall cease and terminate." As before, the names of delinquent members were posted on a bulletin board in the lobby of the Club.

At the same annual meeting the dues were increased $30 a year for all classes except juniors and clergy, and the food minimum raised to $25 per quarter for family members and $12.50 per quarter for singles. Dues and the food minimum were all subject to a 20 per cent Federal excise tax. This special tax had been imposed on clubs during World War II; it was reduced to 10 per cent in 1962 and finally eliminated in 1966, twenty-one years after the end of the war.

At the 1960 meeting Bob Farnsworth stepped down from the presidency after five years in office, and was succeeded by Clifford Brew. In his farewell speech, Bob reviewed the recent progress of the Club and made some predictions of future needs and trends. Among them, he said, would be the necessity to move the Club again in fifteen years—certainly not more than twenty—because by then its land would be far too valuable to developers to justify keeping it for a golf course. He also predicted that the Club would go to a single class of membership.

In 1962 Manager Paul McGraw (Fig. 8-3) was made Recording Secretary and Assistant Treasurer and given authority to sign checks. Dick Dunbar, who had been assistant treasurer since 1944, was made "Internal Auditor," without salary but with dues remitted. Paul was named Assistant Secretary of the Club in 1965.

By late 1962 it was evident that all things did cost more than expected. The Club was operating in the black, but the net income was too small to provide for adequate maintenance, capital expenditures and debt amortization. A 40 per cent increase in dues was proposed at the 1962 annual meeting (now in early December instead of January as heretofore), but after prolonged discussion the increase was voted down

Figure 8-3. Manager Paul McGraw.

and the Board of Managers was asked to consider a single class of membership as proposed by John Harman. To meet current expenses the Board was authorized to borrow an additional $10,000 to be added to the existing indebtedness of a $58,000 mortgage and a $30,000 note.

During the second phase of the settling in, from 1963 through 1969, the Club tried the experiment of a single class of membership (almost a single class, that is; "junior" and "clergy" memberships were retained throughout the period). John Harman, chairman of the Social Committee, evaluated the idea during 1962 and concluded that by combining the family, single, associate and social members into one class of "senior member," with dues for all set at $25 per month, the Club's income should increase considerably. The concept appealed to family members because the large increase in dues would be avoided; it appealed to many of the other members because they would gain full equity with some increase in dues but no additional entrance fee. Another consideration, not openly expressed, was that a number of social members were known to be abusing their privileges and playing golf almost as often as the regular golfing members— for much less money.

The proposal was debated at a special membership meeting on February 11, 1963, and adopted by a vote of 55 to 31. As an accommodation, the dues for continuing single members (but not those who would join in the future) were set at $22.50 per month instead of $25. Dues for junior members and clergy were $6 per month, with no vote and no equity in the Club. The new entrance fee was $250 plus tax for seniors, none for juniors and clergy.

This single membership pattern worked reasonably well for several years. As expected, the Club lost 44 members in 1963, but the "equivalent full membership" (EFM), weighted according to the level of dues for each class, rose from 293 to 311. Membership campaigns were organized to increase the total membership to the limit of 350, but it declined instead. In 1964 it was down to 308 (EFM = 293.5), in part because Agway and General Electric moved their headquarters out of Ithaca. The managers sadly concluded that the membership was never going to reach the desired number.

In 1966 a return to multiple classes of membership, including social members, was considered and rejected. By 1969 the total number of members had fallen to 290 (EFM = 278) and voices were being raised protesting inequities in the system. They asked, "Why should the minorities—the single men and single women, the widowed and divorced members, and all the non-golfers—have to pay the same dues as a golfing family, which gets so much more out of the Club?" The mounting unhappiness among the members, coupled with the Club's falling income and rising expenses, made it clear that another change was, if anything, overdue. In May 1970 a new classification and dues schedule, with six classes of membership, was enthusiastically adopted. The experiment in single membership was over.

This period, 1963 to 1970, was one of rising costs and generally conservative management of the Country Club. Dues were increased five times during the seven years, a total of 70 per cent; even so, insufficient cash necessitated periodic borrowing to pay current expenses. In 1963 the Club's indebtedness was consolidated into a single 25-year mortgage of $100,000, at 5 1/2 per cent interest. The directors* discussed many new projects, even some major ones, but only a few relatively small ones were approved. Some were in response to emergencies—for example, the sewer repair and replacement in 1964 which cost $3,400. In 1963 an

---

*The "Board of Managers" became the "Board of Directors" in January 1965. At the same time, through an amendment to the Certificate of Incorporation, the number of board members was increased from six to nine.

enclosed storm entrance was added to the clubhouse and a causeway constructed across the creek on the 10th hole. A wind-deflecting fence was built in 1964 north of the swimming pool; so was the putting green outside the lounge, the golf shelter near the 16th green, and a storage building for powered golf carts. This last was financed in part by three owners of electric carts who were given free storage for several years in return for their investment.

A small fairway watering system containing 300 feet of pipe was installed in 1963 on the last half of the 9th fairway, where the soil was extremely sandy. In 1965 July and August were unusually dry, and the burned-out fairways prompted serious consideration of artificially watering the rest of the course. Wes White and others studied the possibility and concluded in their September 1966 report that irrigation of the whole course was "out of the question." A test well had shown that there was insufficient natural water on the Club property and purchased water, if available, would be prohibitively expensive.

In August 1965, when George Fry was president, the Club bought back from James Krizek three small lots along Hanshaw Road. The price was $9,500. In October 1966, under Bob Farnsworth, the old Asai house on Pleasant Grove Road was sold to Frank and Mary Gilmore for $13,000. As agreed in 1957, Cornell was given first refusal on this property. It turned down the opportunity, giving up its right of first refusal on this small piece of land—but not on the remainder of the 100 acres owned by the Club.

Bob Farnsworth had stepped down from the presidency in 1960 but had never left the Board: he stayed on in 1961 *ex officio* as past president, was elected to the board in 1962 through 1965, and made president again in 1966, 1967 and 1968. He and the directors proposed a number of forward-looking renovations and additions to the club: to expand the locker rooms; enclose the porches to increase dining space; improve the kitchen; air condition the clubhouse; construct tennis courts, a chipping practice green, and a driveway from Hanshaw Road; and build dressing rooms near the pool. In October they asked the members to increase the debt limit to $300,000 to finance the improvements. The motion failed by a vote of 44 in favor to 39 opposed (a 2/3 favorable vote was required for passage). Two months later a proposal to increase the Club's indebtedness by $150,000 was defeated by a similar margin.

So much for hopes and dreams. Some of the proposed improvements, however, were made piecemeal in later years. In 1969, for example, a chipping practice green was built on the former Krizek property and the clubhouse was air conditioned, financed by a special $50 assessment approved by the membership in August 1968. The driveway from Hanshaw Road was constructed in 1974.

The food minimum was dropped in 1964 when it was determined that it was subject to the 20 per cent Federal excise tax, whether used or not, and the Club had to pay the Internal Revenue Service $6,500 in back taxes and penalties. When the excise tax was eliminated in January 1966 the minimum was re-established at $5 per month. At the same time, leaves of absence with dues remitted were limited to a minimum of twelve months (six-month leaves had become increasingly common), and in August 1967 all leaves were abolished.

Paul McGraw was rehired each year as club manager with substantial increases in salary, an occasional bonus, and a gift of a life insurance policy. In 1966 he became a member of the Club's newly formed Executive Committee. In March 1967 he was awarded the title of "Certified Club Manager" (C.C.M.) by the National Association of Club Managers. Later he served as president of the Central New York Club Managers Association of America (CMAA), vice president of the New York State Association, and vice president and director of the National Association. In October 1967 he became the first General Manager of all aspects of the Club's operations.

Wes White continued as Greens Superintendent, also with yearly salary increases. Several lucrative offers came his way, including one with noted golf architect George Fazio, but he turned them all down. He did design and supervise the construction of several area courses: the 18-hole course at Marathon, the 9-hole Taughannock Golf Club course in Trumansburg, and the course at the Willard State Hospital.

Like the earlier golf professionals, Pat Bucci received only a modest stipend. Much of his income came from such things as lessons and sales of golf balls and equipment, and apparently the directors felt that he should not be encouraged to depend on his allotment from the Club's resources. Salary increases were few, although beginning in 1961 the Club did provide additional funds for a full-time assistant pro. In September 1967 Pat's contract was not renewed, ending his forty years of association with the Club.

A search committee chaired by Jim Clynes received fourteen applications for the vacant position from various parts of the United States. By December they had hired a promising young man, Gary E. Ellis (Fig. 8-4). Gary was born in Rome, New York, in 1941. He graduated from Binghamton Central High School in 1959 and went to Niagara University for two years where he played basketball and golf. A very good golfer, Gary turned professional in 1962, then served as

Figure 8-4. Gary Ellis.

assistant pro at clubs in Syracuse; Pompano Beach, Florida; and Westlake, Ohio. When he was appointed at the Country Club of Ithaca, at age 26, he was a member of the PGA and on the advisory staff of the Wilson Sporting Goods Company. The Club had to pay him a substantially higher stipend than it had ever paid a professional before.

In early 1963 the order of the holes on the front nine of the golf course was changed to the one used now (Figs. 8-5, 8-6). This relieved

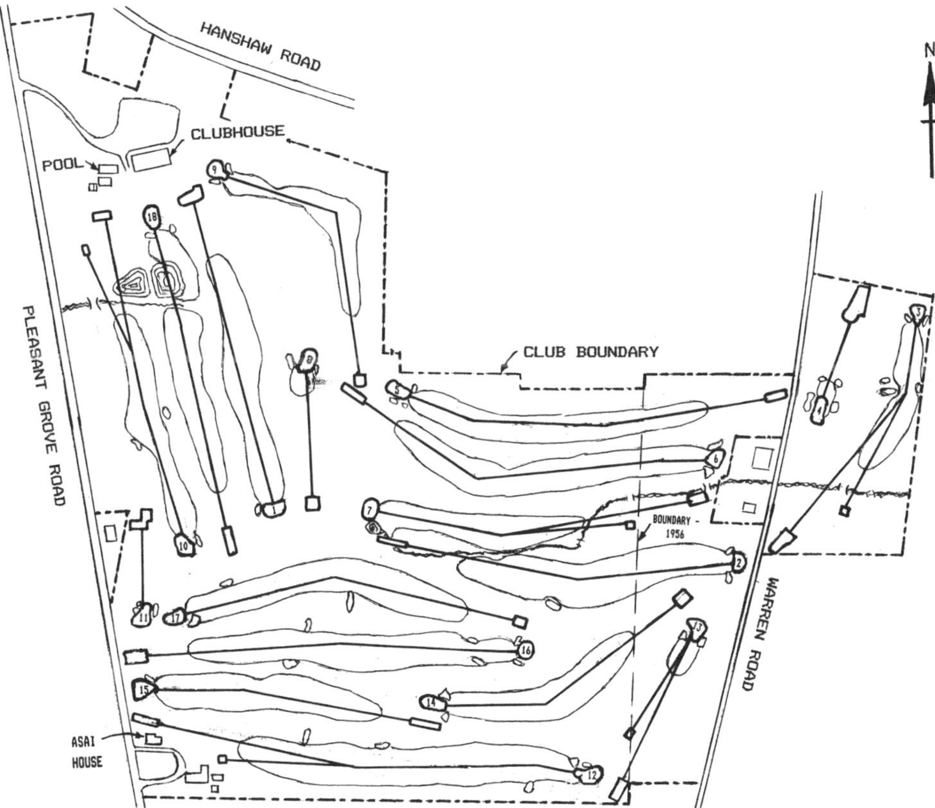

Figure 8-5. Course layout, from 1963 to the present.

the congestion that had occurred on the par-3 second hole (now No. 8) during periods of heavy play. Some traps were enlarged, some reduced in size, some removed. The 3rd tee was moved back twenty yards, and new ladies' tees constructed on Nos. 12 and 13.

HOLE	1	2	3	4	5	6	7	8	9	OUT	10	11	12	13	14	15	16	17	18	IN	TOTAL
CHAMPIONSHIP	385	410	340	150	490	480	390	180	365	3190	425	150	560	220	360	365	495	435	425	3435	6625
REGULAR WHITE	375	385	330	140	480	455	370	170	350	3055	410	140	540	210	350	345	480	425	415	3315	6370
MEN'S PAR	4	4	4	3	5	5	4	3	4	36	4	3	5	3	4	4	5	4	4	36	72
+ − 0																					
LADIES' PAR	4	4	4	3	5	5	4	3	4	36	5	3	6	3	4	4	5	5	5	40	76
LADIES' HANDICAP STROKES	6	14	12	18	4	2	8	16	10		9	17	1	15	13	11	3	7	5		

Signed...

Attested...

Date...

Please Register Guests before starting play.
Replace turf. Repair Punch Marks.
Smooth footprints in traps.
Hold your place on the course or let others through.

Figure 8-6. Scorecard, 1964.

The Club bought a few powered golf carts every year until it built up a considerable fleet. They proved to be a lucrative investment. For a time privately owned carts could be stored and serviced at the Club for $75 a year, but after 1966 no more private carts could be added and after 1969, when the Club had 16 carts of its own, no privately owned carts could be stored or serviced.

Between 1963 and 1968 Jeanne Grover won the women's championship four times. Skip Wallace won his sixth men's championship in 1963 and was Ithaca city champion for the fifth consecutive year. In 1964 Lou Barnard won his *tenth* club championship. In 1965 he came close to winning yet another one, but lost to Herb Broadwell in the finals (Fig. 8-7). The course record of 68 was tied in 1964 by Herb Broadwell and by Hal Hutchinson, Bob Hutchinson's son; on June 23, 1966 Dick Shulman set a new record of 66, with nine birdies and three bogeys. In 1967 Greg Abbott, aged 17 years and three months, beat Don Turcotte to become the youngest person ever to win the Club championship.

Figure 8-7. Lou Barnard (right) and Herb Broadwell, 1965.

The Hester Berry trophy for most points in the TNT League was awarded for the first time in 1967. It is named for one of the daughters of Wilder Bancroft, the Club's first president. She was the wife of Romeyn (Rym) Berry, manager of athletics at Cornell and a well-known local writer. In 1970 Ann Reynolds donated the Eben Reynolds trophy in memory of her husband, a professor of Hotel Administration and a keen golfer. The Clara Durland ladies' tournament was started during this period, in memory of the mother of Lew Durland, former treasurer of Cornell University. Clara (Fig. 8-8) loved golf and would play almost every day, regardless of the weather. She walked a full eighteen holes when she was eighty years old. For years there was no trophy, just the tournament, but in 1985 Clara's daughter-in-law, Barbara Durland Collyer, donated a silver tray as the prize for the winner.

Figure 8-8. Clara Durland in 1964, age 82.

In early 1966 another attempt was made to limit women's golf on weekends. The Golf Committee under Bob Wilkinson proposed a set of restrictive rules which were duly endorsed by the directors. They triggered the same reaction as in 1940 and 1954: letters of protest to the Board and a petition, signed by 47 members, to rescind the action. In May the Board eliminated the restrictions. In the July 1966 *Chip Shots* a note from the Women's Golf Committee said, "We are all happy to have our club privileges back again and the men will know, if they observe carefully, how really considerate we are and will be."

Not all male members, however, shared the majority's attitude toward women's golf. In July 1968 Rita MacDonald lodged a formal complaint with the Board of Directors about a particularly flagrant incident during the Women's Invitational Tournament on Saturday, June 29. Her letter reads:

On this occasion a threesome of men approached a foursome of women, consisting of two single members and their guests, emphatically stating that if the foursome did not allow them to play through, the members of the threesome would hit into them. The foursome agreed to let the threesome play through even though the foursome had themselves been waiting on number 11 tee for another foursome to complete their play and get off the green. When the members of the threesome passed by, they failed to observe the most basic rule of etiquette on the golf course or anywhere else—a simple thank you; instead one member of the threesome took the occasion to deliver a diatribe on the subject of women's playing on Saturday.

She concluded by asking, "Is one Saturday per year for a tournament too much for women to ask? Is it wise for members of our club to present such rude and uneducated behavior to our guests? Is a simple thank you for a courtesy done no longer in vogue?"

Figure 8-9. Pat Bucci coaching his youngest pupil, Chuck Carver, age 6, in 1962.

For a time it looked as though tennis, dormant since 1940, would come back as one of the Club's activities. A Tennis Committee chaired by George and Marcia Poucher promoted the idea among a group of tennis enthusiasts, and after two years of effort asked them for a monetary commitment. It wasn't forthcoming. A few years later Tom Bennett proposed that tennis courts be built on the newly puchased land next to Hanshaw Road, the construction to be financed by a group of 50 persons, mostly non-members, who would have tennis privileges only. The directors rejected this proposal, and appointed a new Tennis Committee to study the matter on behalf of the entire club. Plans were drawn and costs estimated, but other more pressing needs and the lack of available cash, plus the apathy of most of the Club members, kept the project from becoming a reality.

Activities which did flourish included the social program, with many well-attended events every year, and the junior programs: the golf clinics, swimming meets, record hops and live band dances. Darryl Waterman was a most effective Director of Youth and Pool Activities during the 1960s. Swimming and diving lessons for the youngsters were especially popular. In 1963 the Club had its first swim team which competed against, and usually defeated, other teams of teenagers from nearby country clubs—Corning, Cortland and Elmira among them. The Pool and Youth Committee was blessed with a series of able and conscientious chairpersons, often a husband-and-wife team. The 1965 report by John and Betty McManus gives a good picture of that year's successful program: holiday parties for the very small fry, splash parties, hayrides and dances for the junior and senior high-school groups, and barbecues for all ages during the summer months. "A group which needs special attention," said the McManuses, "is composed of college-age young people who are home during holiday periods; there is evidence of a resurgence of interest in this age group in social activities with at least a touch of formality and elegance."

In the world outside the Country Club, of course, college students were soon seeking almost everything but formality and elegance. The mounting social unrest of the late 1960s affected university campuses everywhere, including Cornell's, yet it had surprisingly little effect on the Country Club. Perhaps the "minority revolt" of single members and non-golfing members in 1969, which led to the resumption of multiple classes of membership, reflected the change in public attitude toward real or perceived discrimination. One event which was clearly the result of social disruption was the resignation of James A. Perkins from the Country Club in November 1969. The seventh president of Cornell, Dr. Perkins had joined the Club in 1963; in 1969, a few months after the occupation of Willard Straight Hall by gun-carrying black students, he left the University and resigned from the Club. Overall, however, the Country Club was an island of social calm in a turbulent ocean.

Figure 8-10. From *Chip Shots* cover, October 1968.

The third and last phase of "settling in," the five years between 1970 and 1974, was a period of general stability and growth. Jim Clynes succeeded Bob Farnsworth as president in 1969 and served through 1972. While he was in office the Club Counsel was Joan Harman. (Jim became Counsel again in 1974.) Wally Rogers was elected president in 1973.

Following the return to six classes of membership in 1970, the number of members increased so much that the limit of 350 was raised to 385, then modified to 300 voting members (senior family, single, and associate) with no limit on the other classes. A "retired" class of membership was established in January 1973 for members 65 years of age, or more, who had twenty years of continuous membership in the Club. "Retired" members paid 65 per cent of the senior family dues, set at $510 per year in 1970 and raised to $600 in 1973. Other members paid various percentages of the senior family dues and entrance fee, as follows:

Class		Percentage of:	
		Senior Family Dues	Entrance Fee
1.	Senior family	100	100
2.	Single	70	100
3.	Associate (under 35 years of age)	70	50
4.	Junior (18 through 20 years of age)	5	None
5.	Clergy	15	None
6.	House (clubhouse privileges only)	35	35
7.	Retired (over 65, twenty years membership)	65	—

A family in Class 1 had only one vote at membership meetings. Family memberships included all children under 21 years of age (as they had since 1958). Junior memberships were for young people in the Ithaca area who were not children of Club members. The basic entrance fee was set equal to one year's senior family dues at the time of admission to membership. After 1973 all entrance fees had to be paid in full upon joining the Club.

At first the increase in total membership scarcely affected the number of "equivalent full members," which stayed close to 280 through 1971. Income from dues changed very little. In 1973, however, the EFM reached 308 and dues income increased by about $17,000 per year.

Rising membership and rising income usually signal easy times for a social club. "A financially solvent club is a happy club," said President Rogers. And a happy membership is often favorably disposed toward proposed improvements, even expensive ones; in consequence a great many projects were completed during this period. Some were fairly small—a sauna and a new pool table in the men's locker room (1972); a new 3-meter diving board (1973); a security system for the clubhouse and pro's shop (1974). Some were unplanned, such as the emergency repairs to the sewer line (again) in 1970. In 1973–74 the golf shop was renovated, the sun room winterized, and the sun porch covered with an aluminum awning. Electric baseboard heat and new carpets and draperies were installed in the main rooms of the clubhouse, and the parking lot was extended to the east.

Biggest of all was the bath house project (later called the "pool service facility") to construct men's and women's lockers and changing rooms, new cooking facilities, and a screened-in eating area adjacent to the swimming pool. The membership approved spending $75,000 for this purpose in September 1973. Fred H. Thomas Associates were the architects.

Other major projects were considered and rejected. In 1970–71 a serious proposal was made to erect a large building south of the pool to house apartments and condominiums. In April 1971 the directors considered relocating the Club—moving would soon be inevitable, they agreed, because of the rising value of real estate. They visited two possible sites, one in Freeville and one north of Dryden, and decided that the present location was just fine.

Tennis courts were discussed almost every year, but nothing was done. Tom Bennett turned his attention to all-weather paddle tennis courts, and proposed (successfully) that they be constructed near the swimming pool. In December 1972 the members approved $25,000 for the new courts. The project, supervised by Frank Hanshaw, was completed in May 1973 at a cost of $19,900.

These expenditures were too large to be financed out of operating income, and the Club's indebtedness had to be increased. In 1972 the membership rejected a proposal to increase the mortgage to $225,000, but in September 1973, when funds for the pool service facility were authorized, an increase to $220,000, on a 25-year mortgage at 8 per cent interest, was unanimously approved.

In June 1971, because of a new Federal tax on "unrelated income," the directors resolved that all departments of the Club except the snack shack would be on a charge basis only. No cash would be accepted and voluntary tipping would be replaced by a 15 per cent service charge. This was facilitated by the fact that the Club accounts were being processed—had been since 1968—by an outside computer service. The rules were eased in 1972 to permit cash sales in the pro's shop. The automatic service charge was a continuing source of irritation to the members; it was eliminated in 1976. The "no tipping" rule, however, continued until 1982.

Wages and operating costs began to rise uncontrollably. New words appeared in the minutes: "inflation," "recession," "minimum wage." "Environment," also: concern began to be expressed over the effects of golf-course fertilizers and pesticides. In 1973 Wes White reported that the elm trees were dying, and the burning of wood and brush was no longer lawful. In 1973–74 there was a severe energy crisis following OPEC's manipulation of crude oil prices, and to save fuel the Club was closed all of January 1974 instead of the usual two weeks. An "Energy Problems Committee" under Frank Hanshaw studied the long-term effect on the Club of fuel restrictions and possible gasoline rationing. One idea to save energy was a windmill for charging cart batteries. Fortunately the crisis passed and things returned more or less to normal.

A continuing problem was the food service in the Club dining room—sometimes good but often mediocre. Complaints mounted. At one annual meeting Sam Peter said, "There's room for improvement in the food." Mitch Peter added, "When it comes to food my brother's hard to please!" Paul McGraw and Zelda Johnston, now Food and Beverage Manager, tried their best, but steeply rising food costs and frequent changes of chef made things difficult, to say the least. In 1974 there were four different chefs, with Paul McGraw filling in when none was immediately available. Fortunately, Paul liked to cook.

The practice range parallel to the 9th fairway was opened in 1972. From the start the Club rules say that "no privately owned golf balls may be used on the practice range or the chipping green." The Club provided range balls for practice at 50 cents per bucket. President Clynes was authorized to negotiate with the Club's neighbors for the return of range balls.

In 1974 the ditch across the 18th fairway, south of the pond, was covered over as recommended by Bill Norton, chairman of the Golf Committee. Bill also proposed to cover the ditch between the 2nd and 7th fairways, but this was never done.

Dick Neish twice won the men's golf championship during this period, as did Paul Leurgans. In 1971 Lou Barnard was runner up for the fourth (and last) time. Doris Wright won her second, third and fourth consecutive championships in 1970, 1971 and 1972. The women's Fairway Club was started in 1970, and a new men's golf tournament was added to the schedule—the Skip Wallace Memorial. Skip was killed in a tragic car accident in California in March 1969. This new tournament was dropped in 1973 and the men's regular best-ball event renamed "The Skip Wallace Invitational Tournament."

In December 1971, golf professional Gary Ellis resigned to take a position at the Pittsburgh Field Club in Pittsburgh, Pa. Gordon Richardson of the Vestal Hills Country Club, one of the applicants for the position in 1967, was asked to reapply. He was named professional in early 1972.

A few other events rounded out the "settling in" period. Deane W. Malott, president of Cornell from 1951 to 1963, joined the Club as a house member in 1970. Ezra Cornell and his wife joined in February 1973—Ezra is the great-great-great grandson of the first Ezra, the founder of Cornell University. A testimonial dinner for Bob Farnsworth was held on March 3, 1973. Paul Hahn, a trick-shot artist, gave an exhibition at the Club in June 1974. At the 1973 annual meeting, Bill Norton and John Lowery were nominated from the floor and, unlike most such nominees, they successfully defeated the regular nominees Ann Reynolds and Rita MacDonald. For one year there were no women on the Board of Directors, until Pat Mead was elected in December 1974.

Chapter 9

ONLY YESTERDAY—1975–1989

This final chapter about the most recent fifteen years is different from the previous ones. The events of this period are remembered to some extent by all but the newest members of the Club. The memories remain sharp-edged—they have yet to blur and fade and find their proper place in the historical background. Many of the recent changes are still being evaluated; some current problems are unresolved, some questions unanswered, some trends leading who knows where. This record of the recent years is partly history, partly a discussion of current events, and partly something in between.

In 1975 and 1976 the number of members increased, continuing the trend from the early 1970s. This may have resulted from the growing attractiveness of the facilities, the variety of membership classes, or the effectiveness of the membership campaigns. Whatever the reason, the membership topped 400 during four of the five years between 1975 and 1979. It reached an all-time high of 428 at the end of 1976.

A new class of membership, "Recreation,"was added in 1978; members in this class had the use of all Club facilities except the golf course. The "Nonresident" class, dropped in 1958, was reinstituted in 1979 but restricted to former members whose permanent residence was now more than one hundred miles from Ithaca. Recreation members paid 60 percent of family membership dues; nonresident members paid 50 percent of the dues in their former classification. In 1975 the question arose: Can the children of "single" members use the golf course? The Board decided they could not. In 1979, for purposes of membership classification, "single" was defined to mean "unmarried," including widows, widowers and divorcees, but again without giving golfing privileges to any of their children.

A large membership usually means financial stability for a club, but this was not the case in the late 1970s. It was a time of growing inflation and rising interest rates, both of which ultimately reached unprecedented, frighteningly high levels. In 1976, before the really big increases in inflation, wages were 40 percent higher than in 1970 and the cost of many other items had more than doubled. By 1978 the interest rate on short-term loans had risen from about 6 percent to 9 1/2 percent; by 1980 it was 15 1/2 percent and still going up. The unstable financial picture and the uncertainty about the future certainly contributed to—may even have caused—the multiple changes in management during this period. The Club had four presidents in five years, three greens superintendents and three general managers.

Charles W. Bell succeeded Wally Rogers as president in 1976. Charlie served for two years, and was followed by Mel Passman in 1978 and Scott McRobb in 1979, both of whom served for one year only. Under President Bell in 1976 and 1977, while inflation was still moderate, three ambitious proposals were considered briefly by the Board of Directors and rejected. One was to irrigate the golf course with a Toro system at a cost of $90,000. Another was to relocate the Club to West Hill on land offered for sale by Bruce Babcock. The third was to expand the clubhouse, roughly doubling the size of the kitchen and the dining-room areas. Architect Bob Tallman presented an attractive design for this third project, but the estimated cost of $505,000 was too high to warrant further consideration. The Club's debt was already big enough.

Rising costs put an end to most such dreams during this period. Despite the large number of dues-paying members, costs outran income almost every year. Dues were increased in 1976 and again in 1979; assessments were levied in 1975 and 1976 to cover the operating deficit. Capital projects other than for necessary maintenance were few—but those few were expensive. In 1979, for example, because of the energy shortages the clubhouse roof was insulated and repaired, and the single-pane glass doors replaced—an "energy package" which cost $33,500. A new large freezer and storage facilities in the kitchen added $20,000 and gang mowers for the golf course another $12,000.

The one major project involving completely new construction was the topic of a special membership meeting in May 1979, when Doug Armstrong, chairman of the Tennis Committee, proposed building two tennis courts at a cost of $35,000. Tennis courts had been talked about since 1962 and had been rejected at several earlier membership meetings, but this time things went ahead. The vote was 65 in favor to 25 opposed. The courts, composed of blacktop over crushed stone, were built by Paul Mancini and Sons, Inc. during June and July. The nets, sealer and markings came from Miton of Syracuse. A tennis consultant, William Gauger, reviewed the design and oversaw construction. The new courts were opened for play on August 7, 1979, and for the first time since 1940 the Country Club could offer tennis as an activity for its members.

In April 1980 the driveway from Hanshaw Road was abandoned. Where the driveway had been, a new chipping green and practice trap were built to replace the ones destroyed by the construction of the tennis courts.

Figure 9-1. The tennis courts in 1989.

After twelve years as golf professional and seventeen more as greens superintendent, Wes White decided to retire in the spring of 1975. He was given a testimonial dinner in early May; a few weeks later he and his wife Barbara were made honorary members of the Club. Even in retirement he didn't really leave his beloved golf course, but was retained as consultant to the new superintendent, Larry Albertsen.

Larry came from the Lakeshore Country Club in Council Bluffs, Iowa, where he was employed for over twelve years. His work at the Club was highly satisfactory, but unfortunately he resigned in October 1976

Figure 9-2. Practice chipping green, 1989.

to take a position at the Irondequoit Country Club in Rochester, New York. After an extensive search for his successor, the Greens and Grounds Committee chose Bruce Petrelli from the Milton-Hoosie Club in Canton, Massachusetts. Bruce was 28 years old when he started with the Club in February 1977.

These personnel changes were more or less routine, but those in 1978–79 certainly were not. By then the increasing inflation and the continuing rise in the Club's indebtedness, among other reasons, had led to tensions and dissatisfaction among the members and especially among the directors. Some of the newer board members felt that the management of the Club had fallen into the hands of a few—the "Old Guard"—and that it was time for a change. After a stormy Board meeting on November 14, 1978, General Manager Paul McGraw was asked to resign. He did so on November 26, after twenty-one years of service to the Club. Jim Clynes resigned as Club Counsel to represent him. Following some negotiations, Paul was given the Club's 1975 Chevrolet which he had been driving and the life insurance policy the Club had

Figure 9-3. Zelda Johnston.

taken out in his name. Zelda Johnston (Fig. 9-3) was named interim manager. Fred Beck became Club Counsel.

In January 1979 Richard Cartwright (known as "Hoss" to many of the members) was appointed general manager. Things didn't work out, and he resigned the following August. For a few weeks Zelda Johnston was once again the Interim Manager. In September Cartwright was replaced by George Vignaux, a graduate of Cornell's School of Hotel Administration, who had previously managed clubs in the metropolitan New York area, most recently the Tuxedo Club in Tuxedo Park, New York. With a new general manager on board things became peaceful once again— for a time.

Despite all the turmoil of the late 1970s, the various Club activities, especially golf, continued with great success. Doris Kostrinsky won her second club championship in 1975 and her third in 1978. Dick Shulman won the men's championship in 1975; Tony Treadwell won his first in 1976; Fran Benedict won in 1978. Chad Jacobson was junior champion four times between 1973 and 1976, and men's champion in 1977 and 1979. He and Steve Torrant are the only persons to date to have won both the junior and the men's championships. In February 1977 Vice President Len Kassman died unexpectedly. The men's Tuesday night golf league which he started was renamed the "Kassman League" in his memory.

In 1979 Mike Hulbert of Ithaca and his friend Joey Sindelar of Horseheads teamed together to win the Skip Wallace Invitational Tournament. Both are now among the leading tour professionals—Joey was third on the money list in 1988 and Mike is near the top in 1989.

In the early 1980s the financial problems of the Club reached crisis proportions. For some years the policy of the directors had been to finance capital improvements out of entrance fees, but these were never enough. Between 1974 and 1979 the entrance-fee income totalled $97,800 and capital expenditures $151,700. The difference was made up out of excess operating income—usually nonexistent—or from borrowing. By January 1980 the Club owed $90,000 to the First National Bank on a line of credit, and $190,000 on a mortgage and $15,000 on a short-term note to the Tompkins County Trust Company. Another $25,000 was needed immediately to complete the "energy package." Later in the year the First National Bank required the Club's indebtedness to be secured by collateral mortgages on the former Asai and Sharp properties, land not included in the long-term mortgage with Tompkins County Trust. By November 1980 the total debt was $379,500, structured as follows:

Mortgage, Tompkins County Trust	$191,000	@ 8 1/2 %
Collateral mortgage, First Bank*	95,000	@ 12%
Collateral mortgage, First Bank	93,500	@ prime plus 2%

*The First National Bank had changed its name by then to First Bank. It is now the Norstar Bank.

About $22,000 of the money at the prime rate plus 2 percent had not been used. All the mortgages would come due in December 1983.

Something had to be done. Debt service costs were now $54,000 annually, up from $23,000 in 1977. What they would be after December 1983 was anybody's guess.

In 1980 the dues were raised $10 per month for all classes except clergy, and the food minimum was doubled to $20 per month; even so, an assessment of $125 per member was needed at the end of the year. It was reluctantly approved by the membership, 47 to 46. In January 1981 Dick Shulman proposed to buy the 9th fairway and build condominiums on it, suggesting that the 9th hole be shortened and moved west so it would run through the woods. The Club, he said, could acquire extra land from Cornell University, adjacent to the 3rd tee. The directors found that this might be possible on a long-term lease, but overall the Shulman proposal was not considered attractive and was soon rejected.

In early 1981 President Eben (Bud) Tisdale appointed a Fund Raising Committee to find solutions to the problem of long-term debt. A number of methods were tried. The interest rate on delinquent accounts was raised from 18 percent per year to 24 per cent. With membership approval, dues for retired and nonresident members were increased in February 1981. (At the same membership meeting the dues for house members were actually reduced, but they were restored to their previous level the following December.) Also in February the committee unveiled a plan developed by Frank Speno for voluntary purchases of 6 percent bonds in denominations of $250, $500 and $1,000. It was hoped by this means to raise $50,000 within one year and $100,000 within two, and pay off at least one of the mortgages.

To raise cash early in the year, a ten percent discount was offered in 1979 for prepayment of the annual dues. Members who paid ten months' dues in January received credit for eleven months. This proved popular and did solve the problem of cash flow, but it cost the Club about $2,000 a year. It was discontinued at the end of 1980.

Spearheaded by Tom Bennett in 1981, an extraordinarily successful membership drive brought in 77 new members for a net gain of 30. Part of the success resulted from a temporary suspension of the entrance fee. The membership total, which had slipped to 384 in 1980, rose once more (for the last time to date) to above 400. The 1982 membership drive, again with entrance fees suspended, brought in 40 new members, but there were 83 resignations and membership dropped to 371.

The voluntary bond program was a failure. By August 1982 only $43,500 had been raised, and that would have to be returned to the investors if the minimum goal of $50,000 was not reached by the end of the year. At a special meeting in September the members approved the largest assessment to date—$300 per member—but rejected a complicated, multi-part resolution calling for a dues increase, reinstatement of the entrance fee, and the mandatory purchase of $1,500 bonds. The vote was 60 in favor to 83 against. The problem of debt was becoming crucial, and its solution seemed as distant as ever.

In October 1982 Dick Shulman offered a way out. On behalf of five investors, he made a startling proposal: he would buy the entire Club and its property for a price large enough to discharge the indebtedness. For fifteen years, while paying a yearly fee, the Club would maintain the golf course and other facilities, then have the option to buy back the property for an agreed-upon price. One suggestion was a purchase price of $450,000; rent at 12 percent for five years, 13 for the next five, and 14 for the last five; and a buy-back price of $570,000. The directors quickly rejected the offer.

Other suggestions were made by Board members to raise the needed funds: issue 10 percent bonds, for example, or sell the Club property west of the 4th tee and east of the 13th. Nothing seemed promising. To help in the short term, a special membership meeting was called for November, at which the entrance fee was re-established and family dues raised to $1,548 per year. The directors proposed that the food minimum be eliminated; instead, the members raised it to $30 per month.

The solution came in 1983, less than eight months before the mortgages would come due. On April 15 Dick Jacobson, chairman of the Finance Committee, offered the memership two carefully researched, clearly defined options:

A. Mandatory purchase of $1,500 capital certificates by family, single associate and retired members, and $500 subvention certificates by recreation, nonresident and house members, to be paid in a lump sum on September 1, 1983 or spread over three years at 12 percent interest;

OR

B. A 20-year mortgage of $330,000 at an estimated 14 percent interest, with an annual debt service cost of about $56,500. (This option was clearly less attractive from the directors' point of view.)

The presentation must have been masterful. Somewhat to the directors' surprise, Option A was approved by a vote of 95 to 47. Subsidiary motions were made and carried to amend the Club's certificate of incorporation, and to limit the power of the directors to contract debts at any time to the amount of money in the hands of the treasurer plus $25,000, and an amount equal to the balance outstanding for the purchase of certificates. By the end of the year enough certificate money had been collected to pay off most of the mortgages. A replacement mortgage of $125,000 (20 year life, 12 percent interest with a 5-year balloon) was secured to cover the period while payments were being received on the certificates pledged on a monthly basis. The financial problem had been solved.

With one serious crisis resolved, another appeared almost immediately. This one involved the members' dissatisfaction with the way the Club was being managed. For several years there had been growing complaints about the food. Bill Quinlan resigned from the Board of Directors in 1982 over a disagreement with Manager Vignaux. The directors worked closely with George, making it clear that the members had the ultimate say in how the Club was operated; even so, he continued to be viewed by many as uncooperative and overly possessive of "his" club. In mid-1983, by petition, the members called a meeting to air their concerns. Uninhibited criticisms were made of the poor physical condition of the facilities, the food, and nearly all other aspects of the Club's operation, including the lack of responsiveness by the manager and the directors to members' requests and suggestions. The Board was urged to take immediate action.

One item of contention was the Club's new computer, purchased in 1980. It replaced the outside computer services provided by Radex of Rochester from 1968 to 1976, and after that by the Tompkins County Trust Company. The Club's 64K E.D.P. office computer and accessories cost approximately $18,000. Many felt it had been an unwise investment; others complained that the manager spent too much time working with the new computer and not enough with the members.

Membership began to drop alarmingly. In the early fall more than a hundred members added their names to the original petition, expressing concern over "the poor management of our club and the resultant membership apathy and decline." (Not all members were of the same opinion, of course; more than a few expressed their complete satisfaction with the way things were.)

On October 3, 1983 the Board took action. George Vignaux was informed that his services were terminated as of October 4 and that he would receive pay for 90 days from that date. Immediately Dr. Tisdale resigned the presidency of the Club, saying that he could no longer support the philosophy of the Board.* For the third time in five years Zelda Johnston was named Interim Manager. Vice president Charlie Bell became Acting President for the balance of the year.

Throughout this tumultuous period the Club had a much happier side: its social programs and sports activities. For many members these were by far the more important concerns. They enthusiastically supported the frequent social functions: weekly bridge sessions; poolside barbecues, cookouts and clambakes; masquerades, annual events such as the Awards Dinner, the New Year's Eve Party and the President's Ball. Dances were almost always well attended. Many of the events were "theme parties": King Neptune's Buffet, for example, an After the Hunt

---

*He was the second president to resign over a matter of principle. The first was Professor Lewis Knudson in 1942 over the issue of slot machines.

Dinner, a "Couture de Printemps" Party, a Harvest Moon Dance. Several exchange parties were held with the Ithaca Yacht Club. In 1980–81 two parking lot "Tent Sales" of donated items raised some $2,800 for redecorating the dining room. June Dolph's mural (Fig. 7-9) was painted over at this time; the deteriorated condition of the wall made its restoration impractical.

Lunchtime fashion shows were organized at least once a year by Monique Richardson, Gordon's wife. Most of these shows also had a theme, such as America's Bicentennial; Mickey Mouse's 50th Birthday Party; "The Greatest Show on Earth—Ringling Brothers and Barnum & Bailey." The circus theme was used in 1972 and again eight years later. In the second show George Vignaux was the ringmaster, Charlie Bell the elephant, and Gordon Richardson the lion. Figure 9-4 shows pictures from this happy event.

(a) Bob Head playing the antique calliope.

(b) George Vignaux as ringmaster.

(c) The elephant (Charlie Bell).

(d) The lion (Gordon Richardson).

Figure 9-4. "The Greatest Show on Earth" fashion show, May 1980. (For more conventional pictures of Gordon Richardson and Charlie Bell, see Fig. 9-11.)

Winter sports at the Club had become significant by the 1980s. The Chandler Bowling League, founded in 1960, had ten to twelve teams and an annual schedule of matches. Paddle tennis was played year round. Informal skating on the ponds, sledding, and especially cross-country skiing became more and more popular. The Club provided skiing lessons and a "Ski Lodge" in the pro's shop, where winter sports enthusiasts could change their skis or skates, drink hot chocolate, and get warm.

In the closing months of 1983 a consultant surveyed the dining room procedures and Club facilities and submitted a comprehensive report with recommendations for improvement. Charlie Bell and a search committee interviewed candidates for the general manager's position and selected a young man, Mark H. Davies. In December the membership approved a dues increase to $1,680 for a family membership and a change in the food minimum from $30 per month to $330 per year. They also approved a new membership classification, with single, associate and retired members lumped into a single class, "Class B," all to pay the same annual dues. Reeder Gates was elected president. One proposal—to raise the number of directors to ten and have the Board, not the members, elect the president—was roundly defeated by a vote of 109 to 27.

The most recent six years of the Club's history have been unusually serene. Mark Davies (Fig. 9-5) took over as General Manager on January 1, 1984. He had been Assistant Manager at the Yahnundasis Golf Club in Utica, New York and had experience in restaurant management, a subject in which he holds an AAS degree from Morrisville Agricultural and Technical College. He immediately set out to improve the physical condition of the kitchen and other areas of the clubhouse. With him came a new chef, Andy Mulrennan, and complaints about the food and dining-room service quickly diminished.

Fiscal stability has been achieved by conservative budgeting and careful use of the certificate revenues for capital projects—all coupled with firm control of operating costs by the general manager. The total membership declined in 1984 to 278, its lowest level in twenty-five years, but soon climbed back up to over 300. As of September 1989, it stands at 343.

Policies for the disposition of certificate revenue were adopted at the end of 1984, as follows: (1) Surrendered certificates formerly held by resigning or deceased members would be liquidated as soon as possible, subject to availability of funds, with priority to certificates involved in estate liquidations; (2) a Certificate Liquidation Reserve would be established with a revolving balance of $10,000, to be used for prompt

Figure 9-5. Mark and Lori Davies and daughter Melanie. Courtesy of Mark Davies.

settlement of surrendered certificates; (3) any surplus revenues not needed to satisfy (1) and (2) would be used to finance major capital expenses. Initially, of course, there were no funds for liquidating surrendered certificates; all the revenue went toward paying off the mortgage. The balance owed was quickly reduced, however, and the final payment made in June 1986. The Club had its second mortgage-burning celebration* on September 7, 1986 (see Fig. 9-6).

*The Board of Directors
cordially invite you to attend
a reception
in celebration of our mortgage retirement
Sunday, the seventh of September
nineteen hundred and eighty-six
cocktails and hors d'oeuvres
four-thirty to six-thirty in the afternoon*

members only please

Figure 9-6. Invitation to mortgage retirement reception.

To the pleased surprise of some former members, payments on surrendered certificates began soon after. By October 1988 all outstanding obligations had been discharged. At present the Certificate Liquidation Fund contains the required $10,000 and excess revenues are available for capital expenses. Surrendered certificates, capital or subvention, are normally liquidated one month after they are received.

The years were serene but not uneventful. In late 1984 Zelda Johnston retired; at a reception on November 11, in appreciation for her 31 years of service, she was given a silver tea set and other gifts and an honorary membership in the Club. In July 1985 greens superintendent Bruce Petrelli was dismissed with 120 days severance pay; he was replaced in February 1986 by Peter Wittko, formerly superintendent at Green Acres Golf Club in Bernville, Pennsylvania, near Reading. Clarence Cleveland of the Board of Directors and Ed Bently of the

---

*The first was in November 1946—see Chapter 5.

grounds crew oversaw the course maintenance during the interim between superintendents.

Capital projects, funded out of income or excess certificate revenues, included redecoration of the lounge and bar area; new dining-room chairs; a partition to permit dividing the dining room into formal and informal areas, when desired; and—in 1989—a new roof for the clubhouse. An expensive new sewer line had to be installed in 1985. In late 1986 the office computer and software were replaced by a much more powerful IBM unit and the Arista "Country Club System" of software. New golf carts were purchased every year. The swimming pool was extensively repaired in 1987 (Fig. 9-7).

In 1987–88, yet another comprehensive study of watering the golf course ended with the same conclusions as the earlier ones: a complete irrigation system would be expensive, $250,000 to $300,000, and not enough water is available from ponds and wells on Club property. Purchased water from Bolton Point would be a continuing, escalating expense. In December 1988 the directors allocated $30,000 to irrigate Holes 5, 6 and 7 as the first part of a complete system, but it developed that the Bolton Point water pressure is too low and booster pumps are extremely costly. The project is currently on hold.

Figure 9-7. Swimming pool in 1989.

The current membership classification was adopted in 1984, as follows:

	Class	Percentage of Class A dues
A.	Senior Family, including children under 21	100
B.	Families aged 30–35*; single members 30 and over; retired members (65 or over, with 20 years continuous membership)**	75
C.	Families or single members, aged 25–29	50
D.	Families or single members, aged 21–24	25
E.	Recreation	65
F.	House	35
G.	Clergy	35**
H.	Honorary	None**
I.	Non-resident	Former dues less 270.90**
J.	Junior (aged 18–20, not children of members)	25

*Changed to 39 in March 1985   **No food minimum

There have been no junior members since 1979 and this class of membership will probably be dropped in December 1989. A special 6-month membership for Ithaca Yacht Club members was offered from 1984 through 1986, but no one applied for it. Corporate memberships were considered and rejected, on advice of Counsel, in March 1985. Leaves with dues remitted were briefly reinstituted in 1983 and two requests for leave were approved, but the next year the policy reverted to that of no leaves under any circumstances. A problem arose with family memberships, which could be in the name of either spouse or transferred from one to the other. Thus it was was possible to prolong the stay in a lower, less expensive classification by changing the membership to the younger spouse. In 1989 the directors ruled that after September 1 all new family memberships will be in the name of the older spouse. The certificate, however, can be in both names as joint owners.

In recent years it has become more difficult to define the term "family." What happens to a family membership after a divorce or legal separation? What happens when action is pending but not complete? Does an unmarried couple living together constitute a family? Currently the policy regarding divorces and legal separations is that the family membership continues for both spouses until legal action is completed, after which either spouse may apply for single membership, if desired. In 1986–87 President Fran Benedict and the directors wrestled with the problem of unmarried couples seeking "family" memberships. In May 1987, on a trial basis for the balance of the year, they adopted a policy that a single member could request the Board of Directors to designate another single person of the opposite sex (and his or her minor children) as the member's "guest"—provided the member and designated guest could legally marry each other. Dues would be equal to those for Class A. Two such requests were approved, but the proposal to make the policy statement part of the Club's bylaws was rejected at the 1987 annual meeting by a vote of 51 to 23.

Annual dues for Class A members were raised to $1,800 for 1985, $1,920 for 1986 through 1988, and $2,016 for 1989. The entrance fee, temporarily suspended in 1981 and 1982 and re-established in 1983, was eliminated in December 1985. From 1982 through 1984 anyone who resigned during the year was required to pay a penalty of an extra month's dues for each month during that year in which he or she had been a member, to a maximum of six extra months. This "two-for-one" requirement led to a great deal of contention. It was dropped in February 1985.

Golf during the 1980s saw Tony Treadwell win the men's championship four more times, in 1985–88. Ed Mazza won three times, 1981–83, and Bob Caryl twice, 1980 and 1989. Dom Cafferillo won in 1984. Lise Addis was women's champion four times; Sandy Speno, Bev Wyatt, Judy Dunning and Barbara Collyer each won once. Doris Kostrinsky won her fourth championship in 1989. (See Appendix H.)

In 1980 the Loretta Lewis trophy for the most improved TNT player was donated by Ronald Lewis, owner and operator of Morris' store in Ithaca, in memory of his first wife. The Jean Langdon Memorial Trophy was given in 1981 for the TNT low gross score. Like her sister Hester Berry, Jean was a daughter of the Club's first president, Wilder D. Bancroft. She was club champion in 1950 and 1955.

On September 4, 1983, during the Labor Day tournament, Ed Mazza set a course record of 65 with six birdies and an eagle. The publicity for this round states that Ed Mazza shared the record with Skip Wallace and Dick Shulman, but actually this was a new course record.* In June 1985, just after his first tour victory at the Greater Greensboro Open, long-hitting professional Joey Sindelar gave an exhibition at the Club for the benefit of the Muscular Dystrophy Association. His drive on No. 1 reached the top of

---

*This remains the course record for a member in tournament play. However, Bud Addis recalls that Tom Cleary, a non-member, shot a 65 while qualifying for one of the Skip Wallace tournaments, and that in 1979, when Bud was playing with Mike Hulbert from the blue (championship) tees, Mike shot a 63.

Figure 9-8. TNT and Chandler Leagues, 1981. Courtesy of Sterling Mac Adam.

the hill, about 300 yards out. He reached No. 12 green with a drive and a 2-iron, and on No. 16 he was over the green with his second shot, a 7-iron. He shot even par 72, with three 3-putt greens.

Since 1974 there have been more than forty holes-in-one by members of the Club. Bud Addis had four of them, including two in one year (1978). One of these, a 3-wood shot on No.13, hit the hole on the fly with such force that it broke the cup. At least three double eagles have been recorded on the present course: Harold Smith (Smiling Smitty) and Herb Broadwell both had twos on No. 6, and in 1978 Charles Becker sank his second shot on No. 16.

In 1984 the annual member-guest tournament was renamed in honor of W. Robert Farnsworth. Long-time member and director of the Club, president for a total of eight years, and negotiator *par excellence* with Cornell University during the land deals of the late 1950s, Bob was made an Honorary Member in December 1988.

The golf course (Fig. 9-9) has continued to mature. Trees, once small and spindly, have grown tall and easy to hit. Fairways seem narrower every

Figure 9-9. Air photo map of course area, April 22, 1980. Courtesy of Tompkins County Division of Assessment.

season, especially on the first nine holes. The battle against snow mold and poa on the greens, especially those shaded by trees, continues without end. In 1984 a professional trapper caught ten raccoons and eleven skunks living near the first tee and moved them to a distant home.

There have been few changes in the course itself in recent years, other than the construction of new ladies' tees and modification of some sand traps. The USGA "slope" ratings were determined in 1987 and 1988: for women it is 125 from the red markers, 131 from the white; for men it is 125. The handicap rating for men is 70.9. To obtain the men's rating it was necessary to install a permanent marker on each tee and measure accurately the horizontal yardage to the green.

The Club currently has reciprocal arrangements with thirteen clubs in upstate New York, plus one—very rarely used—in Elgin, Scotland (see Appendix J). The arrangements with the clubs in Cortland, Elmira, and Waverly (Shepard Hills) date back to 1921. In permitting play at Ithaca by members of a reciprocal club, the Club imposes the same restrictions on women—and sometimes men—as exist at the other club.

Because of its size and location, the practice range (Fig. 9-10) has been a constant problem. Range balls find their way to the 9th fairway or into neighboring back yards. Despite nets and fences along the property

Figure 9-10. Practice range, 1989

line, hundreds of balls are lost every year. Some have been returned to the Club, or sold back; others have been sold to a driving range in Lansing. The Golf Committee has tried a variety of limitations on the use of the range, with very modest success. What the Club really needs is more land for a larger practice range. If only it hadn't sold the property along the south side of Hanshaw Road, or had kept the 40 acres it once owned to the north...

Figure 9-11. Gordon Richardson, center, with (from left) Fran Benedict, Joe Bugliari, Charlie Bell and Keith Schaufler, 1988.

Gordon B. Richardson, the Club's golf professional since 1972, was born in 1931 in Winnipeg, Canada. There he learned to play golf and to ski. Originally attracted to the United States by opportunities in the skiing business, he gained professional golfing experience as an assistant at the Sunnehanna Country Club in Johnstown, Pennsyvania and the Vestal Hills Country Club in Binghamton, New York. To complement his summer position, in 1962 he became Ski School Director at Greek Peak in Virgil, New York. At the Club Gordon and his wife Monique have provided the members with superior services and merchandise, and instituted a number of innovative programs.

The tennis courts are well used by a moderate number of club members. Matches are informal; there are no club champions. "If there

Figure 9-12. Platform tennis courts and recreation center, 1989.

were a tennis champion," said a tennis-playing member recently, "it would probably be Tom Bennett." Platform tennis is perhaps even more popular than regular tennis, with several tournaments each year.

Especially during the last ten years or so, the Club has been subject to increasingly stringent and complicated governmental regulations. Acronyms such as IRS, EPA, and OSHA appear over and over in the minutes of the board meetings. The Internal Revenue Service recently adopted regulations regarding "outside business" by private, non-profit clubs. For example, revenue from dinners or parties for more than eight people, unless three-fourths of them are club members, may constitute taxable "outside business." All income from the use of the course and facilities by members of reciprocal clubs is "outside" and taxable. Any club with more than 400 members and which serves regular meals has to be especially careful or it may lose its status as a private club. A federal audit in 1988 found that the Club owed the IRS $1,238 in taxes on "outside business income."

The federal Environmental Protection Agency and the New York State Department of Environmental Conservation have limited the use of pesticides and other chemicals on the golf course. In 1988 the diving boards had to be removed from the swimming pool because regulations

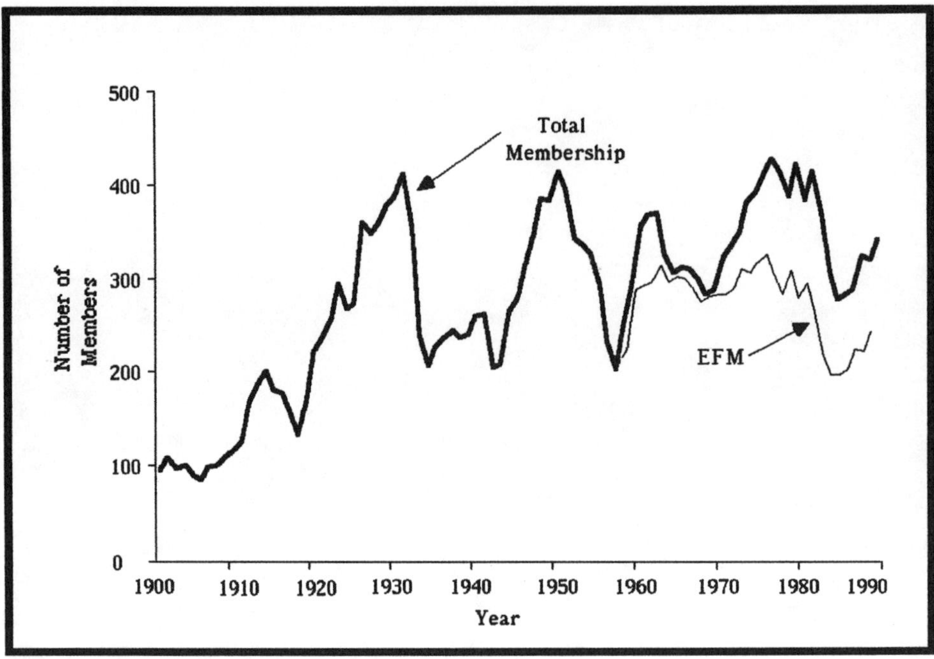

Figure 9-13. Graph of membership, 1900 to 1989.

by the New York State Department of Health for new pool construction were suddenly applied to existing pools, many of which (including the Club's) were not in compliance. A new board will probably be installed in 1990.

Perhaps most burdensome have been the Department of Health regulations regarding the kitchen and dining room. To comply with some of them would have been almost impossible. Fortunately the more unreasonable regulations have largely been relaxed.

In ninety years the Country Club of Ithaca has changed enormously from its very modest beginnings. Professors Dennis and Bancroft and the other founders, could they see it now, would be impressed and perhaps amazed to find their dreams so fully realized. The golf course has grown from nine short holes on Franklin Cornell's field to a demanding championship layout. The primitive wooden clubhouse has been replaced by the attractive structure shown on the front cover of this book. Other facilities—the tennis courts, paddle tennis, swimming pool and recreation center—have been added over the years.

Membership has fluctuated as shown in Fig. 9-13 and Appendix E. It has never been very large, as country clubs go; its all-time high was 428 in 1976. The average for the seventy years since 1920 is 317. The membership lists in Appendixes C and D contain 2,332 names, but many other people, members for short periods only, are not included. Based on an annual membership turnover of ten to twelve percent, it is safe to say that over 3,000 people have belonged to the Club during its ninety years.

The members, in the main, have been extraordinarily loyal and supportive. Only rarely have they rejected proposals, even costly ones, made by the Board of Directors, and almost never when the proposal was carefully worked out and well presented. The Club has also benefited greatly from its dedicated officers and directors and its outstanding managers, greenskeepers and golf professionals. A host of talented individuals made the Club what it is today.

The Club has become a substantial, complex business operation. In ninety years the annual budget has risen from about $1,000 to over $900,000. Dues have increased from $15 to over $2,000, but the entrance fee has decreased—from $5 to zero. (It reached $600, however, before it was eliminated.) The Club has been through some very hard times financially, especially in 1906, the 1930s, the mid-1950s and the early 1980s. It has survived two world wars, the Great Depression, and growing governmental regulation and control. It has accommodated to enormous changes in social attitudes.

All the signs point to a promising future. The Club is financially stable, with top-notch management and no long-term debt. Membership has risen steadily during the recent past and participation in the various activities has been excellent. It seems entirely reasonable to suppose that in ten more years the Club will celebrate its centennial and—at the opening of the twenty-first century—begin the long road through its second hundred years.

EPILOGUE

Ninety times the swift seasons have rolled over the Country Club of Ithaca. Ninety times in the endless annual cycle the golfers have enjoyed the golfing weather and endured the long wintry periods of anticipation. "Maybe next year I'll break 90 (or 80, or 120)..."

In its time the Club has had seven distinctly new golf courses and many minor changes in layout. Four of the courses were designed by prominent architects. The clubhouse has been destroyed by fire, rebuilt, demolished and replaced. It has been in four different locations, moving ever east and north as land was bought and sold. (Appendix F is a complete list of the land transactions.)

Every ten to twelve years or so, on an irregular cycle, the Club membership has peaked and then declined—sometimes slowly, sometimes precipitately. The most rapid gains in membership accompanied the opening of a new golf course or expanded facilities. Steep drops occurred during the world wars and the great depression, but also at other times (for less global reasons) in 1954-7, 1962-3 and 1981-4.

Rising membership and increasing income have often led to overspending, growing debt and sometimes near disaster. In periods of falling membership, strict economy—sometimes overstrict—has been imposed, to the point that the Club lost some of its attractiveness to new members. It takes careful yet far-sighted management for any club to balance its short-range commitments against its long-term needs, and to keep its members reasonably happy while so doing.

Change is inevitable, and must be planned for. Key personnel, sooner or later, will leave and have to be replaced. Equipment and facilities wear out. Social attitudes toward private clubs may well continue to change. Possibly the day will come when the Club's land will be valuable enough to warrant selling it and moving elsewhere, but if it were put up for sale the first option to purchase, by the 1957 agreement, would have to be given to Cornell University.

The early history of the Club is closely related to the development of Cornell Heights and the Village of Cayuga Heights, but even more closely linked to that of Cornell University. The Club was founded by two Cornell professors, and half the charter members were affiliated with the University. The first courses were on land owned by Ezra Cornell's son. Five of Cornell's nine presidents have belonged to the Club; one (Deane Malott) is still a member. From 1900 until the 1950s a great many members were Cornell employees—faculty, administrators, and staff—and fees from students made up a substantial fraction of the Club's income. This changed after Cornell opened its own 18-hole course in 1954. Today about ten percent of the Club's 343 members are employed by, or have retired from, the university.

A few things have remained constant over the years. Complaints about the golf course, for example: the condition of the greens, the rough, the fairways; the unfairness of the layout; the lack of golfing etiquette. The longing for watered fairways, for another, and the difficulty of providing them. And—periodically—the food. "Of all the positions at a private club," said Paul McGraw, "the most difficult to fill is that of the chef." A good chef is usually something of a prima donna, and few are willing or able to accommodate to the whims of the members. The manager's job is also a hard one, as are those of the greenskeeper and the golf professional, yet good people in these key positions are essential if the Club is to prosper.

Fortunately the Club has had many more-than-competent employees, some of whom have survived the demands put on them for very long periods of time. Walter Bells worked for the Club for more than thirty years. So did greenskeeper Albert Collins, dining-room manager Zelda Johnston, and golf professional/greens superintendent Wes White. Chan Chandler gave golf lessons at the Club for 21 seasons and was Club professional for fifteen of them. Pat Bucci was a Club employee in various capacities for a total of 26 years. Paul McGraw was manager for 21. Gordon Richardson, recovering from an emergency operation in August 1989, is completing his eighteenth year as the Club's golf professional. A list of the present employees of the Club is in Appendix I.

Zelda Johnston (Mrs. James Johnston, Jr.) is now Kitchen Supervisor at the McGraw House in Ithaca. She was a gracious hostess for the Club—and made what were probably the best pies the Club has ever known. Paul McGraw is retired and living in Ithaca; after he left the Club he was consultant and manager at the Elmira Country Club for a few years, and was later manager of Joe's Restaurant on Meadow Street in Ithaca. Pat Bucci, also retired, is living in Varna; his wife Thelma died in November 1987 after a very long illness. Wes White is spending his retirement years in Freeville writing a book on the craft of the early American gunsmiths.

Gary Ellis is now head professional at the Harbour Town Golf Links on Hilton Head Island, South Carolina, and Director of Golf Operations in Alaqua, a 1,400-acre development near Orlando, Florida. He has been National Junior Chairman, National Vice President, and President of the Tri-State Section of the PGA. In 1979 he was named Club Professional of the Year and inducted into the World Golf Hall of Fame in Pinehurst, North Carolina. In 1987 he was elected "Master Professional" by the PGA.

Of the 343 Club members in 1989, 48 percent were members in 1975; 20 percent in 1960; and 11 percent in 1950. Nine of the 343 were members in 1936, and eight in 1930. Two of the present members are children of charter members: Charles Treman, Jr. and Betty Wyckoff Balderston, daughter of Clarence Wyckoff. An Ithaca resident who remembers the Highland Road course is Margaret Thilly Raynolds, whose father, Professor Frank Thilly, joined the Club in 1907, when Margaret was eight. Two Club members lived to be centenarians— Professor Walter Willcox, who died at 103 in 1964, and Lucy Stephens, widow of Fitch H. Stephens, who was member in the 1920s and again after 1960. She died in 1989 at the age of 104.

Many prominent people have belonged to the Country Club of Ithaca. To name but a few, they include Andrew D. White, first president of Cornell, Minister and Ambassador to Germany, and Minister to Russia; dancer and movie star Irene Castle (Treman); artist Louis Agassiz Fuertes; inventors Everett and Frank Morse (automobile timing chains) and William Geer (airplane wing de-icer; balata golf ball cover). Also William Dillon, Sr. who wrote the song "I Want a Girl Just Like the Girl..." And a host of civic and academic leaders from the Ithaca area.

In many ways the Country Club of Ithaca is a very special club. It is fairly small and only twice has the membership limit been reached. (The limit was almost immediately raised in both cases.) It is financially secure— it owns its own land and has no long-term debt. Perhaps because of its origins it has always had a liberal attitude and a broader membership base than many other private clubs. (A southern "society" wife once made her husband resign from the Club when she learned that some of the members were tradespeople and store owners.) In one respect it is almost unique among private clubs: except for very short periods, it has never had rules restricting women's golf play on weekends.

Writing this history of the Club has been a rewarding and educational experience— tedious at times, but enjoyable. I will be interested to see what happens next, as the Club approaches its hundredth birthday. Another historian, however, will have to write the next volume of this history for the Club's bicentennial in the year 2100, for I doubt if I'll be up to reading the next 110 years of minutes of the Board of Directors' meetings.

Someone else can have that pleasure.

APPENDIX A

CHARTER MEMBERS OF
THE COUNTRY CLUB OF ITHACA

Family Members

Almy, Bradford	County Judge and surrogate
Bancroft, Wilder D.	CU Chemistry
Banks, S. Edwin	Lawyer
Beaman, Charles P.	Physician and surgeon
Beckwith, Mrs. Lucretia M.	Widow of Henry C. Beckwith
Blair, Mrs. Charles H.	Ezra Cornell's daughter Emma; husband a lawyer in New York City
Bostwick, Herman V.	Manufacturer of staves, barrels, etc
Boynton, Frank D.	Superintendent of schools
Carpenter, Rolla C.	CU Prof. Mech. Engr.; vice pres. Ithaca Street Railway Co., etc.
Comstock, John Henry	CU Entomology
Cooper, H. S.	
Crane, Thomas Frederick	CU Romance Languages; Dean of Arts & Sciences
Creighton, James E.	CU Philosophy
Dann, Hollis E.	Dir. of music, Ithaca Public Schools
Durand, William F.	CU Prof. Marine Engr.
Elmer, Herbert Charles	CU Latin
Fairbanks, Arthur	CU Acting Ass't. Prof. Philosophy
Finch, Dudley F.	Started Corner Book Store
Finch, Francis M.	CU Law; dean
Fuertes, Estevan A.	CU Civil Engr.
Gauntlett, John C.	Vice president Tompkins County National Bank
Gibb, Arthur N.	Architect
Halliday, Samuel D.	Lawyer (Halliday and Denton)
Hart, James M.	CU English
Hinckley, Henry L.	Cashier, Tompkins County National Bank
Hull, Charles H.	CU History; Secretary of University Faculty

Family Members (Cont'd)

Jenks, Jeremiah W.	CU Prof. Political Economy
King, Leander R.	Treman, King & Co.
Law, James	CU Veterinary; Director Vet. College
Lee, Duncan C.	CU Ass't Prof., Elocution and Oratory
Metcalf, William, Jr.	CU junior Law Student
Miller, Willam Henry	Architect
Morris, John L.	CU Prof. Practical Mechanics
Newman, Jared T.	Lawyer (Newman and Blood)
Nichols, Edward L.	CU Physics
Redfield, Henry Stephen	CU Prof. Law
Schurman, Jacob Gould	CU President
Stephens, Henry Morse	CU History
Stewart, Edwin C.	D. B. Stewart & Co.; New York State senator, 40th district
Stowell, Calvin D.	J. C. Stowell, Son, and Co.
Tanner, John H.	CU Mathematics
Tarr, Ralph S.	CU Geology
Treman, Ebenezer M.	Pres. and sec., Ithaca Water Works
Treman, Robert H.	Pres. Tompkins County National Bank
Trowbridge, Alexander B.	CU Prof. in charge, College of Agriculture
Van Cleef, Mynderse	Lawyer
Van Vleet, DeForest	Lawyer
White, Horatio Stevens	CU German; Dean of Univ. Faculty
Williams, George R.	President First National Bank
Williams, Mrs. Josiah Butler	Widow
Williams, Roger B.	Partner Williams Bros.; president Ithaca Savings Bank
Wyckoff, Edward G.	E.G. Wyckoff Co.; President Ithaca Street Railway Co., etc.

Single Ladies

Brownell, Miss L. S.	
Cornell, Miss Mary	
Drake, Miss Jane	
Frisbie, Miss Alice	
Gardiner, Miss H. L.	
Hall, Miss E. R.	
MacBeth, Miss Marie Louise	Ass't to warden, Sage College
Rankin, Miss Mary	
Rogers, Miss Isabel	
Schuyler, Mrs. Walter S.	Wife of Maj. Schuyler, US Army
St. John, Mrs. Henry A.	Husband president Autophone Co. and insurance
Swan, Miss Isabelle T.	
Thompson, Mrs.	
Valentine, Miss	
Wilder, Miss Bertha	

Single Men

Albee, Ernest	CU Instr. Philosophy
Andrews, Eugene P.	CU Instr. Archeology
Bennett, Charles E.	CU Latin
Blood, Charles H.	District att'y (Newman and Blood)
Borden, G. M.	
Bostwick, Charles D.	Lawyer; ass't to treasurer of CU
Carveth, Hector R.	CU Instr. Chemistry
Cobb, Fordyce A.	Tompkins, Cobb and Cobb
DeGarmo, Charles	CU Prof. Education
Dennis, Louis M.	CU Chemistry, department head.
Drake, Allen N.	Secretary R.T.Booth Co., Ithaca Street Railway Co., etc.
Durham, Charles L.	CU Instr. Latin & Greek
Foote, George Franklin	Manager of Sage College
Gaston, Charles R.	CU Assistant in English
Howe, Herbert C.	CU, President Schurman's secretary
Huffcut, Ernest W.	CU Prof. Law
Martin, Clarence A.	CU Architecture
McMahon, James	CU Mathematics
Merritt, Ernest	CU Ass't Prof. Physics
Moore, Alfred A.	CU Instr.
Mott, William E.	CU Prof.
Murray, Daniel A.	CU Instr.
Olmsted, Everett W.	CU Prof. Romance Languages
Prescott, Frederick C.	CU English
Shearer, John S.	CU Instr. Physics
Treman, Charles E.	Treman, King & Co.
Turner, Samuel B.	Lawyer
Van Pelt, John V.	CU Prof. Architecture
Williams, Roger B., jr.	CU Student, junior in Civil Engr.
Wyckoff, Clarence F.	President R.T.Booth Co., C.F. Wyckoff Co.

Sources: Country Club booklet, May 1900; Norton & Hanford's *Ithaca City Directories*, 1899, 1901; Bishop, *A History of Cornell*, Cornell Univ. Press, 1962; Sisler, *Enterprising Families*, Enterprise Publishing, Ithaca, N.Y., 1986

APPENDIX B

1900 BOOKLET

Board of Managers

Wilder D. Bancroft

Charles H. Blood

Louis M. Dennis

Ernest W. Huffcut

John H. Tanner

Charles E. Treman

Clarence F. Wyckoff

Committees

House
W. D. Bancroft
C. H. Blood
J. H. Tanner

Grounds
W. D. Bancroft
C. E. Treman
C. F. Wyckoff

Tournament
J. H. Tanner
A. W. Church*
L. M. Dennis
F. C. Prescott

Auditing
S. E. Banks
C. D. Bostwick

Entertainment
W. D. Bancroft
Mrs. Bancroft
C. H. Blood
E. W. Huffcut
D. C. Lee
Mrs. Lee
Miss Stowell
C. E. Treman
Mrs. Trowbridge
Mrs. Van Cleef
Mrs. White
R. B. Williams, Jr.

*A Cornell student member, Alfred Whiting Church, a freshman in Mechanical Engineering. He did not return to Cornell in 1900–01, or later.

CONSTITUTION

ARTICLE I Name: The name of this organization shall be The Country Club of Ithaca, N. Y.

ARTICLE II Object: This Club is organized for social and athletic purposes, and with a view to promote interest in the game of Golf, and the maintenance of links for the benefit of its members.

ARTICLE III Membership: Section 1. The members of this Club shall be composed of four classes: (a) Family Members whose initiation fee shall be five dollars and whose annual dues shall be fifteen dollars, and who shall be entitled to enroll, as associate members of the Club, all the members of their immediate families except children under fourteen years of age, and young men over twenty-one years of age; (b) Single Members, whose initiation fee shall be five dollars and whose annual dues shall be ten dollars for men and five dollars for women; (c) Associate Members, who shall be designated as such by family members of the Club as specified in (a) above; young men who are associate members on becoming twenty-one years of age may, at their own option, qualify as members under class a or class b but their associate membership shall not be renewed after they have become twenty-one years of age; (d) Non-resident Members whose dues shall be ten dollars per year; this class may include persons pursuing a course of study in Cornell University, who are in the City of Ithaca but are not legal residents of the city.

Dues shall be payable in March of each year. The Board of Managers may remit half the annual dues for the current year of members joining after September fifteenth. The Board of Managers may also fix the terms on which non-residents may be granted the privileges of the club for a shorter period than one year.

Sect. 2. Associate and non-resident members shall not be entitled to vote or hold office, and in the event of the dissolution of the Club shall not be entitled to any interest in its property.

Sect. 3. All persons whose names appear on the subscription roll used in the formation of the Club, are hereby made members of this Club and shall be considered as charter members, and may be required to pay the same entrance fees and annual dues as other members. Proposals for membership other than associate membership shall be made in writing by two active members of the Club and handed to the Secretary of the Club accompanied by a detailed letter of information concerning the proposed candidate; but in the case of students of Cornell University proposals for non-resident membership may be submitted by the Membership Committee of the Cornell Golf Club. Proposals for membership shall be passed upon by the Board of Managers of the Club at any regular or special meeting of such Board of Managers. Two negative votes cast at such meeting shall prevent admission, and no person hereafter elected by said Board of Managers shall be entitled to the privileges of the Club until he shall have paid the sum fixed for initiation fee and the dues.

ARTICLE IV Board of Managers: Section 1. The Board of Managers shall consist of the president and vice-president of the Club and five other managers who shall be elected from and by the voting members of the Club at their annual meeting for the term of one year, or until their successors have been duly chosen.

Sect. 2. A majority of the Board of Managers shall constitute a quorum for the transaction of business.

Sect. 3. The Board of Managers shall have power in full to manage all affairs of the Club; to make by-laws and rules and regulations for the use of the property of the Club and for the preservation of said property; to employ such servants and make such contracts respecting the management and custody of the affairs of the Club as may be needful; to formulate plans for the improvement of the grounds, and have charge of the laying out of the same; and to appoint, from among their own number, or among other members of the Club, such committees for the custody of the grounds, the entertainment of the members of the Club or otherwise as they shall deem needful to facilitate the carrying out of the duties of said Board.

Sect. 4. The Board of Managers shall make at the annual meeting of the Club a report in writing of the affairs of the Club.

Sect. 5. The Board of Managers has no power to contract debts or incur liabilities beyond the amount of money in the hands of the treasurer and the collectible sums due the Club during the year for which the said Board of Managers shall have been elected. Nothing in this section contained, however, shall limit the power of the Board of Managers in making additional expenditures, providing special authority shall have been given them by a two-thirds vote of the voting members present at any regular or special meeting of the Club, duly called as hereinafter provided.

Sect. 6. The Board of Managers shall meet at any time upon the call of the president or of three managers.

ARTICLE V Officers: Section 1. The officers of the Club shall be a president and vice-president elected by the Club at its annual meeting; a secretary and treasurer elected by the Board of Managers from their number at the first meeting of such Board (which shall be held on the day of and immediately after the annual meeting of the Club) and shall hold office for one year, or until their successors are elected and have accepted and qualified.

Sect. 2. In case of vacancy in any office or in the Board of Managers, the Board shall supply the vacancy for the remainder of the current year, or until a successor is elected.

Sect. 3. The president, or in his absence, the vice-president, shall preside at each meeting of the Club and of the Board of Managers. He shall, with the secretary, sign all written contracts and obligations of the Club and perform such other duties as may be required of him by the Board of Managers, and shall at the annual meeting appoint two auditors, who shall audit the accounts of the treasurer.

Sect. 4. The secretary shall keep minutes of the Club and of the Board of Managers; shall notify all members of their election, issue notices for all meetings, conduct the correspondence and keep records of the Club, which records and correspondence shall be open to the inspection of the members at all reasonable times; he shall perform such other duties as may be required by the Board of Managers or by the by-laws.

Sect. 5. The treasurer shall collect, and under the directions of the Board of Managers disburse the funds; he shall report at the annual meeting, or oftener if required by the Board of Managers, the state of the funds. He shall deposit the funds in one of the banks of the city to the credit of the Country Club of Ithaca, N. Y.; he shall send out bills for dues on the 1st day of March of each year, and at other times at his discretion.

ARTICLE VI Meetings: Section 1. The regular annual meeting of the Club shall be held for the election of officers and any other business, on some day in February each year at such time and place as may be designated by the president.

Sect. 2. A special meeting may be called by the direction of the Board of Managers or by the secretary upon the written request of ten members stating the object and the purpose of the meeting.

Sect. 3. A quorum at either regular or special meeting of the Club shall consist of those members who attend.

Sect. 4. Meetings both of the Board of Managers and of the Club shall be called by a notice mailed by the secretary to each manager or member at least twenty-four hours before the day of such meeting; which said notice in case of a special meeting of the Club, shall state the object of such meeting.

ARTICLE VII Resignation and loss of membership: Section 1. Resignation of members shall be made in writing addressed to the secretary and shall be presented at the first meeting of the Board of Managers thereafter, but shall not take effect until all outstanding dues and debts to the Club shall have been paid.

Sect. 2. Failure to pay the dues imposed by this constitution for one month after the same become due, shall deprive a member of his membership, subject, however, to the power of the Board of Managers to excuse default on subsequent payment.

Sect. 3. Members leaving the city of Ithaca for the term of one year or longer may, upon notice to the secretary, retain their membership and have their dues remitted for that time.

ARTICLE VIII Amendments: This constitution may be amended by the majority vote of those present and voting at any regular or special meeting of the Club, provided due notice be given in writing to each voting member that an amendment of the specific article or section proposed to be amended will be considered at such meeting.

BY-LAWS

1. Committees: The following committees shall be appointed by the Board of Managers as soon as possible after the general election:

1. Greens Committee	-	3 members
2. House Committee	-	3 members
3. Entertainment Committee	-	
4. Tournament Committee	-	4 members
5. Auditing Committee	-	2 members

To serve during the pleasure of the Board. Each committee shall make reports to the Board of Managers whenever required by such Board.

2. Greens Committee: The Greens Committee shall have charge of the links and golf grounds, tennis courts and other athletic grounds, and shall employ a green keeper and such assistants as may be necessary. It shall have power to order the purchase of necessary tools and materials. It shall select the Caddies who shall be admitted to the links and shall fix the rates at which they shall be paid. It shall have the power to draw up a special set of rules of play and also rules of etiquette and precedence to be observed on the links, which said rules when prepared shall be posted conspicuously in the Club House.

3. House Committee: The House Committee shall have full charge of the Club House and buildings and grounds other than those reserved for the Greens Committee. It shall order the purchase of necessary supplies for the Club, and shall have charge of the lockers, and shall employ and control all servants except those under the control of the Greens Committee. It shall establish locker charges and house rules, which same shall be posted by them in the Club House.

4. Complaints: The Greens Committee and House Committee shall redress all errors and abuses, and supply all defects in the matters under their charge. All complaints must be in writing and must be addressed to the Secretary of the Club and by him referred to the committee having the matter to which they refer in charge. In case any Committee shall fail to act after complaint duly made, the matter may be brought before the Board of Managers through the Secretary of the Club.

5. Entertainment Committee: The Entertainment Committee shall provide for and have charge of entertainments for the members of the Club, subject to such restrictions as may be imposed by the Board of Managers.

6. Tournament Committee: The Tournament Committee shall have charge of all Club Matches; shall provide a score book and may establish handicaps. It shall arrange and send notices of all club matches; provide for the award of prizes; select the players to represent the Club in Inter-Club Matches, and generally have charge of all competitive contests or exhibitions, subject to such restrictions as may be placed on it by the Board of Managers.

7. Auditing Committee: The Auditing Committee shall examine all books of account of the Treasurer and bills which were paid by him, and see that they have been approved by the committee or officer from whom they emanated. Prior to the annual meeting, it shall assist the Treasurer in compiling a complete statement showing receipts from initiation fees, dues, donations and entertainments, and expenditures of the various committees and officers for the year.

8. Appropriations: No funds of the Club shall be expended and no debt contracted for any purpose except for incidental and ordinary expenses of maintenance, unless the Board of Managers shall have first made the appropriation for that purpose.

9. Guests: No resident of Ithaca and no student in Cornell University who is not a member of the Club shall be granted any of the privileges of the Club unless by vote of the Board of Managers. Persons residing more than ten miles from Ithaca, may be received as guests for not to exceed two weeks at a time without charge. The names and residences of guests and the names of the members introducing them, must be recorded in the guest book as supplied by the House Committee, and the persons introducing guests shall be responsible for them and shall obtain cards for them from the Secretary.

10. Membership: Names proposed for membership shall be posted by the Secretary in the Club House for two weeks prior to action being taken thereon by the Board of Managers, during which time any member may file with the Secretary of the Club written objections to the candidate.

11. Miscellaneous: The rules of the game of golf of the United States Golf Association are adopted as rules of this Club, except as modified by local rules.

Members playing upon the links are requested to register in a book provided by the House Committee for that purpose, on each occasion when the links are used.

The Club House and grounds shall be open to members of the Club and their guests during seven days of the week, but no game shall be played on Sunday.

No member or guest shall give any fee or gratuity to a Club Servant, Caddie or Professional; nor shall any member pay a larger amount to a Caddie for his services than the price fixed by the Greens Committee.

The Board of Managers may, for such compensation as they deem adequate, permit a member to engage the club house for a private entertainment, to be held any evening after seven o'clock. Notice of the granting of such permit must be posted in the club house at least three days prior to the evening for which the permit is granted.

12. Amendment: The By-Laws of the Club may be amended by a majority vote of the Board of Managers at any regular meeting thereof.

ETIQUETTE OF GOLF

The following customs belong to the established etiquette of golf, and should be observed by all golfers.

1. No player, caddie or onlooker should move or talk during a stroke.

2. No player should play from the tee until the party in front have played their second strokes and are out of range, nor play to the putting green until the party in front have holed out and moved away.

3. The player who leads from the tee should be allowed to play before his opponent tees his ball.

4. Players who have holed out should not try their puts [sic] over again when other players are following them.

5. Players looking for a lost ball must allow any other match coming up to pass them.

6. A party playing three or more balls must allow a two-ball match to pass them.

7. A party playing a shorter round must allow a two-ball match playing the whole round to pass them.

8. A player should not put at the hole when the flag is in it.

9. The reckoning of strokes is kept by the terms "the odd," "two more," "three more," etc., "one off three," "one off two," "the like." The reckoning of the holes is kept by the terms - so many "holes up," or "all even," and so many "to play."

10. Turf cut or displaced by a stroke in playing should be at once replaced.

APPENDIX C

COUNTRY CLUB MEMBERS—1900-1919

Key to Membership Symbols:
F = Family member; SL = Single lady; SM = Single man;
NR = Non-resident; ST = Student; TM = Temporary

NAME	00	02	03	04	05	06	07	08	09	10	11	12	13	14	15	16	17	18	19
Adams, F. S.	-	-	-	-	-	-	-	-	-	-	-	-	-	-	SM	SM	-	-	-
Albee, Ernest	SM	SM	SM	SM	SM	SM	SM	SM	SM	SM	SM	F	F	F	-	-	-	-	-
Albert, Mrs. C. D.	-	-	-	-	-	-	-	-	-	-	-	-	SL	SL	-	-	-	-	-
Alexander, D. C., Jr.	-	-	-	-	-	-	-	-	-	-	-	-	SM	SM	-	-	-	-	-
Alexander, Miss Katherine	-	-	-	-	-	-	-	-	SL	SL	SL	SL	SL	SL	SL	SL	SL	SL	SL
Alexander, Miss Virginia W.	-	-	-	-	-	-	-	SL	-	-	-	-	-	-	-	-	-	-	-
Allen, R. G.	-	F	F	F	-	-	-	-	-	-	-	-	-	-	-	-	-	-	-
Almy, Bradford	F	F	F	-	-	-	-	-	-	-	-	-	-	-	-	-	-	-	-
Anderson, E. I. A.	-	-	-	SM	-	-	-	-	-	-	-	-	-	-	-	-	-	-	-
Andrews, Eugene P.	SM	SM	SM	SM	SM	SM	SM	-	-	-	-	SM	SM	SM	SM	SM	SM	SM	F
Atkinson, George F.	-	-	-	-	-	-	-	-	-	-	-	-	-	-	SM	SM	SM	-	-
Atkinson, Ruth V.	-	-	-	-	-	-	-	-	-	-	-	-	-	-	-	-	SL	-	-
Atwater, Frieda	-	-	-	-	-	-	-	-	-	-	-	-	SL	SL	-	-	-	-	-
Austen, Willard H.	-	-	-	-	-	-	-	F	-	-	-	-	-	-	-	-	-	-	-
Bailey, Austin	-	-	-	-	-	-	-	-	-	-	-	-	-	-	-	-	-	-	SM
Baker, G. R.	-	-	-	-	-	-	-	-	-	-	-	-	-	-	-	F	F	F	-
Baker, John W.	-	-	-	-	-	-	-	-	-	-	-	-	-	-	-	-	-	SM	F
Bancroft, Wilder D.	F	F	F	F	F	F	F	F	F	F	F	F	F	F	F	F	F	F	F
Banks, Morris F.	-	-	-	-	-	-	-	-	-	-	F	F	F	F	F	F	F	-	-
Banks, S. Edwin	F	F	F	F	-	-	-	-	-	-	-	F	F	F	F	F	F	-	-
Barbour, Mrs. Elizabeth H.	-	-	-	-	-	-	-	-	SL	SL	SL	SL	SL	-	-	-	-	-	-
Bargun, Ruth	-	-	-	-	SL	-	-	-	-	-	-	-	-	-	-	-	-	-	-
Barr, J. H.	-	F	-	-	-	-	-	-	-	-	-	-	-	-	-	-	-	-	-
Barr, Joseph S.	-	-	-	-	-	-	-	-	-	-	-	-	-	-	-	-	-	-	SM
Barr, Mrs.	-	-	SL	-	-	-	-	-	-	-	-	-	-	-	-	-	-	-	-
Barsham, E. N.	-	-	-	-	-	-	-	-	-	-	-	-	-	F	F	F	F	-	-
Barton, Frank A.	-	-	-	F	F	F	F	-	-	-	-	-	-	-	-	-	-	F	F
Bates, Laura	-	-	-	-	-	-	-	-	-	-	-	-	-	-	SL	-	-	-	-
Bates, W. J.	-	-	-	-	-	-	-	-	-	-	-	-	F	F	-	-	-	-	-
Beaman, Charles P.	F	F	F	F	F	F	F	F	F	-	-	-	-	-	-	-	-	-	-
Beaman, Mrs. Charles P.	-	-	-	-	-	-	-	-	-	-	-	-	F	F	F	F	F	-	-
Beardsley, D. P.	-	-	-	-	-	-	-	-	-	-	-	-	-	-	-	SM	F	-	-
Beckwith, Mrs. Lucretia M.	F	SL	-	-	-	-	-	-	-	-	-	-	-	-	-	-	-	-	-
Bedell, Frederick	-	F	F	F	F	SM	SM	F	F	-	F	F	F	F	F	F	F	F	F
Bement, Louis C.	-	-	-	-	-	-	-	-	SM	SM	F	F	F	F	F	F	F	F	F
Benjamin, Earl W.	-	-	-	-	-	-	-	-	-	-	-	-	-	-	-	-	F	F	-
Bennett, Charles E.	SM	SM	SM	SM	SM	SM	-	-	-	-	-	-	-	-	-	-	-	-	-
Bentley, G. M.	-	-	SM	SM	-	-	-	-	-	-	-	-	-	-	-	-	-	-	-
Bentley, John, Jr.	-	-	-	-	-	-	-	-	-	-	-	-	-	-	-	-	-	F	-
Bergen, John R.	-	-	-	-	-	-	-	F	F	F	F	-	-	SM	-	-	-	-	-
Bergen, Ruth	-	-	-	-	-	-	SL	-	-	-	-	-	SL	-	-	-	-	-	-
Bernstein, Isaac K.	-	-	-	-	-	-	-	-	-	-	-	F	F	F	-	-	-	-	-
Berry, Romeyn	-	-	-	-	-	-	-	-	-	-	-	-	-	-	-	-	-	-	F
Bingham, L.	-	-	-	-	-	-	-	-	-	-	-	-	-	-	SM	SM	SM	-	-
Bishop, Miss Eva E.	-	SL	SL	SL	-	-	-	-	-	SL	SL	SL	SL	SL	-	-	-	-	-
Blackstone, J. H.	-	-	-	-	-	-	-	-	-	-	-	-	-	-	F	-	-	-	-
Blair, John H.	-	SM	-	SM	SM	SM	SM	SM	SM	-	F	F	F	SM	-	-	-	-	-
Blair, Mrs. Charles H.	F	SL	-	SL	SL	SL	SL	SL	SL	-	-	-	SL	-	-	-	-	-	-
Blair, W. D.	-	-	SM	-	-	-	-	-	-	-	-	-	-	-	-	-	-	-	-
Blaker, E.	-	-	-	-	-	-	-	-	-	-	-	F	-	-	-	-	-	-	-
Blood, Charles H.	SM	SM	SM	SM	SM	F	F	F	F	F	F	F	F	F	F	F	F	F	F
Bodley, Mrs. C. F.	-	-	-	-	-	-	-	-	-	-	-	-	-	-	-	SL	SL	SL	SL
Bogert, George G.	-	-	-	-	-	-	-	-	-	-	-	-	-	SM	SM	SM	-	-	F
Borden, G. M.	SM	SM	-	-	-	-	-	-	-	-	-	-	-	-	-	-	-	-	-

NAME	00	02	03	04	05	06	07	08	09	10	11	12	13	14	15	16	17	18	19
Bossange, P. R.	-	-	-	-	-	-	-	-	-	-	-	-	F	F	F	-	-	-	-
Bostwick, Charles D.	SM	-	-	F	F	F	F	F	F	-	-	-	-	-	F	F	F	F	F
Bostwick, Edward H.	-	-	-	-	-	-	-	-	-	F	F	F	F	F	-	-	-	-	-
Bostwick, Herman V.	F	F	F	F	F	F	F	-	-	-	-	-	-	-	-	-	-	-	-
Bostwick, Miss Ada T.	-	-	-	-	-	-	-	-	-	-	-	-	-	-	-	-	-	-	SL
Bostwick, Miss Sarah	-	-	-	-	-	-	-	SL	SL	SL	SL	SL	SL	SL	-	SL	SL	-	SL
Bosworth, Frank H.	-	-	-	-	-	-	-	-	-	-	-	-	-	-	-	-	-	-	F
Boynton, Frank D.	F	F	F	-	-	-	F	F	F	F	F	F	F	F	F	-	F	F	F
Brauner, Olaf M.	-	F	F	F	F	F	F	F	F	F	F	F	F	F	F	F	F	F	F
Breckenridge, Mrs. R. W.	-	-	-	-	-	-	-	-	-	-	-	-	-	-	F	SL	SL	-	-
Bretz, Julian P.	-	-	-	-	-	-	-	-	SM	SM	-	-	-	SM	SM	SM	SM	SM	SM
Brooks, Alice	-	-	-	-	-	-	-	-	-	-	-	-	-	SL	-	-	-	-	-
Brooks, F. W.	-	-	-	-	-	-	-	-	-	-	-	F	F	-	-	-	-	-	-
Brooks, Miss Carolyn	-	-	-	-	-	-	-	-	-	-	-	-	-	-	-	-	-	SL	SL
Brooks, Mrs. John G.	-	-	-	-	-	-	-	-	-	-	-	-	-	-	-	-	-	-	SL
Brown, G. G.	-	-	-	-	-	-	-	-	-	-	-	-	-	-	-	F	-	-	-
Brown, G. H.	-	-	-	-	-	-	-	-	-	-	-	-	-	-	SM	SM	-	-	-
Brown, Samuel A. R.	-	-	-	-	F	F	F	-	-	-	-	-	-	-	-	-	-	-	-
Brownell, Miss L. S.	SL	-	-	-	-	-	-	-	-	-	-	-	-	-	-	-	-	-	-
Bruce, Miss Margaret	-	SL	SL	-	-	-	-	-	-	-	-	-	-	-	-	-	-	-	-
Bryant, Laura	-	-	-	-	-	-	-	-	-	-	-	-	-	-	-	SL	SL	SL	SL
Buckingham, Charles L.	-	SM	SM	-	-	-	-	-	-	-	-	-	-	-	-	-	-	-	-
Bull, Edward L.	-	-	-	-	-	-	-	-	-	-	-	-	-	-	-	-	-	-	F
Bull, Lieut. H. T.	-	-	-	-	-	-	-	-	-	-	-	-	F	F	F	-	-	-	-
Burdick, Charles K.	-	-	-	-	-	-	-	-	-	-	-	-	-	-	-	F	-	-	F
Burnham, Leroy P.	-	-	-	-	-	-	-	-	-	-	-	-	-	SM	SM	SM	SM	-	F
Caldwell, Mrs. F. E.	-	-	-	-	-	-	-	-	-	-	-	-	-	-	F	F	-	-	-
Campbell, Robert A.	-	-	-	-	-	-	-	-	-	-	-	-	-	-	SM	F	F	F	F
Carney, Margaret	-	-	-	SL	-	-	-	-	-	-	-	-	-	-	-	-	-	-	-
Carpenter, H. G.	-	-	-	-	-	-	-	-	-	-	-	-	F	-	-	-	-	-	-
Carpenter, Rolla C.	F	F	F	F	F	-	-	-	-	-	-	-	-	-	-	-	-	-	-
Carr, Lorna D.	-	-	-	-	-	-	-	-	-	-	-	-	-	-	-	SL	-	-	-
Carroll, Charles H.	-	-	-	-	-	-	-	-	-	-	-	-	-	-	-	SM	-	-	F
Carver, Walter B.	-	-	-	-	-	-	-	-	-	-	-	-	-	-	-	F	F	F	F
Carveth, Hector R.	SM	SM	SM	-	-	-	-	-	-	-	-	-	-	-	-	-	-	-	-
Case, Don G.	-	-	-	-	-	-	-	-	-	-	-	-	SM	SM	-	-	-	-	-
Cassard, Mrs. F. Herbert	-	-	-	-	-	-	-	-	SL	SL	SL	-	-	-	-	-	-	-	-
Castle, S. N.	-	-	F	F	-	-	-	-	-	-	-	-	-	-	-	-	-	-	-
Catterall, Ralph C. H.	-	-	F	F	F	F	F	F	F	F	F	F	F	F	-	-	-	-	-
Causer, James A.	-	-	-	-	-	-	-	-	-	-	-	-	-	-	-	F	-	-	-
Chamberlain, J. Mark	-	-	-	-	-	-	-	-	-	-	-	-	-	-	-	-	-	-	F
Chase, Mrs. M. Haney	-	-	-	-	SL	-	-	-	-	-	-	-	-	-	-	-	-	-	-
Chipman, John	-	-	-	-	-	-	-	-	-	-	-	-	-	-	-	-	-	-	F
Church, Irving P.	-	-	-	-	-	-	-	-	F	F	F	F	F	F	F	F	F	F	-
Clapp, Ester	-	-	-	-	-	-	-	-	-	-	-	-	SL	SL	-	-	-	-	-
Clapp, Julius M.	-	-	-	-	-	-	F	F	-	-	-	F	-	-	-	-	-	-	-
Clapp, Miss Helen	-	-	-	-	-	-	-	-	SL	-	-	-	-	-	-	-	-	-	-
Clapp, R. D. W.	-	-	-	-	-	-	-	-	-	-	-	-	-	-	-	-	-	F	-
Cleveland, F. A.	-	-	-	-	-	-	-	F	-	-	-	-	-	-	-	-	-	-	-
Clinton, C. Lewis	-	-	-	-	-	-	-	-	-	-	-	-	-	-	-	-	-	SM	SM
Clymer, Paul K.	-	-	-	-	-	-	F	F	F	F	F	F	F	F	-	-	-	-	-
Clymer, Pauline	-	-	-	-	-	-	-	-	-	-	-	-	-	-	SL	-	-	-	-
Cobb, Fordyce A.	SM	-	-	-	-	-	-	-	-	-	-	-	-	-	-	-	-	-	-
Cockran, Miss Julia A.	-	SL	-	-	-	-	-	-	-	-	-	-	-	-	-	-	-	-	-
Coleman, George L.	-	-	-	-	-	-	-	-	-	-	F	F	SM	SM	SM	SM	SM	SM	-
Comfort, William W.	-	-	-	-	-	-	-	-	-	F	F	F	F	-	-	F	-	-	-
Comstock, John Henry	F	F	F	-	-	-	-	-	-	-	-	-	-	-	-	-	-	-	-
Cook, Miss Laura A.	-	-	-	-	-	-	-	-	SL	SL	SL	-	-	-	-	-	-	-	-
Cooper, H. S.	F	-	-	-	-	-	-	-	-	-	-	-	-	-	-	-	-	-	-
Cornell, Charles E.	-	-	-	-	-	-	-	-	-	-	F	-	-	F	F	F	-	-	-
Cornell, Franklin C., Jr.	-	-	-	-	-	-	F	F	F	F	F	F	F	F	F	F	F	-	-
Cornell, Mrs. Franklin C.	-	-	-	-	-	-	-	-	-	-	-	-	-	-	-	-	-	-	SL
Cornell, Miss Mary E.	SL	SL	SL	SL	SL	SL	SL	SL	SL	-	-	-	-	SL	-	-	-	-	-
Coville, Luzerne	-	-	-	-	-	-	-	-	-	-	-	F	F	F	F	F	-	-	-
Craig, John	-	-	F	-	-	-	-	F	F	F	F	F	-	-	-	-	-	-	F
Crane, Thomas Frederick	F	F	F	F	F	F	F	F	F	F	F	F	F	F	F	F	F	F	F
Crawford, Miss Caroline	-	-	-	-	-	-	SL	-	-	-	-	-	-	-	-	-	-	-	-
Creighton, James E.	F	F	F	F	F	F	F	F	F	-	F	F	F	F	F	F	F	-	-
Crosby, D. J.	-	-	-	-	-	-	-	-	-	-	-	-	-	-	-	-	-	SM	SM
Crowell, W. H.	-	-	-	-	-	-	-	-	-	-	-	F	F	F	F	F	-	-	-
Culver, George W.	-	-	-	-	-	-	-	-	-	SM	SM	SM	SM	F	F	F	F	F	F
Curtis, Charles E.	-	-	-	-	-	-	-	-	-	-	-	-	-	-	-	-	-	-	F
Cuthbert, Miss Margaret Ross	-	-	-	-	-	-	-	-	-	-	-	-	-	-	-	-	-	-	SL

NAME	00	02	03	04	05	06	07	08	09	10	11	12	13	14	15	16	17	18	19
Dann, Hollis E.	F	-	-	-	-	-	-	-	-	F	F	F	F	F	F	-	F	F	F
Davidsen, Hermann C.	-	-	-	-	-	-	-	-	-	-	F	F	F	F	-	-	-	-	-
Davidson, Mrs. Archibald R.	-	-	-	-	-	-	-	-	-	-	SL	-	-	-	-	-	-	-	-
Davis, Faith	-	-	-	-	-	-	-	-	SL	-	-	-	-	-	-	-	-	-	-
Davis, George B.	-	F	F	-	-	-	-	-	-	-	-	-	-	-	-	-	-	-	-
Davis, Mrs. K. I.	-	-	-	-	-	-	-	F	-	-	-	-	-	-	-	-	-	-	-
Davis, W. J.	-	-	-	-	-	-	-	-	-	-	-	F	F	F	F	F	-	-	-
de Grassi, Georgio	-	-	-	-	-	-	-	-	-	-	-	-	F	F	F	-	-	-	-
de Grassi, Mrs. Giorgio	-	-	-	-	-	-	-	-	-	SL	SL	-	-	-	-	-	-	-	-
DeGarmo, Charles	SM	F	F	F	F	F	F	F	F	F	F	F	F	F	-	F	-	-	-
Delano, Victor M.	-	-	-	-	-	-	-	SM	-	-	SM	SM	-	-	-	-	-	-	-
Denman, C. F.	-	-	-	-	-	-	-	-	-	-	-	-	-	F	F	SM	SM	SM	SM
Dennis, C. M.	-	-	-	-	-	-	-	-	-	-	-	-	SM	SM	-	-	-	-	-
Dennis, Louis M.	SM	F	F	F	F	F	F	F	F	F	F	F	F	F	F	F	F	F	F
Dibble, Miss Evelyn	-	-	-	-	-	-	-	SL	SL	SL	-	SL	SL	SL	SL	-	-	-	-
Dixon, Miss Margery	-	-	-	-	-	-	-	-	-	-	-	-	-	-	-	-	-	SL	SL
Donahue, E. J.	-	-	-	-	-	-	-	-	-	-	-	-	-	-	-	-	-	-	SM
Dowd, Thomas H.	-	-	-	-	-	-	-	-	-	-	-	-	SM	SM	SM	-	-	-	-
Drake, Allen N.	SM	-	-	-	-	-	-	-	-	-	-	-	-	-	-	-	-	-	-
Drake, Miss Jane	SL	-	-	-	-	-	-	-	-	-	-	-	-	-	-	-	-	-	-
Drew, W. L.	-	-	-	-	F	F	F	-	-	-	-	-	-	-	-	-	-	-	-
Dudley, Eric	-	-	-	-	-	-	-	-	-	F	F	F	F	F	F	F	F	F	F
Dugan, William J.	-	-	-	-	-	-	-	SM	SM	SM	F	F	F	-	-	-	-	-	-
Duggar, Benjamin M.	-	-	-	-	-	-	-	-	F	F	F	F	-	-	-	-	-	-	-
Durand, William F.	F	-	-	-	-	-	-	-	-	-	-	-	-	-	-	-	-	-	-
Durham, Charles L.	SM	F	F	SM	SM	F	F	F	F	F	F	F	F	F	F	F	F	F	F
Elmer, Herbert Charles	F	-	-	-	-	-	-	-	-	-	F	F	F	F	F	F	F	F	F
English, Donald	-	-	-	-	-	-	-	-	-	-	-	-	-	-	-	-	-	-	SM
Evans, Cadwallader	-	-	-	-	-	-	-	-	-	-	-	-	-	-	-	-	-	-	F
Fairbanks, Arthur	F	-	-	-	-	-	-	-	-	-	-	-	-	-	-	-	-	-	-
Fassett, Truman E.	-	-	-	-	-	-	-	F	-	-	-	-	-	-	-	-	-	-	-
Faust, Albert B.	-	-	-	-	-	-	-	SM	SM	SM	SM	F	-	F	F	SM	SM	SM	SM
Ferdon, Miss Adele F.	-	SL	-	-	-	-	-	-	-	-	-	-	-	-	-	-	-	-	-
Fetter, Frank A.	-	F	F	F	F	F	-	-	-	-	-	-	-	-	-	-	-	-	-
Field, Arthur	-	-	-	-	-	-	-	-	-	-	-	-	F	-	-	-	-	-	-
Finch, Dudley F.	F	F	F	F	F	F	F	F	F	F	F	F	F	F	F	F	F	F	F
Finch, Francis M.	F	F	F	F	F	F	F	-	-	-	-	-	-	-	-	-	-	-	-
Finch, Miss H. E.	-	-	-	-	-	-	SL	-	-	-	-	-	-	-	-	-	-	-	-
Finch, Miss Mary	-	-	-	-	-	-	-	-	-	-	-	-	-	-	-	-	-	-	SL
Fisher, John C.	-	-	-	-	-	-	-	-	-	-	-	-	-	-	-	-	-	-	F
Fiske, Miss C.	-	-	-	-	-	-	-	-	-	-	-	-	SL	-	-	-	-	-	-
Fiske, Rev. A. S.	-	-	-	-	-	-	-	-	F	-	-	-	SM	-	-	-	-	-	-
Fite, William B.	-	-	-	-	-	-	F	F	F	-	-	-	-	-	-	-	-	-	-
Flack, Harold	-	-	-	-	-	-	-	-	-	-	-	-	-	-	-	SM	SM	-	-
Fletcher, C. W.	-	-	-	-	-	-	-	-	-	-	-	-	-	-	SM	-	-	-	-
Fletcher, Charles W.	-	-	-	-	-	-	F	F	F	-	-	-	-	-	-	-	-	-	-
Fluegel, Ernst J.	-	-	-	-	-	-	-	-	-	-	F	F	-	-	-	-	-	-	-
Foote, George Franklin	SM	SM	SM	SM	-	SM	SM	-	-	-	-	-	-	-	-	-	-	-	-
Fraser, D. Kennedy	-	-	-	-	-	-	-	-	-	-	-	-	-	-	F	SM	-	-	SM
Freeman, S. B.	-	SM	-	-	-	-	-	-	-	-	-	-	-	-	-	-	-	-	-
Fried, Jerome K.	-	-	-	-	-	-	-	-	-	-	-	-	-	-	SM	SM	SM	SM	SM
Frisbie, Miss Alice	SL	-	-	-	-	-	-	-	-	-	-	-	-	-	-	-	-	-	-
Fuertes, Estevan A.	F	F	-	-	-	-	-	-	-	-	-	-	-	-	-	-	-	-	-
Fuertes, Katherine	-	-	SL	-	-	-	-	-	-	-	-	-	-	-	-	-	-	-	-
Fuertes, Louis Agassiz	-	-	-	-	-	-	-	F	-	F	F	F	F	F	-	-	-	-	-
Gannett, Frank E.	-	-	-	-	-	-	-	-	-	-	-	SM	-	-	-	-	-	-	-
Gardiner, Miss Henrietta S.	SL	-	-	-	SL	SL	SL	-	-	-	-	-	-	-	-	-	-	-	-
Gaston, Charles R.	SM	-	-	-	-	-	-	-	-	-	-	-	-	-	-	-	-	-	-
Gauntlett, John C.	F	F	F	F	F	F	F	F	F	-	F	F	F	F	-	-	-	-	-
Gauntlett, Mrs. J. C.	-	-	-	-	-	-	-	-	-	-	-	-	-	-	F	SL	SL	SL	SL
Gauntlett, John M.	-	-	-	-	-	-	-	-	-	-	-	-	SM	SM	SM	SM	F	F	-	F
Genung, Harold	-	-	-	-	-	-	-	-	-	-	-	-	SM	-	-	-	-	-	-
George, Edward A.	-	-	-	F	F	F	F	F	F	F	F	F	F	F	F	F	F	F	-
Gibb, Arthur N.	F	-	-	-	-	-	-	-	-	-	F	F	F	F	F	F	F	F	F
Gill, A. Capen	-	F	F	F	F	SM	SM	SM	SM	SM	SM	SM	SM	F	F	F	F	F	F
Gillespie, D. C.	-	-	-	-	-	-	-	-	-	-	-	-	-	-	-	-	F	F	F
Gillette, Edwin	-	-	F	-	-	-	-	-	-	-	-	F	F	F	-	-	-	-	-
Gillmore, W. E.	-	-	-	-	-	-	-	-	-	-	-	F	-	-	-	-	-	-	-
Gilman, R. E.	-	-	-	-	-	-	-	-	-	-	-	-	-	-	-	SM	-	-	-
Gluck, Miss	-	SL	-	-	-	-	-	-	-	-	-	-	-	-	-	-	-	-	-
Gordon, Arthur	-	-	-	-	-	-	-	-	-	-	F	F	-	-	-	-	-	-	-
Gould, Alan J.	-	-	-	-	-	-	-	-	-	-	-	-	-	-	-	-	-	SM	-
Gould, G. M.	-	-	-	-	-	-	-	-	F	-	-	-	-	-	-	-	-	-	-

NAME	00	02	03	04	05	06	07	08	09	10	11	12	13	14	15	16	17	18	19
Gowan, Miss	-	-	-	-	-	-	-	F	-	-	-	-	-	-	-	-	-	-	-
Grant, Frank W.	-	-	-	-	-	-	-	-	-	-	-	F	F	F	F	F	F	-	-
Grant, Mrs. Frank W.	-	-	-	-	-	-	-	-	SL	SL	SL	-	-	-	-	-	-	-	-
Gray, Mrs. C. J.	-	-	-	F	-	-	-	-	-	-	-	-	-	-	-	-	-	-	-
Greene, Miss Antoinette	-	-	SL	-	-	-	-	-	-	-	-	-	-	-	-	-	-	-	-
Griffis, Mrs. William E.	-	-	-	-	-	-	-	-	-	-	SL	SL	SL	SL	SL	SL	SL	-	-
Guerlac, Othon G.	-	-	-	-	-	-	SM	SM	F	F	F	F	-	F	F	-	-	F	F
Guerlac, Mrs. O. G.	-	-	-	-	-	-	-	-	-	-	-	-	-	-	-	SL	SL	-	-
Hall, Gordon	-	-	-	-	-	-	-	-	-	-	-	SM	SM	-	-	-	-	-	-
Hall, Miss E. R.	SL	-	-	-	-	-	-	-	-	-	-	-	-	-	-	-	-	-	-
Halliday, Samuel D.	F	F	F	-	-	-	-	-	-	-	-	-	-	-	-	-	-	-	-
Halliday, Mrs. Samuel D.	-	-	-	-	-	-	-	-	-	-	-	F	-	-	-	-	-	-	-
Hammond, William A.	-	F	F	F	F	F	F	F	F	F	F	F	F	F	F	F	F	F	F
Hanford, Nathan	-	-	-	-	-	-	-	-	-	-	-	SM	F	F	F	-	F	F	F
Hart, James M.	F	F	F	F	F	F	-	-	-	-	-	-	-	-	-	-	-	-	-
Harvey, Miss Margaret	-	SL	SL	-	-	-	-	-	-	-	-	-	-	-	-	-	-	-	-
Haskell, Eugene E.	-	-	-	-	-	-	F	F	F	F	F	F	-	F	F	F	F	F	-
Hayes, Alfred, Jr.	-	-	-	-	-	-	-	F	F	F	F	F	F	F	F	-	-	-	-
Hayes, L. D.	-	-	-	-	-	-	-	-	-	-	-	-	-	F	F	-	-	-	-
Hayes, Rutherford B.	-	-	-	-	-	-	-	-	-	-	-	F	F	F	-	-	-	-	-
Hayes, Mrs. R. B.	-	-	-	-	-	-	-	-	-	-	-	-	-	-	SL	-	-	-	-
Hazeltine, R. H.	-	F	F	F	-	F	F	-	-	-	-	-	-	-	-	-	-	-	-
Hebrard, Jean	-	-	-	-	-	-	-	-	SM	SM	SM	-	-	-	-	-	-	-	-
Hermannson, H.	-	-	-	-	-	-	-	-	-	-	-	-	SM	-	SM	SM	SM	SM	SM
Herrick, Glenn W.	-	-	-	-	-	-	-	-	-	-	-	-	-	-	-	F	F	F	F
Hewett, W. Thomas	-	-	-	-	F	F	F	-	-	-	-	-	-	-	-	-	-	-	-
Heyl, Miss F. M.	-	-	-	-	-	-	-	-	-	-	-	-	-	-	-	-	-	-	SL
Hibbard, Horace M.	-	F	F	F	F	F	F	F	F	F	F	F	F	-	-	-	-	-	-
Hill, A. Ross	-	-	-	-	-	-	F	-	-	-	-	-	-	-	-	-	-	-	-
Hill, O. Wendell	-	-	-	-	SM	-	-	-	-	-	-	-	-	-	-	-	-	-	-
Hilliard, Herbert B.	-	-	-	-	-	-	-	-	F	F	F	F	F	F	-	-	-	-	-
Hinckley, Henry L.	F	F	F	F	F	-	-	-	-	-	-	-	-	-	-	-	-	-	-
Hinckley, Henry N.	-	-	-	-	-	-	-	-	SM	SM	SM	SM	SM	SM	SM	SM	SM	-	-
Hitchcock, H. A.	-	-	-	-	-	-	-	-	-	-	-	-	-	-	-	F	F	-	-
Hitchcock, Mrs. Edward, Jr.	-	SL	SL	-	-	-	-	-	-	-	-	-	-	-	-	-	-	-	-
Hoagland, Ernest B.	-	-	-	-	-	-	-	-	-	-	SM	SM	SM	SM	SM	-	-	-	-
Hoard, Mrs. P. D.	-	-	SL	SL	-	-	-	-	-	-	-	-	-	-	-	-	-	-	-
Holbert, Miss Alice	-	-	-	-	-	SL	-	-	-	-	-	-	-	-	-	-	-	-	-
Horton, George William	-	-	-	-	-	-	-	-	-	-	-	-	-	-	-	-	F	F	F
Horton, Henry P.	-	-	-	-	-	-	-	-	-	-	-	F	F	F	F	F	SM	SM	SM
Horton, Miss Q. N.	-	-	-	-	-	-	SL	-	SL	-	-	-	-	-	-	-	-	-	-
Horton, Randolph	-	-	-	-	-	-	-	-	-	-	-	F	F	F	F	-	-	-	-
Hostetter, E. Byron	-	-	-	-	-	-	-	-	-	F	-	-	-	-	-	-	-	-	-
Hovanus, George	-	-	-	-	-	-	-	-	-	-	-	-	-	-	-	-	-	F	-
Howard, Miss Clara	-	-	-	-	-	-	-	-	-	-	-	-	-	-	-	-	-	-	SL
Howard, Mrs.	-	-	-	-	SL	-	-	-	-	-	-	-	-	-	-	-	-	-	-
Howe, Fred B.	-	-	-	-	-	-	-	-	-	-	-	-	F	F	F	F	-	-	-
Howe, Herbert C.	SM	-	-	-	-	-	-	-	-	-	-	-	-	-	-	-	-	-	-
Howe, John B.	-	-	-	-	-	-	-	-	-	-	-	F	F	F	F	F	F	F	F
Howell, George B.	-	-	-	-	-	-	-	-	-	-	-	-	SM	SM	SM	-	-	-	F
Hoy, David F.	-	-	-	-	-	-	-	-	-	-	-	-	-	F	F	F	F	F	F
Huffcut, Ernest W.	SM	SM	SM	-	-	-	-	-	-	-	-	-	-	-	-	-	-	-	-
Hull, Albert M.	-	SM	SM	SM	SM	SM	SM	SM	SM	SM	SM	SM	-	-	-	-	-	-	-
Hull, Charles H.	F	F	F	F	F	F	F	F	F	F	F	F	F	F	F	F	F	F	F
Hunter, Andrew	-	-	-	-	-	-	-	-	-	-	-	F	F	F	-	-	-	-	-
Hunter, Mabel D.	-	-	-	-	-	-	F	-	-	-	-	-	-	-	-	-	-	-	-
Hutchinson, J. I.	-	-	F	-	-	-	-	-	-	-	-	-	-	-	-	-	-	-	-
Hutchinson, Mrs. J. I.	-	-	-	F	-	-	-	-	SL	-	-	-	-	-	-	-	-	-	-
Hutchinson, Robert A.	-	-	-	-	-	-	-	-	-	-	-	-	-	-	SM	SM	SM	-	SM
Hutchinson, William Herbert	-	-	-	-	F	F	F	F	F	-	F	-	-	-	-	-	-	-	-
Hyde, Paul H.	-	-	-	-	-	-	-	-	-	-	-	-	-	-	-	-	-	F	-
Ingersoll, Miss Elizabeth S.	-	-	-	-	-	-	-	-	SL	SL	SL	SL	SL	SL	SL	SL	SL	SL	SL
Irvine, Mrs. Frank	-	-	-	-	SL	SL	SL	-	-	-	-	-	F	F	F	F	F	F	F
Jackson, Donald	-	-	-	-	-	-	-	-	-	-	-	-	-	-	SM	-	-	-	-
Jelke, W. F.	-	-	-	-	SM	-	-	-	-	-	-	-	-	-	-	-	-	-	-
Jenks, E.	-	-	-	-	-	-	-	-	-	-	-	-	SM	SM	-	-	-	-	-
Jenks, Jeremiah W.	F	F	F	F	F	F	F	F	F	F	F	F	F	-	-	-	-	-	-
Jenson, G. E.	-	-	-	-	-	-	-	-	-	-	-	-	-	F	-	-	-	-	-
Johns, Miss J. P.	-	-	-	-	-	-	-	-	-	-	-	-	-	-	-	-	-	-	SL
Johnson, Miss Louise	-	-	-	-	-	-	SL	SL	-	-	-	-	-	-	-	-	-	-	-
Jones, Alfred H.	-	-	-	-	-	-	-	-	-	-	SM	-	-	-	-	-	-	-	-
Jones, Forrest R.	-	-	-	-	F	-	-	-	-	-	-	-	-	-	-	-	-	-	-
Jones, George W.	-	-	-	-	F	SM	-	-	-	-	-	-	-	-	-	-	-	-	-

NAME	00	02	03	04	05	06	07	08	09	10	11	12	13	14	15	16	17	18	19
Jones, R. F.	-	-	-	-	-	-	-	-	-	-	-	-	-	-	-	-	-	SM	-
Kahn, E. J.	-	-	-	-	-	-	-	-	-	-	-	-	-	F	-	-	-	-	-
Kemmerer, E. Walter	-	-	-	-	-	-	-	-	-	-	F	F	-	-	-	-	-	-	-
Keniston, R. H.	-	-	-	-	-	-	-	-	-	-	-	-	-	-	F	F	F	F	F
Kent, G. Ervin	-	-	-	-	-	-	-	-	-	-	SM	SM	SM	F	F	F	F	-	-
Kent, Mrs. G. Ervin	-	-	-	-	-	-	-	-	-	-	-	-	-	-	-	-	-	SL	-
Kerl, Thomas T.	-	-	-	-	-	-	-	-	-	-	F	F	F	-	-	-	-	-	-
King, Leander R.	F	-	-	-	-	-	-	-	-	-	-	-	-	-	-	-	-	-	-
King, Miss Alice F.	-	SL	-	-	SL	SL	SL	SL	SL	-	-	-	-	-	-	-	-	-	-
Kingsbury, Benjamin F.	-	-	-	-	-	-	-	-	-	-	F	F	F	F	-	-	-	-	-
Kirk, Richard R.	-	-	-	-	-	-	-	-	-	-	SM	SM	-	-	-	-	-	-	-
Lacy, Mrs. M. A.	-	F	-	-	-	-	-	-	-	-	-	-	-	-	-	-	-	-	-
Ladd, Mrs. Carolyn	-	-	-	-	-	-	-	-	-	-	-	F	F	F	F	F	SL	-	SL
Lambert, A. R.	-	-	-	-	-	-	-	-	-	-	-	-	F	F	-	-	-	-	-
Law, James	F	F	F	F	F	-	F	F	F	F	F	F	F	-	-	-	-	-	-
Leaman, T. P.	-	-	-	-	-	-	-	-	-	-	-	-	-	-	-	-	F	-	-
Lee, Duncan C.	F	F	F	F	-	-	-	-	-	-	-	-	-	-	-	-	-	-	-
Lee, W. F.	-	-	-	-	-	-	-	-	-	-	-	-	-	-	SM	SM	-	-	SM
Lemon, B. J.	-	-	-	-	-	-	-	-	-	-	-	-	SM	SM	SM	-	-	-	-
Lent, B. F.	-	-	-	-	-	-	-	-	-	-	-	-	-	-	-	F	F	-	-
Leonard, A. K.	-	-	-	-	-	-	-	-	-	-	-	-	-	-	SM	SM	-	-	-
Livermore, Paul S.	-	-	-	-	-	-	F	F	F	F	F	F	F	F	F	F	F	F	F
Loeb, R. H.	-	-	-	-	-	-	-	-	-	-	-	-	-	F	-	-	-	-	-
Long, Eleanor T.	-	-	-	-	-	-	-	-	-	-	-	-	-	-	-	SL	SL	SL	SL
Loomis, Miss L. R.	-	-	-	-	-	-	SL	-	-	-	-	-	-	-	-	-	-	-	-
Lovett, Charles H.	-	-	-	-	-	-	-	-	-	-	F	-	-	-	-	-	-	-	-
Lunt, W. E.	-	-	-	-	-	-	-	-	-	-	-	-	F	F	F	F	-	-	-
Lyon, Thomas L.	-	-	-	-	-	-	-	-	-	-	F	F	F	F	F	-	-	-	-
Lyon, Mrs. Thomas L.	-	-	-	-	-	-	-	-	-	-	-	-	-	-	SL	-	SL	-	-
MacBeth, Miss Marie Louise	SL	-	-	-	-	-	-	-	-	-	-	-	-	-	-	-	-	-	-
MacGill, F. C.	-	-	-	SM	-	-	-	-	-	-	-	-	-	-	-	-	-	-	-
MacIntosh, John A.	-	-	-	-	-	-	-	-	-	-	-	F	F	F	F	F	F	F	F
MacLaughlin, Donald H.	-	-	-	-	-	-	-	-	-	-	-	-	-	-	-	-	-	-	F
MacRae, D. A.	-	-	F	-	-	-	-	-	-	-	-	-	-	-	-	-	-	-	-
Mahan, A. A.	-	-	-	-	-	-	-	-	-	-	-	-	SM	SM	-	-	-	-	-
Major, Miss Marion	-	-	-	-	-	-	-	SL	-	-	-	-	-	-	-	-	-	-	-
Mallory, Philip	-	-	-	-	-	-	-	-	-	-	-	-	SM	SM	-	SM	-	-	-
Mange, John I.	-	-	-	-	-	-	-	-	-	-	-	-	-	-	-	-	F	F	F
Manning, George L.	-	F	-	F	F	-	-	-	-	-	-	-	-	-	-	-	-	-	-
Marsh, Daniel E.	-	-	-	-	-	-	-	-	-	-	-	F	F	F	F	F	F	-	-
Martin, Clarence A.	SM	SM	SM	SM	-	-	-	-	-	-	-	-	-	-	F	F	F	-	-
Matthews, Robertson	-	-	-	-	-	-	-	-	-	-	-	-	-	-	-	-	-	-	SM
Mauxion, Georges R.	-	-	-	-	-	-	-	-	-	-	-	SM	F	F	-	-	-	-	-
Mazzonovich, Mrs. J. G.	-	SL	-	-	-	-	-	-	-	-	-	-	-	-	-	-	-	-	-
McAllister, Peter F.	-	-	-	-	-	-	SM	SM	SM	F	F	F	F	F	F	F	F	F	-
McConnell, Murray	-	-	-	-	-	-	-	-	-	-	-	-	-	-	-	F	-	-	-
McCormick, Miss J.	-	-	-	-	-	-	-	-	-	-	-	SL	-	-	-	-	-	-	-
McDermott, Jean	-	-	-	-	-	-	-	-	-	-	-	-	SL	SL	SL	SL	-	-	-
McDermott, Lawrence	-	-	-	-	-	-	-	-	SM	SM	-	-	-	-	-	-	-	-	-
McGilvary, E. B.	-	SM	SM	SM	SM	-	-	-	-	-	-	-	-	-	-	-	-	-	-
McKinney, J. A.	-	-	-	-	-	-	-	-	-	-	:	F	F	F	F	-	-	-	-
McKnight, C. H.	-	SM	SM	SM	-	-	-	-	-	-	-	-	-	-	-	-	-	-	-
McMahon, James	SM	SM	SM	SM	SM	SM	SM	SM	SM	SM	SM	SM	SM	SM	-	-	-	-	-
Melotte, Miss Julia L.	-	-	-	-	-	-	-	-	-	-	-	-	-	-	-	-	-	-	SL
Merriam, Henry E.	-	-	-	-	-	-	-	-	-	F	F	F	F	F	F	F	-	-	-
Merritt, Ernest	SM	SM	SM	SM	-	-	-	-	-	-	-	-	-	-	-	-	-	-	-
Metcalf, William, Jr.	F	-	-	-	-	-	-	-	-	-	-	-	-	-	-	-	-	-	-
Miller, Miss Gladys	-	-	-	-	-	-	-	SL	-	-	-	-	-	-	-	-	-	-	-
Miller, Miss Ruth	-	-	-	-	-	-	-	-	SL	-	-	-	-	-	-	-	-	-	-
Miller, Nathan L.	-	-	-	-	-	-	-	-	-	-	-	F	F	F	F	F	-	-	-
Miller, William Henry	F	F	F	-	-	-	-	-	-	-	-	-	-	-	-	-	-	-	-
Mitchell, B. R.	-	-	-	-	-	-	-	-	-	-	-	F	F	F	-	-	-	-	-
Mitchell, C. M.	-	-	-	-	-	-	-	-	-	-	-	-	-	-	-	-	-	-	F
Moakley, John F.	-	-	-	-	-	-	-	-	-	-	-	F	F	F	F	F	F	F	F
Monroe, B. S.	-	-	-	-	-	-	-	-	-	-	-	F	F	F	-	-	-	-	-
Montgomery, E. G.	-	-	-	-	-	-	-	-	-	-	-	F	-	-	-	-	-	-	-
Montgomery, Mrs. E. G.	-	-	-	-	-	-	-	-	-	-	-	-	-	SL	-	SL	-	-	-
Montillon, Eugene D.	-	-	-	-	-	-	-	-	-	-	-	-	-	-	-	SM	SM	-	-
Moore, Alfred A.	SM	SM	SM	SM	SM	-	-	-	-	-	-	-	-	-	-	-	-	-	-
Moore, H. M.	-	-	-	-	-	-	-	-	-	-	-	-	-	F	F	SM	SM	SM	-
Morris, John L.	F	-	-	-	-	-	-	-	-	-	-	-	-	-	-	-	-	-	-
Morris, William T.	-	SM	SM	SM	SM	SM	SM	SM	SM	SM	SM	SM	SM	SM	-	SM	SM	-	-
Morrison, J. M.	-	-	-	-	-	-	-	-	-	-	-	F	F	F	F	-	F	-	-

NAME	00	02	03	04	05	06	07	08	09	10	11	12	13	14	15	16	17	18	19
Morrison, William H.	-	-	-	-	-	-	-	-	-	-	-	-	-	-	-	F	F	F	F
Morse, Clarence F.	-	-	-	-	-	-	-	-	-	-	-	SM	SM	F	-	-	-	-	-
Morse, Everett F.	-	-	-	-	-	-	-	-	-	F	F	F	F	-	-	-	-	-	-
Morse, Everett R.	-	-	-	-	-	-	-	-	-	-	-	-	SM	SM	F	SM	-	-	-
Morse, Frank L.	-	-	-	-	-	-	-	-	-	F	F	-	F	F	F	F	F	F	F
Morse, Miss Dorothy	-	-	-	-	-	-	-	SL	SL	SL	-	-	-	-	-	-	-	-	-
Morse, Robert V.	-	-	-	-	-	-	-	-	-	-	-	-	SM	SM	SM	SM	SM	F	F
Morse, Virgil D.	-	-	-	-	-	-	-	-	-	F	F	F	F	F	F	SM	-	-	-
Mott, William E.	SM	F	F	F	F	-	-	-	-	-	-	-	-	-	-	-	-	-	-
Muchmore, G. B.	-	-	-	-	-	-	-	-	-	-	-	-	-	-	-	SM	SM	SM	SM
Muggens, Pauline	-	-	-	-	-	-	-	-	-	-	-	-	-	-	-	SL	SL	-	-
Murdock, Carlton C.	-	-	-	-	-	-	-	-	-	-	-	-	-	-	-	-	-	-	SM
Murdock, Raymond L.	-	-	-	-	-	-	-	-	-	-	-	-	-	SM	-	-	-	-	-
Murray, Daniel A.	SM	-	-	-	-	-	-	-	-	-	-	-	-	-	-	-	-	-	-
Nash, A. C.	-	SM	-	-	-	-	-	-	-	-	-	-	-	-	-	-	-	-	-
Needham, Mrs. Mabel A.	-	-	-	-	-	-	-	-	-	-	SL	SL	SL	SL	SL	SL	SL	SL	SL
Newberry, Mrs. Clara W.	-	F	F	SL	SL	SL	-	-	-	-	-	-	-	-	-	-	-	-	-
Newman, Charles H.	-	-	-	-	-	-	-	-	-	-	-	-	-	SM	SM	SM	SM	-	SM
Newman, Jared T.	F	F	F	F	F	F	F	F	F	F	F	F	F	-	F	-	F	F	F
Nichols, Edward L.	F	F	F	F	-	-	-	-	-	-	-	-	-	-	-	-	-	-	-
Nye, Miss Gertrude H.	-	-	SL	SL	SL	SL	SL	SL	SL	SL	SL	SL	SL	SL	SL	SL	SL	SL	SL
O'Connell, Mrs. Mary W.	-	-	-	-	-	-	-	-	SL	SL	SL	SL	SL	SL	SL	SL	SL	SL	F
Olmsted, Everett W.	SM	-	-	-	-	-	-	-	-	F	F	F	F	F	-	-	-	-	-
Orndorff, William R.	-	-	-	-	-	-	-	-	-	-	-	F	-	-	-	-	-	-	-
Orth, L. P.	-	-	-	-	-	-	-	-	-	-	-	-	-	-	-	F	F	F	F
Paine, Ernest T.	-	-	-	-	-	-	-	-	-	-	-	-	-	F	-	-	-	-	-
Parker, Esther	-	-	-	-	-	-	-	-	-	-	-	-	SL	SL	SL	SL	SL	SL	SL
Parsell, C. V.	-	-	-	-	-	-	-	-	-	-	-	F	F	F	F	-	-	-	-
Paton, David	-	SM	-	-	-	-	-	-	-	-	-	-	-	-	-	-	-	-	-
Patterson, G. C.	-	-	-	SM	-	-	-	-	-	-	-	-	-	-	-	-	-	-	-
Patterson, Woodford	-	-	-	-	-	-	SM	SM	SM	SM	SM	SM	SM	SM	SM	SM	SM	SM	SM
Pearson, R. A.	-	-	-	-	F	-	-	-	-	-	-	-	-	-	-	-	-	-	-
Peer, Sherman S.	-	-	-	F	-	-	-	-	-	-	-	SM	SM	SM	SM	SM	SM	SM	-
Peirce, Miss H. L.	-	-	-	-	-	-	-	SL	-	-	-	-	-	-	-	-	-	-	-
Perez, Mrs. P. E.	-	-	-	-	-	-	-	-	-	-	-	-	-	-	-	-	-	-	F
Perky, Scott H.	-	-	-	-	F	F	F	TM	-	-	-	-	-	-	-	-	-	-	-
Perry, Helen	-	-	-	-	SL	SL	-	-	-	-	-	-	-	-	-	-	-	-	-
Peters, H. W.	-	-	-	-	-	-	-	-	-	-	-	-	-	-	SM	-	-	-	-
Peters, Russell H.	-	-	-	-	-	-	-	-	-	-	-	-	-	-	-	-	-	SM	-
Phelps, A. C.	-	-	-	-	-	-	-	-	-	-	-	-	-	-	-	F	F	-	F
Philips, Capt. E. L.	-	-	-	-	-	-	-	-	F	F	-	-	-	-	-	-	-	-	-
Pierce, C. A.	-	-	-	-	-	-	-	-	-	-	-	-	-	-	-	-	F	-	-
Pope, P. R.	-	-	-	-	-	-	-	-	-	F	-	-	-	-	-	-	-	-	-
Pound, Cuthbert W.	-	-	-	F	-	-	-	-	-	-	-	-	-	-	-	-	-	-	-
Pratt, Miss Helen L.	-	-	-	-	-	-	-	-	-	-	-	-	-	-	-	SL	SL	SL	SL
Prescott, Frederick C.	SM	SM	SM	SM	F	F	F	F	F	F	F	F	F	F	F	F	F	F	F
Pringle, M. N.	-	-	-	-	-	-	-	-	-	-	-	-	-	-	-	-	SM	-	-
Publow, C. A.	-	-	-	-	-	-	-	-	-	F	-	-	-	-	-	-	-	-	-
Pumpelly, Lawrence	-	-	-	ST	-	-	-	SM	SM	SM	SM	SM	SM	SM	SM	SM	SM	SM	SM
Putnam, H. S.	-	-	-	-	SM	-	-	-	-	-	-	-	-	-	-	-	-	-	-
Quarles, James T.	-	-	-	-	-	-	-	-	-	-	-	-	-	F	F	F	F	F	F
Rankin, George S.	-	F	F	F	F	F	F	F	F	F	F	F	F	F	F	-	-	-	-
Rankin, Miss Mary	SL	-	-	-	-	-	-	-	-	-	-	-	-	-	-	-	-	-	-
Ranum, Arthur	-	-	-	-	-	-	-	-	F	F	F	-	-	-	-	-	-	-	-
Reddington, Miss C. A.	-	-	-	SL	-	SL	SL	-	-	-	-	-	-	-	-	-	-	-	-
Redfield, Henry Stephen	F	-	-	-	-	-	-	-	-	-	-	-	-	-	-	-	-	-	-
Reed, Harold L.	-	-	-	-	-	-	-	-	-	-	-	-	-	SM	SM	-	SM	SM	SM
Rice, Frank E.	-	-	-	-	-	-	-	-	-	-	-	-	-	-	-	-	F	F	SM
Ricker, C. S.	-	-	-	-	-	-	-	F	-	-	-	-	-	-	-	-	-	-	-
Riker, T. W.	-	-	-	-	-	-	-	-	SM	-	-	-	-	-	-	-	-	-	-
Rites, Mrs. Frank M.	-	-	-	-	-	-	-	-	-	-	-	-	-	-	-	F	F	F	F
Robbins, W. M.	-	-	-	-	-	-	-	-	-	-	-	-	-	-	-	-	-	SM	-
Robinson, James R.	-	-	-	-	-	-	-	-	-	-	-	F	F	F	F	F	F	F	F
Roe, David, Jr.	-	F	-	-	-	F	-	F	F	-	-	-	-	-	-	-	-	-	-
Rogalsky, George F.	-	-	-	-	-	-	-	-	-	-	-	SM	SM	SM	SM	SM	SM	SM	F
Rogers, Miss Isabel	SL	-	-	-	-	-	-	-	-	-	-	-	-	-	-	-	-	-	-
Rose, Miss Flora	-	-	-	-	-	-	-	-	-	-	-	SL	SL	-	-	-	-	-	-
Rothschild, Jacob	-	-	-	-	-	-	-	-	-	-	-	F	F	F	F	F	F	F	F
Rothschild, Leon D.	-	-	-	-	-	-	-	-	-	-	-	SM	SM	SM	SM	SM	SM	SM	SM
Routh, Mrs. W. W.	-	-	-	-	-	-	-	-	-	-	F	-	-	-	-	-	-	-	-
Royce, Edward	-	-	-	-	-	-	-	-	-	-	-	-	-	-	-	-	F	F	F
Rust, Ethel	-	-	-	-	-	-	-	-	-	-	-	-	SL	SL	SL	-	-	-	-
Rust, Wilbur	-	-	-	-	-	-	-	-	-	-	-	-	SM	SM	-	-	-	-	-

NAME	00	02	03	04	05	06	07	08	09	10	11	12	13	14	15	16	17	18	19
Sailor, R. Warren	-	-	-	-	-	-	-	-	-	-	-	-	-	-	-	-	F	F	F
Sampson, Martin W.	-	-	-	-	-	-	-	F	SM	SM	F	F	F	F	F	F	F	F	F
Sanford, Benjamin E.	-	TM	TM	-	-	-	-	-	-	-	-	-	-	-	-	-	-	F	F
Schaub, Edward L.	-	-	-	-	-	-	-	-	SM	SM	-	-	-	-	-	-	-	-	-
Schively, Mrs. F. C.	-	-	-	-	-	-	-	-	-	-	-	-	F	F	F	-	-	-	F
Schurman, Jacob Gould	F	F	F	F	F	F	F	F	F	F	F	F	F	F	F	F	F	F	F
Schurman, Robert	-	-	-	-	-	F	SM	-	-	-	-	-	-	-	-	-	-	-	-
Schuyler, Mrs. Walter S.	SL	-	-	-	-	-	-	-	-	-	-	-	-	-	-	-	-	-	-
Scott, John H.	-	-	-	-	-	-	-	-	SM	SM	SM	-	-	-	-	-	-	-	-
Seeley, Miss Grace	-	-	-	-	-	-	-	-	-	-	-	-	-	-	-	-	-	-	SL
Sharpe, A. H.	-	-	-	-	-	-	-	-	-	-	-	-	F	F	F	F	F	F	F
Shearer, John S.	SM	-	-	-	-	-	-	-	-	-	-	-	-	-	-	-	-	-	-
Sheldon, C. L., Jr.	-	-	-	-	-	F	F	-	-	-	-	-	-	-	-	-	-	-	-
Sheppard, George S.	-	F	-	-	-	-	-	-	-	-	-	-	-	-	-	-	-	-	-
Sherwood, Mrs. C. R.	-	-	-	-	-	-	-	-	-	-	-	F	F	F	-	-	-	-	-
Sill, Henry A.	-	-	SM	SM	-	-	-	-	F	F	F	-	-	-	-	-	-	-	-
Smith, Albert W.	-	-	-	-	SM	-	-	-	-	-	-	F	F	F	F	F	F	-	F
Smith, Claude H.	-	-	-	-	-	-	-	-	-	F	F	F	F	F	F	F	F	F	F
Smith, Fred Hayes	-	-	-	-	-	-	-	-	-	-	-	F	-	-	-	-	-	-	-
Smith, Frederick M.	-	-	-	-	-	-	-	-	-	-	-	-	F	-	-	-	-	-	-
Smith, L. P.	-	-	-	-	-	-	-	-	-	-	-	-	F	F	F	F	F	F	F
Snowdon, Florence	-	-	-	-	-	-	-	-	-	-	-	-	SL	SL	-	-	-	-	-
Southworth, Fred.	-	SM	-	-	-	-	-	-	-	-	-	-	-	-	-	-	-	-	-
Southworth, John H.	-	-	-	-	-	F	F	-	-	-	-	-	-	-	-	-	-	-	-
Southworth, Mrs. John H (Ella)	-	SL	-	SL	SL	SL	-	-	SL	SL	-	-	-	-	-	-	-	-	-
St.John, Henry A.	-	-	-	-	-	-	-	-	-	-	-	F	F	F	SM	-	-	-	-
St.John, Mrs. Henry A.	SL	SL	SL	SL	SL	SL	SL	SL	SL	SL	SL	-	-	-	-	-	-	-	-
St.John, Sheila	-	-	-	-	-	-	-	-	-	-	-	-	-	-	-	SL	SL	SL	SL
Stagg, C. Tracy	-	-	-	-	-	-	-	-	-	-	-	-	-	-	-	-	-	-	F
Stanton, Robert B., Jr.	-	-	-	-	-	F	F	-	-	-	-	-	-	-	-	-	-	-	-
Stanton, Mrs. Robert B., Jr.	-	-	-	-	-	-	-	-	-	F	-	-	-	-	-	-	-	-	-
Stephens, Henry Morse	F	-	-	-	-	-	-	-	-	-	-	-	-	-	-	-	-	-	-
Sterrett, J. R .S.	-	F	SM	SM	-	-	-	-	-	-	-	-	-	-	-	-	-	-	-
Stevens, F. H.	-	-	-	-	-	-	-	-	-	-	-	-	-	-	-	-	-	-	F
Stevens, Irvine R.	-	-	-	-	-	-	-	-	-	-	-	-	-	-	SM	SM	-	-	SM
Stevens, Shepherd	-	-	-	-	-	-	-	-	-	-	-	-	-	-	SM	SM	SM	F	F
Stevenson, Hermann	-	-	-	-	-	-	-	-	-	-	-	-	-	-	-	SM	-	-	-
Stewart, Edwin C.	F	F	F	F	F	F	F	F	F	F	F	F	F	F	F	F	F	F	F
Stiles, Charles A.	-	-	F	F	F	F	F	-	F	-	-	-	-	-	-	-	-	-	-
Stoddard, E. G.	-	-	-	-	-	-	-	-	-	-	-	F	F	F	F	F	-	-	-
Stone, Albert G.	-	-	-	-	-	-	F	F	F	F	F	F	F	F	F	F	F	F	F
Stone, Delia	-	-	-	-	-	-	-	-	-	-	-	-	-	-	-	SL	-	SL	SL
Stone, John L.	-	-	-	-	-	-	-	-	-	-	-	-	-	-	-	F	-	-	-
Stone, Julia	-	-	-	-	-	-	-	-	-	-	-	-	-	-	-	SL	-	-	-
Storms, William H.	-	-	-	-	-	-	-	-	-	-	-	-	-	SM	SM	SM	SM	SM	SM
Stowell, Calvin D.	F	-	-	-	-	-	-	-	-	-	-	-	-	-	-	-	-	-	-
Stowell, Miss Mary E.	-	-	-	SL	SL	SL	SL	SL	-	SL	-	-	-	-	-	-	-	-	-
Stowell, Mrs. Amelia E.	-	F	F	-	-	-	-	-	-	-	-	-	-	-	-	-	-	-	-
Strunk, W., Jr.	-	-	-	F	-	F	F	F	F	F	-	-	-	SM	SM	SM	-	-	-
Sturgis, Cony	-	-	-	-	-	-	-	-	-	-	-	-	-	-	F	F	F	TM	SM
Stutz, H. G.	-	-	-	-	-	-	-	-	-	-	-	F	F	SM	-	-	-	-	-
Swan, Miss Isabelle T.	SL	SL	SL	SL	SL	SL	SL	-	-	-	-	-	-	-	-	-	-	-	-
Swan, Norman	-	-	-	-	-	-	-	SM	-	-	-	-	-	-	-	-	-	-	-
Sweetland, Mrs. M. M.	-	-	-	-	-	-	-	-	-	-	-	SL	SL	SL	-	-	-	-	-
Tanner, John Henry	F	F	F	F	F	F	F	F	F	F	F	F	F	F	F	F	F	F	F
Tarbell, George S.	-	F	F	F	F	F	F	F	F	F	F	F	F	F	F	F	F	F	F
Tarr, Ralph S.	F	F	F	-	-	-	F	F	F	F	F	-	-	-	-	-	-	-	-
Tarr, Mrs. Ralph S. (Kate)	-	-	-	-	-	-	-	-	-	-	-	F	F	F	F	F	F	F	SL
Taylor, James B., Jr.	-	-	-	-	-	F	F	F	F	F	F	F	-	-	F	F	-	-	-
Taylor, W. W.	-	-	-	-	-	-	-	-	-	-	-	-	-	-	-	-	-	-	NR
Thilly, Frank	-	-	-	-	-	-	F	F	F	F	F	F	F	F	F	F	F	F	F
Thomas, Oliver W.	-	-	-	-	-	-	-	-	-	-	-	-	-	-	-	-	-	SM	-
Thomas, William T.	-	-	-	-	-	-	-	-	-	-	-	-	-	-	-	F	-	-	F
Thompson, Mrs. Carrie W.	SL	SL	-	-	-	-	-	-	-	-	-	-	-	-	-	-	-	-	-
Thompson, Lieut. Charles F.	-	-	-	-	-	-	-	-	-	-	-	-	-	-	-	F	F	-	-
Thompson, Mrs. Charles F.	-	-	-	-	-	-	-	-	-	-	-	-	-	-	-	-	-	-	SL
Thurber, Raymond D.	-	-	-	-	-	-	-	F	F	F	F	-	-	-	-	-	-	-	-
Thurston, Miss L.	-	SL	-	-	-	-	-	-	-	-	-	-	-	-	-	-	-	-	-
Thurston, Mrs. L. B.	-	-	-	-	F	-	-	-	-	-	-	-	-	-	-	-	-	-	-
Thurston, Robert Henry	-	F	F	-	-	-	-	-	-	-	-	-	-	-	-	-	-	-	-
Tibbetts, H. B.	-	SM	-	-	-	-	-	-	-	-	-	-	-	-	-	-	-	-	-
Tinker, Martin B.	-	-	-	-	-	-	-	-	-	-	-	-	F	F	F	F	-	-	-
Todd, Mrs. L. G.	-	-	-	-	-	-	-	-	-	-	-	-	SL	SL	-	SL	-	-	-

NAME	00	02	03	04	05	06	07	08	09	10	11	12	13	14	15	16	17	18	19
Townley, John H.	-	-	-	-	-	-	-	-	-	-	-	-	-	SM	-	-	-	-	-
Townley, Lucy	-	-	-	-	-	-	-	-	-	-	-	-	SL	SL	SL	-	-	-	-
Treman, Charles E.	SM	F	F	F	F	F	F	F	F	F	F	F	F	F	F	F	F	F	F
Treman, Ebenezer M.	F	F	F	F	F	F	F	F	F	F	F	F	F	F	-	-	-	-	-
Treman, Mrs. Ebenezer M.	-	-	-	-	-	-	-	-	-	-	-	-	-	-	SL	-	-	-	-
Treman, Robert E.	-	-	-	-	-	-	-	-	-	-	-	SM	SM	SM	SM	SM	-	SM	F
Treman, Robert H.	F	F	F	F	F	F	F	F	F	F	F	F	F	F	F	F	F	F	F
Trevor, Mrs. Joseph E. (Margaret)	-	-	SL	SL	SL	SL	SL	SL	SL	-	SL	-	-	SL	SL	SL	SL	-	SL
Trowbridge, Alexander B.	F	F	-	-	-	-	-	-	-	-	-	-	-	-	-	-	-	-	-
Turner, Samuel B.	SM	SM	SM	SM	SM	SM	-	-	-	-	-	-	-	-	-	-	-	-	-
Urquhart, L. C.	-	-	-	-	-	-	-	-	-	-	-	-	-	-	F	SM	-	-	-
Usher, A. P.	-	-	-	-	-	-	-	-	-	-	-	-	-	F	F	F	F	-	SM
Valentine, Miss	SL	-	-	-	-	-	-	-	-	-	-	-	-	-	-	-	-	-	-
Van Buren, Charles B.	-	-	-	-	-	-	-	-	F	-	-	-	-	-	-	-	-	-	-
Van Cleef, Mynderse	F	F	F	F	F	F	F	F	F	F	F	F	F	F	F	F	F	F	F
Van Pelt, John V.	SM	F	-	F	F	F	-	-	-	-	-	-	-	-	-	-	-	-	-
Van Rensselaer, Miss Martha	-	-	-	-	-	-	-	-	-	-	-	-	SL	SL	-	-	-	-	-
Van Valzah, W. W.	-	-	-	-	-	-	-	-	-	SM	-	-	-	-	-	-	-	-	-
Van Vleet, DeForest	F	-	-	-	-	-	-	-	-	-	-	-	-	-	-	-	-	-	-
Vant, George H.	-	-	-	-	SM	-	-	-	-	-	-	-	-	-	-	-	-	-	-
Victor, William H.	-	-	-	-	-	-	-	-	-	-	-	-	F	-	-	-	-	-	-
Vietor, Mrs. Hermann	-	-	-	-	-	-	-	-	F	F	F	-	F	-	-	-	-	-	-
Wait, L. A.	-	-	-	-	SM	-	-	-	-	-	-	-	-	-	-	-	-	-	-
Walker, G. L.	-	-	-	-	-	-	-	-	-	-	-	-	-	-	F	-	-	-	-
Waltz, Orman H.	-	-	-	-	-	-	-	-	-	-	-	-	-	-	-	-	-	-	F
Ward, A. L.	-	-	-	-	-	-	SM	-	-	-	-	-	-	-	-	-	-	-	-
Ware, Raymond	-	-	-	-	-	-	-	-	-	-	-	-	-	-	-	-	-	SM	SM
Warner, A. P.	-	-	-	-	-	-	-	-	-	-	-	-	F	F	-	-	-	-	-
Warren, Mrs. Maud R.	-	-	-	-	-	-	-	-	-	-	-	-	-	-	-	-	-	-	SL
Washburn, Miss M. F.	-	SL	-	-	-	-	-	-	-	-	-	-	-	-	-	-	-	-	-
Webb, Charles W.	-	-	-	-	-	-	-	-	-	-	-	-	SM	SM	-	-	-	-	-
Weiss, Alma	-	-	-	-	-	-	-	-	-	-	-	-	-	-	-	-	SL	-	-
Weld, H. P.	-	-	-	-	-	-	-	-	-	-	-	-	F	F	F	-	F	F	F
Wellar, Arthur B.	-	-	-	-	-	-	-	F	F	F	F	F	F	-	-	-	-	-	-
Westinghouse, Henry H.	-	-	F	F	F	F	F	F	F	F	F	F	F	F	F	F	F	F	F
Whipple, G. M.	-	-	SM	SM	-	-	-	-	-	-	-	-	-	-	-	-	-	-	-
White, Andrew D.	-	-	-	F	F	F	-	F	F	F	F	F	F	F	F	F	F	F	-
White, Horatio Stevens	F	F	-	-	-	-	-	-	-	-	-	-	-	-	-	-	-	-	-
White, Miss Francis C.	-	-	-	-	-	-	-	-	-	-	-	-	-	-	-	-	-	-	SL
White, Miss Georgia L.	-	-	-	-	-	-	-	-	-	-	-	-	-	-	-	-	-	-	SL
White, Mrs. Andrew D.	-	-	-	-	-	-	-	-	-	-	-	-	-	-	-	-	-	-	SL
Wickwire, J. R.	-	-	-	-	-	-	-	-	-	-	-	-	F	F	-	-	-	-	-
Wickwire, T. H.	-	-	-	-	-	-	-	-	-	-	-	F	F	F	F	-	-	-	-
Wightman, Gordon E.	-	-	-	-	-	-	-	-	-	-	-	-	-	F	F	F	-	-	-
Wilder, Miss Bertha	SL	SL	SL	SL	SL	SL	SL	SL	SL	SL	SL	SL	SL	SL	SL	SL	SL	SL	SL
Willcox, Walter F.	-	F	F	F	F	F	F	F	F	F	F	F	F	F	F	F	F	F	F
Williams, C. W.	-	-	-	-	-	-	F	F	F	F	-	-	F	F	F	F	F	F	F
Williams, Emmons L.	-	-	-	F	F	SM	SM	F	F	F	F	F	F	F	F	F	F	F	F
Williams, Ethel	-	-	-	-	-	-	-	-	-	-	-	-	-	SL	SL	SL	-	-	-
Williams, George R.	F	F	F	F	F	F	F	-	-	-	-	-	-	-	-	-	-	-	-
Williams, Henry Shaler	-	-	-	F	F	F	F	F	F	F	F	F	F	F	F	F	F	F	-
Williams, Mrs. Josiah Butler	F	F	F	F	-	-	-	-	-	-	-	-	-	-	-	-	-	-	-
Williams, Percy A.	-	-	-	-	-	-	SM	-	-	-	-	-	-	-	-	-	-	-	-
Williams, Roger B.	F	F	F	F	F	F	F	F	F	F	F	F	F	F	F	F	F	F	F
Williams, Roger B., jr.	SM	-	-	-	-	-	-	-	-	-	-	F	F	F	F	F	F	F	-
Willis, Miss Marjorie	-	-	-	-	-	-	-	-	-	-	-	-	-	-	-	-	-	-	SL
Wilson, Wilford M.	-	-	-	-	-	-	-	-	SM	SM	SM	F	F	F	F	F	F	F	F
Winans, James A.	-	-	-	-	-	-	-	-	-	-	-	F	F	SM	SM	SM	SM	SM	SM
Wood, Merritt L.	-	-	-	-	-	-	SM	SM	-	SM	SM	SM	SM	SM	SM	SM	SM	SM	SM
Wood, Miss Mary C.	-	-	-	-	-	-	-	-	SL	SL	SL	SL	SL	SL	SL	SL	SL	SL	SL
Wood, William Lutan	-	SM	SM	SM	SM	-	-	SM	SM	-	-	-	-	-	-	-	-	-	-
Wooding, E. R.	-	-	-	-	-	-	-	-	-	-	-	-	-	-	-	-	F	-	-
Woodruff, Dorothy	-	-	-	-	-	-	-	-	-	-	-	-	-	SL	SL	SL	SL	-	-
Woodward, Julian L.	-	-	-	-	-	-	-	-	-	-	-	-	-	-	-	-	-	-	SM
Wray, A. B.	-	-	-	-	-	-	-	-	-	-	-	F	F	F	SM	F	-	-	-
Wright, Henry W.	-	-	-	F	F	F	-	-	-	-	-	-	-	-	-	-	-	-	-
Wyckoff, Clarence F.	SM	F	F	F	F	F	F	F	-	-	-	-	F	F	-	F	F	F	F
Wyckoff, E. F.	-	-	-	-	-	-	-	-	-	-	-	F	-	-	-	-	-	-	-
Wyckoff, Edward G.	F	F	F	F	F	F	F	F	-	-	-	F	-	F	F	F	F	-	-
Wyckoff, Mrs. Edward G.	-	-	-	-	-	-	-	-	-	-	-	-	-	-	-	-	-	SL	SL
Young, Allyn A.	-	-	-	-	-	-	-	-	-	-	-	-	-	F	F	F	F	F	F
Young, Charles V. P.	-	-	-	-	-	-	-	-	F	F	F	F	F	F	F	F	F	F	F
Young, George, Jr.	-	-	-	-	-	-	-	-	-	-	-	-	-	-	SM	SM	-	-	-

APPENDIX D

Members of the Country Club of Ithaca
Selected Years, 1920-1989

Key to Membership Symbols:

AS = Associate	B = (AS + S + R)	C = Under 30
CL = Clergy	D = Under 25	F = Family
HS = House	HON = Honorary	JR = Junior
L = Leave	NR = Nonresident	R = Retired
REC = Recreation	S = Single	SL = Single lady
SM = Single man	SOC = Social	TN = Tennis

NAME	1920	'25	'30	'36	'50	'60	'75	'89
Abbott, David M.	-	-	-	-	-	F	-	-
Abbott, George	-	-	-	-	-	F	-	-
Abbott, Robert	-	-	-	-	SM	-	-	-
Abt, Henry E.	-	-	-	-	F	F	-	-
Ackerman, Henry	-	-	-	-	F	-	-	-
Adams, Bristow	F	F	-	-	-	-	-	-
Adams, John C.	-	-	-	-	-	-	HS	-
Adams, Mrs. John C.	-	-	-	-	-	-	-	REC
Addis, Bernard F.	-	-	-	-	-	-	F	F
Affeld, F. O., Jr.	-	-	SM	-	-	-	-	-
Agard, Merritt M.	-	-	-	-	-	F	F	-
Albert, C. D.	-	-	F	-	-	-	-	-
Albree, Fred W.	F	F	F	-	-	-	-	-
Aldridge, John S.	-	-	-	-	-	-	F	-
Alemany, J. B.	-	F	-	-	-	-	-	-
Alexander, Bernard J.	-	-	-	-	-	-	JR	-
Alexander, Miss Katherine	SL	SL	-	-	-	-	-	-
Allanson, C. A.	-	-	-	F	F	-	-	-
Allen, Francis P.	-	-	JR	-	-	-	-	-
Allen, Mrs. N. M.	-	-	SL	-	-	-	-	-
Allen, R. B.	F	-	-	-	-	-	-	-
Allen, Robert N.	-	-	-	-	-	SOC	-	-
Aloi, Thomas A.	-	-	-	-	-	-	S	-
Alspach, Miss Evelyn	SL	-	-	-	-	-	-	-
Altman, William C.	-	-	-	-	-	-	HS	-
Ames, Donald	-	-	JR	-	-	-	-	-
Ames, H. L.	-	-	F	-	-	-	-	-
Ames, Helen L.	-	-	JR	-	-	-	-	-
Amter, Robert F.	-	-	-	-	-	-	-	F
Anderson, W. A.	-	-	-	SM	SM	-	-	-
Andree, Robert	-	-	-	-	-	-	-	NR
Andrew, Walter M.	-	-	-	-	NR	-	-	-
Andrews, Eugene P.	F	-	SM	L	-	-	-	-
Andrews, Miss M.	-	-	-	NR	-	-	-	-
Apgar, Clara S.	SL	SL	SL	SL	-	-	-	-
Appleton, R. W.	-	-	-	L	-	-	-	-
Armstrong, Douglas H.	-	-	-	-	-	-	F	-
Arnett, Martha B.	-	-	-	-	-	-	-	S
Arnold, Edward F.	-	-	-	-	-	-	HS	-
Arquette, Gordon J.	-	-	-	-	-	-	F	HS

NAME	1920	'25	'30	'36	'50	'60	'75	'89
Ash, Suzanne	-	-	-	-	-	-	-	AS
Ashberry, Ray S.	-	-	SM	L	F	-	-	-
Ashman, Curt	-	-	-	-	-	-	-	AS
Atwood, W. G.	-	-	-	F	-	-	-	-
Avery, M. C.	-	-	-	-	F	-	-	-
Avery, Ralph C.	-	-	SM	-	F	-	-	-
Avramis, Bill	-	-	-	-	-	-	-	HS
Babbage, Jack K.	-	-	-	-	-	-	F	R
Babbage, Mark K.	-	-	-	-	-	-	F	-
Babcock, Bruce M.	-	-	-	-	-	-	F	-
Babcock, John B.	-	-	-	-	-	-	F	R
Babcock, Monroe C.	-	-	-	-	-	F	F	NR
Bagnardi, Mrs. Elizabeth	-	-	-	-	-	-	HS	-
Bailey, Austin	SM	-	-	-	-	-	-	-
Bailey, David A.	-	-	-	-	-	-	AS	-
Bailey, E. E.	-	-	-	-	F	-	-	-
Bailey, Edward H.	SM	-	-	-	-	-	-	-
Bailliere, M. V., Jr	-	-	-	-	-	F	-	-
Baker, Bert T.	-	-	-	-	SOC	-	-	-
Baker, Robert W.	-	-	-	-	-	SOC	F	HS
Bakko, R. Norman	-	-	-	F	F	-	-	-
Balderston, Betty	-	-	-	-	-	-	R	R
Baldini, Martje J.	-	-	-	-	-	-	-	R
Baldini, William Q.	-	-	-	-	-	-	F	-
Baldridge, J. Lakin	-	F	F	F	-	-	-	-
Baldwin, H. C.	-	F	F	F	-	-	-	-
Ballard, Donald W.	-	-	-	-	-	F	-	-
Ballenstedt, George H.	-	-	-	F	-	-	-	-
Balliett, Fargo, Jr.	-	-	-	-	F	-	-	F
Bancroft, Gene	-	-	JR	-	-	-	-	-
Bancroft, George	-	SM	F	-	-	-	-	-
Bancroft, Hester	-	-	JR	-	-	-	-	-
Bancroft, John C.	-	SM	SM	NR	-	-	-	-
Bancroft, Wilder D.	F	F	F	F	-	-	-	-
Banfield, Geoffrey	-	-	-	-	-	-	-	F
Bangs, John F.	-	-	-	-	F	-	-	-
Banner, L. William	-	-	-	-	-	SOC	F	-
Barkee, Bernice A.	-	-	SL	-	-	-	-	-
Barker, Charles S.	-	-	-	-	F	-	-	-
Barlow, Mary L.	-	-	JR	-	-	-	-	-
Barlow, Mrs. Bertha H.	-	SL	SL	-	-	-	-	-
Barnard, Louis B.	-	-	-	SM	F	F	-	-
Baron, Edward	-	-	-	-	-	-	F	F
Barr, Charles R., Jr.	-	-	-	-	-	-	AS	-
Barr, J. H.	-	F	F	-	-	-	-	-
Barr, Joseph S.	F	F	F	-	-	SOC	-	-
Barr, Mrs. J. S.	-	-	-	SOC	-	-	-	-
Barrett, E. J.	-	-	SM	-	-	-	-	-
Barrett, Roland	-	-	-	-	SOC	-	-	-
Barrett, William C.	-	-	-	-	-	-	F	HS
Barry, James A.	-	-	-	-	-	F	-	-
Barstow, Dorothy	-	-	SL	NR	-	-	-	-
Barton, Frank A.	F	-	-	-	-	-	-	-
Barton, H. A.	-	-	SM	-	-	-	-	-
Barton, Miss	-	JR	-	-	-	-	-	-
Barton, Mrs. L. W.	-	SL	-	-	-	-	-	-
Barton, Roger W.	-	-	-	-	-	-	F	-
Barton, Mrs. Roger W.	-	-	-	-	-	-	-	HS
Bass, Robert O.	-	-	-	-	-	F	-	-
Bass, W. C.	-	-	-	-	F	-	-	-
Bauerlein, A., Jr.	-	-	-	-	-	F	-	-
Baxter, H. E.	-	SM	-	-	-	-	-	-
Bayer, Barbara S.	-	-	-	-	-	-	-	HS

NAME	1920	'25	'30	'36	'50	'60	'75	'89
Beach, U. E.	-	-	F	-	-	-	-	-
Beacham, J. W.	-	-	F	-	-	-	-	-
Beam, Edward B.	-	-	-	-	-	F	-	-
Beaudry, G. F.	-	-	-	-	NR	-	-	-
Beck, Frederick	-	-	-	-	SM	-	-	-
Beck, Frederick, Jr.	-	-	-	-	-	-	F	F
Beckwith, C. A.	-	-	SM	-	-	-	-	-
Bedell, Caroline	-	JR	-	-	-	-	-	-
Bedell, Frederick	F	F	-	-	-	-	-	-
Begent, Gordon	-	-	-	-	F	-	-	-
Begent, Mrs. Gordon	-	-	-	-	-	SL	-	-
Belcher, Donald J.	-	-	-	-	-	SOC	-	-
Bell, A. H.	-	-	-	-	SOC	-	-	-
Bell, Charles W.	-	-	-	-	-	-	F	F
Bell, Lewis	-	-	-	-	NR	-	-	-
Bement, A.	-	JR	-	-	-	-	-	-
Bement, Louis C.	F	F	SM	-	-	-	-	-
Bement, N.	-	JR	-	-	-	-	-	-
Bemont, Mrs. Isabel L.	-	-	-	-	SL	-	-	-
Benedict, Francis E.	-	-	-	-	-	-	F	F
Benedict, Timothy & Anne	-	-	-	-	-	-	-	AS
Benedict, Valentine & Dorothy	-	-	-	-	-	-	-	F
Benjamin, Charles	-	-	-	-	SOC	-	-	-
Benjamin, Charles S.	-	-	-	-	-	F	-	-
Benjamin, Earl W.	F	-	-	-	-	-	-	-
Bennett, Thomas H.	-	-	-	-	-	-	F	R
Benscoter, C. A.	-	-	-	-	F	-	-	-
Bergmann, Frederick G.	-	-	-	-	-	SM	-	-
Bero, James D.	-	-	-	-	-	F	-	-
Berry, Hilda	-	-	JR	-	-	-	-	-
Berry, Miss	-	-	JR	-	-	-	-	-
Berry, Romeyn	F	F	SM	-	-	-	-	-
Berry, Mrs. Romeyn	-	-	-	-	-	SL	-	-
Berth, Donald F.	-	-	-	-	-	-	HS	-
Bertram, W. W.	-	-	-	SM	-	-	-	-
Besancon, Phillip H.	-	-	-	-	-	SOC	-	F
Best, Judith A.	-	-	-	-	-	-	F	S
Betten, Cornelius	-	-	F	-	-	-	-	-
Betten, Cornelius, Jr.	-	-	SM	-	-	-	-	-
Beyer, Glen H.	-	-	-	-	SM	-	-	-
Bicknell, Harrison C.	-	-	-	-	-	SOC	-	-
Binzel, Miss Cora E.	SL	-	-	-	-	-	-	-
Bird, Maura W.	-	-	-	-	-	-	-	AS
Bird, Miss P. G.	-	-	-	SL	-	-	-	-
Bishop, Miss Alison	-	-	-	-	JR	-	-	-
Bishop, Miss Eva	-	SL	-	-	-	-	-	-
Bishop, Morris G.	-	-	F	-	SM	-	-	-
Bishop, Mrs. Morris (Alison K.)	-	-	-	-	-	-	HS	-
Blair, Charles H.	-	-	-	-	NR	-	-	-
Blanchard, Raymond E.	-	-	-	-	-	-	F	-
Blasko, Stella	-	-	-	-	-	-	S	S
Blinn, Miss Alice	SL	-	-	-	-	-	-	-
Bloetjes, Mrs. Mary	-	-	-	-	-	SOC	-	-
Blomquist, A. T., Jr.	-	-	-	-	JR	-	-	-
Blomquist, Alfred T.	-	-	-	-	F	SOC	-	-
Blood, Charles H.	F	F	F	F	-	-	-	-
Bodine, C. P.	-	-	-	-	SOC	-	-	-
Bodley, Mrs. C. F.	SL	-	-	-	-	-	-	-
Bogert, George G.	F	F	-	-	-	-	-	-
Boggess, William T.	-	-	-	-	-	-	-	F
Bohland, Bernhard S.	-	-	-	-	F	F	F	R
Boice, Ned G.	-	-	-	-	-	SOC	-	-
Bolger, Mary L.	-	-	SL	-	-	-	-	-

NAME	1920	'25	'30	'36	'50	'60	'75	'89
Bond, M.	-	F	-	-	-	-	-	-
Boochever, L. C.	-	-	F	F	-	-	-	-
Boochever, L. C., Jr.	-	-	-	JR	-	-	-	-
Bookholder, W. H.	-	SM	-	-	-	-	-	-
Booraem, R. M.	-	-	SM	-	-	-	-	-
Booth, Mrs. M. Van Cleef	-	-	-	-	-	-	F	S
Boothroyd, Robert L.	-	-	-	-	-	-	HS	HS
Boothroyd, Robert S.	-	-	-	-	-	SOC	F	-
Boothroyd, Mrs. Robert S.	-	-	-	-	-	-	-	NR
Borst, Victor D., Jr.	-	-	-	-	-	-	HS	-
Bostwick, Charles D.	F	F	F	-	-	-	-	-
Bostwick, Emily	-	-	JR	-	-	-	-	-
Bostwick, Julia B.	-	SL	-	-	-	-	-	-
Bostwick, Miss Ada T.	SL	-	-	-	-	-	-	-
Bostwick, Miss Sarah	SL	SL	SL	L	-	-	-	-
Bosworth, Frank H.	F	F	F	F	-	-	-	-
Bower, C. W.	-	SM	-	-	-	-	-	-
Bowman, John J.	-	-	-	-	-	-	F	-
Boyd, W. A.	-	F	-	-	-	-	-	-
Boynton, Frank D.	F	-	-	-	-	-	-	-
Boynton, H. G.	-	-	-	-	F	-	-	-
Boynton, Mrs. J.	-	-	-	SL	-	-	-	-
Bradley, Jane Lee	-	-	-	-	-	-	HS	-
Bradley, Richard C.	-	-	-	-	-	SOC	-	-
Bradt, Elizabeth B.	-	-	-	-	-	-	-	S
Brainard, Paul	-	-	-	-	F	SOC	-	-
Brand, Walter N.	-	-	F	L	-	-	-	-
Brand, Mrs. Walter N.	-	-	-	-	-	SOC	-	-
Bransman, H. C.	-	SM	-	-	-	-	-	-
Brashear, H. R.	-	-	SM	SM	-	-	-	-
Brauner, Olaf M.	F	SM	F	-	-	-	-	-
Bredbenner, Edgar E.	-	-	SM	F	F	-	-	-
Bretz, Julian P.	SM	-	-	-	-	-	-	-
Brew, Clifford E.	-	-	-	-	F	F	-	-
Brewer, R. Selden	-	-	-	-	-	F	-	-
Broadwell, Herbert E.	-	-	-	-	F	F	F	R
Brock, Harry W.	-	-	-	-	-	F	-	-
Brooks, Miss Carolyn	SL	SL	-	-	-	-	-	-
Brooks, Mrs. B. E. (Lucy T.)	-	-	-	SL	SOC	-	HS	-
Brooks, Mrs. John G. (Maude S.)	SL	SL	SL	-	-	-	-	-
Brown, F. L., Jr.	-	-	F	F	F	F	-	-
Brown, Mrs. F. L.	-	-	-	-	-	-	S	-
Brown, Frederick S.	-	-	-	-	-	-	F	F
Brown, H. McD.	-	F	-	-	-	-	-	-
Brown, H. S.	-	-	SM	SM	-	-	-	-
Brown, Mrs. Bertha	-	-	-	-	SL	-	-	-
Brucher, Miss O. P.	-	-	-	SL	-	-	-	-
Brundage, Edward F.	-	-	-	-	F	SOC	-	-
Brunett, E. L.	-	-	-	F	-	-	-	-
Brunk, Max E.	-	-	-	-	SM	-	F	-
Bryant, Fred B.	-	-	-	-	SOC	SOC	-	-
Bryant, Laura	SL	-	-	-	-	-	-	-
Bryant, Winifred M.	-	-	SL	SL	SOC	-	-	-
Bucci, Adam	-	-	-	-	L	-	-	-
Bucci, Patrick	-	-	-	-	F	SM	-	-
Buchanan, N. S.	-	-	SM	-	-	-	-	-
Bueche, Arthur M.	-	-	-	-	F	-	-	-
Bugliari, Joseph B.	-	-	-	-	-	-	F	F
Buhl, Timothy C.	-	-	-	-	-	-	AS	-
Bull, Edward L.	F	-	-	-	-	-	-	-
Burch, Miss Betty	-	-	-	-	SL	-	-	-
Burchard, Seth W.	-	-	-	-	-	-	HS	HS
Burdick, Charles K.	F	F	-	-	-	-	-	-

NAME	1920	'25	'30	'36	'50	'60	'75	'89
Burke, Edmund J., Jr.	-	-	-	-	-	-	AS	-
Burkholder, W. H.	-	-	SM	-	-	-	-	-
Burness, Charles S.	-	-	-	-	-	-	F	-
Burnham, Leroy P.	F	F	F	-	-	-	-	-
Burns, Miss Elizabeth	-	-	-	-	SOC	-	-	-
Burns, Robert M.	-	-	-	-	-	-	HS	-
Burns, Ruth	-	-	-	-	SOC	SOC	HS	-
Burrell, Margaret	-	-	SL	-	-	-	-	-
Burrows, E. N.	-	-	-	F	SOC	-	-	-
Burrows, Mrs. E. N.	-	-	SL	-	-	-	-	-
Burruss, Clay	-	-	-	-	-	-	-	AS
Burton, John E.	-	-	-	-	-	SOC	-	-
Butler, Karl D.	-	-	-	-	-	SOC	-	-
Butterworth, J. E.	-	-	F	F	-	-	-	-
Butterworth, J. Scott	-	-	SM	-	-	-	-	-
Button, E. D.	F	-	-	-	-	-	-	-
Buzzell, Gordon C.	-	-	-	-	-	F	-	-
Byrne, William	-	-	-	SM	SM	-	-	-
Byrnes, James J.	-	-	-	-	-	-	-	REC
Cady, L. E.	-	-	-	F	-	-	-	-
Cafferillo, Sheila H.	-	-	-	-	-	-	-	F
Caldwell, Howard R.	-	-	-	-	-	-	-	CL
Caldwell, Lawrence B.	-	-	-	-	-	-	F	F
Calkins, H. F.	-	-	F	-	-	-	-	-
Cameron, H. S.	-	-	-	F	-	-	-	-
Campbell, Fanny	-	SL	-	-	-	-	-	-
Campbell, Joseph B.	-	-	-	-	NR	F	-	-
Campbell, M. E. (Scotty)	-	-	-	SM	F	-	-	-
Campbell, Mrs. Charles H.	-	-	SL	-	-	-	-	-
Canders, Phillip J.	-	-	-	-	-	-	AS	-
Canfield, Thomas H.	-	-	-	-	-	SOC	-	-
Capece, Michael J.	-	-	-	-	NR	-	-	-
Carey, Henry A.	-	-	F	-	-	SOC	-	-
Carlson, Leo S.	-	-	-	-	SM	-	-	-
Carlyon, Harold R.	-	-	-	-	-	F	-	-
Carpenter, Mrs. C. M.	-	-	SL	-	-	-	-	-
Carrigg, James A.	-	-	-	-	-	-	F	-
Carroll, Charles H.	F	-	-	-	-	-	-	-
Carver, Arthur	-	-	-	SM	-	-	-	-
Carver, John	-	-	JR	SM	F	-	-	-
Carver, W. W.	-	-	JR	SM	-	-	-	-
Carver, Walter B.	F	F	F	F	SM	-	-	-
Caryl, Robert J.	-	-	-	-	-	-	AS	F
Case, C. F.	-	F	F	NR	-	-	-	-
Case, Louise	-	-	JR	-	-	-	-	-
Cashman, C. J.	-	-	-	-	SOC	-	-	-
Catherwood, M. P.	-	-	-	-	F	-	HS	-
Causer, James A.	F	F	F	-	-	-	-	-
Causer, Mrs. Laura H.	-	-	-	SL	SL	SOC	-	-
Causer, Robert L.	-	SM	SM	SM	SM	-	-	-
Ceurvels, Ronald F.	-	-	-	-	-	-	-	AS
Chamberlain, A. W.	-	-	-	SM	-	-	-	-
Chamberlain, Floyd B.	SM	-	-	-	-	-	-	-
Chamberlain, J. Mark	F	-	-	-	-	-	-	-
Chamberlain, P. R.	-	-	SM	-	-	-	-	-
Chamberlain, R. F.	-	-	-	-	F	-	-	-
Chambers, R. E.	-	-	F	F	-	-	-	-
Chambers, W. E.	-	-	-	-	L	-	-	-
Chambers, William	-	-	JR	-	-	-	-	-
Champaign, L. M.	-	-	-	F	F	-	-	-
Champaign, Mrs. K.	-	SL	-	-	-	-	-	-
Champlin, O. K.	-	-	-	-	SOC	-	-	-
Chandler, Donald F.	-	-	-	-	-	-	-	F

NAME	1920	'25	'30	'36	'50	'60	'75	'89
Chandler, John C.	-	-	-	-	-	SOC	-	-
Chandler, Mrs. J. Halsey	-	-	-	-	SL	-	-	-
Chapman, John	-	-	-	-	JR	-	-	-
Charton, Paul W.	-	-	-	-	-	SOC	-	-
Chase, Miss Dorothy C.	-	-	-	-	SL	-	-	-
Chase, R. M.	-	-	NR	-	-	-	-	-
Chick, Mrs. F. E.	-	-	-	-	-	-	S	-
Childers, William B.	-	-	-	-	-	-	-	AS
Christenat, H. B.	-	-	SM	L	-	-	-	-
Christian, Cahrles R.	-	-	-	-	-	F	-	-
Christiansen, Robert	-	-	-	-	-	F	F	-
Church, Corinne	-	-	-	-	-	-	-	AS
Church, Miss Elsie S.	SL	-	-	-	-	-	-	-
Clapper, Lynn M.	-	-	-	-	F	-	-	-
Clarey, B. M.	-	-	-	F	F	F	-	-
Clark, H. G.	-	-	-	F	F	-	-	-
Clark, J. S.	-	-	-	-	SM	-	-	-
Clark, J. T.	-	-	-	F	-	-	-	-
Clark, J. T., Jr.	-	-	-	JR	-	-	-	-
Clark, Mrs. Carolyn M.	-	-	-	-	-	SL	-	-
Clarke, T. J.	-	-	-	-	F	-	-	-
Cleary, Donald M.	-	-	-	-	SM	CL	-	-
Cleary, S. F.	-	SM	SM	-	-	-	-	-
Cleary, Thomas K.	-	-	-	-	-	CL	CL	-
Cleveland, Clarence	-	-	-	-	-	-	-	F
Clifford, Frank R.	-	-	-	-	-	-	F	R
Clines, Mrs. James	-	-	-	-	SOC	-	-	-
Clinton, C. Lewis	SM	-	-	-	-	-	-	-
Clynes, James J.	-	-	-	-	F	F	-	-
Clynes, James J., Jr.	-	-	-	-	JR	F	S	S
Coe, Willis G.	-	-	-	-	-	-	F	-
Coffin, Foster M.	F	SM	F	L	-	-	-	-
Colbert, Betsy M.	-	-	-	-	-	-	-	AS
Colbert, Robert R., Sr.	-	-	-	-	-	SOC	-	HS
Cole, Ernest J., Jr.	-	-	-	-	-	SOC	-	-
Cole, S. A.	-	-	-	F	-	-	-	-
Coleman, George L.	SM	-	-	-	-	-	-	-
Coles, Haines	-	-	-	-	F	-	-	-
Collins, John J., Jr.	-	-	-	-	-	F	-	-
Collyer, Frank	-	-	-	-	-	-	-	F
Comar, Miss Ann P.	-	-	-	-	-	SL	-	-
Comber, Stewart M.	-	-	-	-	-	-	F	-
Compagni, Frederick G.	-	-	-	-	-	-	F	-
Comstock, John A.	-	-	-	-	F	-	-	-
Comstock, John, Jr.	-	-	-	-	JR	-	-	-
Condon, George E.	-	F	-	-	-	-	-	-
Conley, J. W.	-	-	F	-	-	-	-	-
Conley, Joseph T.	-	-	-	-	-	SOC	-	-
Conley, Miss Alice K.	-	-	-	-	SL	SL	-	-
Conlin, Miss Katherine M.	SL	-	-	-	-	-	-	-
Conneman, George J.	-	-	-	-	-	-	-	HS
Connor, C. A.	-	SM	-	-	-	-	-	-
Conta, Bart	-	-	-	-	-	SOC	-	-
Conta, Claire	-	-	-	-	-	-	-	F
Conway, Frank	-	-	-	-	SM	-	-	-
Conwell, Walter L.	-	-	SM	SM	SM	-	-	-
Cook, Junius F.	F	-	-	-	-	-	-	-
Cook, Junius F., Jr.	SM	-	-	-	-	-	-	-
Cooke, Mrs. William (Mary)	-	-	-	-	-	-	F	-
Cooke, W. P.	-	SM	SM	-	-	-	-	-
Cooke, William E.	-	-	-	-	-	-	AS	-
Coon, Ernest, Jr.	-	-	-	-	-	F	-	-
Coors, Mrs. Dorothea M.	-	-	-	-	-	SOC	-	-

NAME	1920	'25	'30	'36	'50	'60	'75	'89
Copeland, Harry C.	-	-	-	-	F	-	-	-
Corcoran, W. B.	-	-	-	-	SOC	-	-	-
Corless, Ruth	-	-	-	-	-	-	S	-
Cornelius, Archie B.	-	-	-	-	-	SOC	-	-
Cornelius, Mrs. Archie B.	-	-	-	-	-	-	S	R
Cornelius, Harold J.	-	-	-	-	-	-	F	-
Cornell, Ezra	-	-	-	-	-	-	AS	HS
Cornell, Franklin C., Jr.	F	F	-	-	-	-	-	-
Cornish, Elizabeth	-	-	-	-	-	-	-	HS
Cosentini, Joseph	-	-	-	-	-	F	R	-
Cosentini, Joseph P.	-	-	-	-	-	F	F	-
Costello, John E.	-	-	-	-	-	-	F	-
Court, H. W.	-	-	-	-	-	F	-	-
Cramton, Robert C.	-	-	-	-	-	-	-	REC
Crandall, Carl	-	-	-	-	F	SOC	-	-
Crane, Thomas Frederick	F	-	-	-	-	-	-	-
Crispell, Leslie, Jr.	-	-	-	-	-	SM	-	-
Crissey, Jack	-	-	-	-	F	SOC	-	-
Crosby, D. J.	SM	SM	-	-	-	-	-	-
Crosby, Richard	-	JR	-	-	-	-	-	-
Cross, A. A.	-	-	SM	-	-	-	-	-
Cross, George E.	-	-	F	F	F	F	-	-
Cross, Mrs. George E. (Blanche)	-	-	-	-	-	-	HS	HON
Crouch, Helen B.	-	-	SL	-	-	-	-	-
Crouse, N. M.	-	F	-	TN	-	-	-	-
Crowley, A. W.	-	F	F	F	F	-	-	-
Crowley, Daniel	-	F	-	-	-	-	-	-
Crowley, Miss Margaret C.	-	-	-	-	-	SL	-	-
Crowley, Robert L.	-	-	-	-	-	-	F	F
Cullen, Robert L.	-	-	-	-	SM	F	F	R
Cullen, Terence M.	-	-	-	-	-	-	-	F
Culver, George W.	F	-	-	-	-	-	-	-
Curchin, M. M.	-	-	F	F	SM	-	-	-
Curran, Richard C.	-	-	-	-	-	F	F	NR
Currey, Charles T.	-	-	-	-	-	-	AS	-
Curtis, Charles E.	F	F	-	-	-	-	-	-
Cusick, John C.	-	-	-	-	-	-	-	F
Cuthbert, Miss Margaret Ross	SL	-	-	-	-	-	-	-
Cynoske, David E.	-	-	-	-	F	F	F	HS
Dahmen, Ernest A., Jr.	-	-	-	-	F	F	-	-
Dahmen, H. B.	-	-	-	-	F	-	-	-
Daino, Joseph F.	-	-	-	-	F	F	HS	HS
Dale, A. C.	-	-	-	-	F	-	-	-
Dale, Marjorie	-	-	-	JR	-	-	-	-
Dale, Mrs. G. I.	-	-	SL	SL	-	-	-	-
Daley, Richard	-	-	-	-	-	-	F	-
Dall, J. J., Jr.	-	F	F	F	-	-	-	-
Daniels, C. W.	-	SM	SM	F	-	-	-	-
Daniels, Thomas F.	-	-	-	-	-	-	-	F
Dann, Hollis E.	F	-	-	-	-	-	-	-
Dates, Miss H.	-	-	-	NR	-	-	-	-
Davis, E. Gorton	F	-	-	-	-	-	-	-
Davis, Herman B.	-	-	-	-	-	-	F	-
Davis, Miss R.	-	-	-	SL	-	-	-	-
Davis, Mrs. A. C.	-	-	-	-	SL	-	-	-
Davis, R. Wendell	-	-	-	-	-	F	F	-
Davis, Mrs. R. Wendell	-	-	-	-	-	-	-	R
Daw, Lawrence	-	SM	SM	-	-	-	-	-
Dayton, C. Edwin	-	-	-	-	F	F	-	-
Dayton, Frances H.	-	-	-	-	-	-	-	HS
Dean, Frank S.	-	-	-	F	F	-	-	-
Dean, Gertrude	-	-	SL	-	-	-	-	-
Dean, Robert T.	-	-	-	-	F	F	F	R

NAME	1920	'25	'30	'36	'50	'60	'75	'89
Dean, William T.	-	-	-	-	-	SOC	-	-
Deck, E. W.	-	-	-	-	F	-	-	-
Deibler, Gordon	-	-	-	-	-	-	-	HS
Del Rosso, Victor	-	-	-	-	-	-	F	HS
Dembitski, Peter H.	-	-	-	-	-	-	AS	-
Denman, C. E.	SM	F	F	L	-	-	-	-
Dennis, Louis M.	F	F	F	L	-	-	-	-
Denniston, H. P.	-	-	F	F	-	-	-	-
DeSanto, Martin J.	-	-	-	-	-	-	-	F
Devricks, R. K.	-	-	-	-	F	-	-	-
DiGiacomo, Angelo R.	-	-	-	-	-	-	F	-
DiGiacomo, Anthony C.	-	-	-	-	-	SOC	F	REC
Dillenbeck, W. E.	-	-	-	F	-	-	-	-
Dillingham, H. I.	-	-	-	-	-	SOC	-	-
Dillon, William A.	-	F	-	-	-	-	-	-
Dillon, William A., Jr.	-	-	-	-	SM	F	F	-
DiPasquale, Raymond A.	-	-	-	-	-	-	F	-
Dixon, C. R.	-	-	-	F	-	-	-	-
Dixon, Miss Margery	SL	SL	-	-	-	-	-	-
Dobie, Gilmour	SM	SM	SM	-	-	-	-	-
Dodge, W. W.	-	F	-	-	-	-	-	-
Doebler, Lawrence	-	-	-	-	-	-	-	F
Doepke, Charles W.	-	-	-	-	-	F	-	-
Doig, Russell I.	-	-	-	NR	SM	-	-	-
Dolph, June P.	-	-	-	-	-	-	-	R
Dolph, Ormsby	-	-	-	-	-	F	F	-
Donald, Jack	-	-	-	-	-	SM	-	-
Donohue, Florence	-	-	SL	-	-	-	-	-
Donohue, Ralph E.	-	-	-	-	-	SOC	-	-
Doremus, Mabel	-	-	-	-	-	-	HS	-
Dorsey, J. F.	-	F	F	-	-	-	-	-
Dorst, Mrs. Frederick W.	-	-	-	-	-	-	-	CL
Downey, J. J. C.	-	-	-	-	F	-	-	-
Downing, Marshall	-	-	-	-	-	-	-	HS
Downing, William S., Jr.	-	-	-	-	-	F	F	R
Drinkwater, David	-	-	-	-	-	-	-	F
Driscoll, E. J.	-	-	-	SM	-	-	-	-
Driscoll, R. P.	-	-	SM	-	-	-	-	-
Driscoll, R. P., Jr.	-	-	-	-	-	-	S	-
Driscoll, Susan	-	-	SL	-	-	-	-	-
Dudley, Eric	F	F	F	-	-	-	-	-
Dudley, Ralph	-	-	-	-	F	-	-	-
Dudley, William	-	-	-	-	JR	-	-	-
Dunbar, C. L.	-	-	-	-	F	F	-	-
Dunbar, Mrs. Carrie S.	-	-	-	-	-	-	HON	-
Dunning, Franklin W.	-	-	-	-	-	-	-	F
Dunphy, Cornelia	-	-	SL	-	-	-	-	-
Durham, A. G.	-	-	SM	-	-	-	-	-
Durham, A. L.	-	-	SM	-	-	-	-	-
Durham, Charles L.	F	F	SM	F	-	-	-	-
Durham, David H.	-	-	JR	SM	F	-	-	-
Durham, G. E.	-	-	SM	-	-	-	-	-
Durland, Lewis H.	-	-	SM	SM	F	F	R	-
Durland, Mrs. Clara J.	-	-	-	SL	SL	SL	-	-
Durland, Mrs. Margaret	-	-	-	-	-	-	S	R
Dusinberre, Mrs. A. B. (Rhea)	-	-	-	-	SL	SL	S	-
Dykema, Norman D.	-	-	-	-	-	-	F	-
Dykes, Charles E.	-	-	-	-	F	-	-	-
Earle, Jeffery	-	-	-	-	-	-	-	AS
Eaton, Miss Ethel G.	-	-	-	-	SL	-	-	-
Eckelmann, Herman J.	-	-	-	-	-	-	CL	-
Eckley, P. W.	-	-	F	F	-	-	-	-
Edelman, Audrey	-	-	-	-	-	-	-	F

NAME	1920	'25	'30	'36	'50	'60	'75	'89
Edson, Miss I. E.	-	-	-	-	SL	SL	-	-
Egan, Jack	-	-	-	-	NR	-	-	-
Egan, William M.	-	-	-	-	-	SOC	-	-
Egbert, Mrs. Alice G.	-	-	-	-	-	-	HS	-
Egbert, Perry T.	-	-	-	-	-	F	-	-
Elkins, Leonard	-	-	-	-	-	SOC	F	R
Ellenwood, F. O.	-	F	SM	F	-	-	-	-
Elles, Edward S., Jr.	-	-	-	-	-	-	-	F
Elliott, R. W. B.	-	SM	-	NR	-	-	-	-
Elliott, Mrs. R. W. B.	-	SL	-	-	-	-	-	-
Elliott, Roswell	-	-	-	-	F	F	F	-
Ellsworth, William S.	-	-	-	-	F	-	-	-
Elmer, C. J.	-	SM	F	-	-	-	-	-
Elmer, Herbert Charles	F	F	F	-	-	-	-	-
Embody, Dan	-	-	JR	-	-	-	-	-
Embody, G. C.	-	-	SM	-	-	-	-	-
Emerson, R. A.	-	-	SM	SM	-	-	-	-
Emerson, Willard I.	-	-	-	-	-	SOC	-	-
Emmanuel, Victor	-	-	-	-	-	SOC	-	-
Engdahl, Serena	-	-	-	-	SL	-	-	-
English, Donald	SM	SM	SM	L	-	-	-	-
Eno, A. M.	-	-	-	-	F	-	-	-
Ensworth, Herbert K.	-	-	-	-	-	-	-	HS
Enzian, Henry F.	-	-	-	-	-	F	F	-
Enzian, Mrs. Henry F.	-	-	-	-	-	-	-	R
Erdman, Ellis E.	-	-	-	-	-	F	-	-
Ericson, Myrtle H.	-	-	-	-	-	-	-	HS
Euvrard, Alan D.	-	-	-	-	-	-	-	REC
Evans, Cadwallader	F	-	-	-	-	-	-	-
Everett, Miss Dorothy G.	-	-	-	-	SOC	SOC	-	-
Ewanicki, John	-	-	-	-	-	-	F	R
Exo, Miss F.	-	-	-	SL	-	-	-	-
Fagan, Charles F.	-	-	-	-	F	-	-	-
Faigin, Stanley	-	-	-	-	-	-	F	F
Fallon, Edmund H.	-	-	-	-	F	F	-	-
Farinella, Paul J.	-	-	-	-	-	-	F	-
Farley, E. J.	-	-	F	-	-	-	-	-
Farley, Joseph F.	-	-	-	SM	F	-	-	-
Farnham, Miss Janet	-	-	-	-	JR	-	-	-
Farnham, William H.	-	-	SM	TN	F	-	HS	-
Farnham, Mrs. William H.	-	-	-	-	-	-	-	HS
Farnsworth, W. Robert	-	-	-	-	F	F	R	HON
Farrand, Livingston	-	F	F	F	-	-	-	-
Faust, Albert B.	SM	-	-	-	-	-	-	-
Federer, Walter R.	-	-	-	-	F	-	-	-
Felton, Garrett J.	-	-	-	-	-	SOC	-	-
Fennell, Mary K.	-	SL	-	-	-	-	-	-
Fenner, J. Hubert	-	SM	F	-	-	-	-	-
Fenton, George E.	-	-	-	-	F	-	-	-
Ferris, J. David	-	-	-	-	-	-	-	F
Fertik, Harry	-	-	-	-	-	-	F	-
Fey, William H.	-	-	-	-	-	SOC	-	-
Fields, William J.	-	-	-	-	-	SOC	-	-
Filios, Achilles M.	-	-	-	-	-	-	HS	-
Finch, Dudley F.	F	-	-	-	-	-	-	-
Finch, Katherine	-	SL	SL	-	-	-	-	-
Finch, Miss Mary S.	SL	SL	-	-	-	-	-	-
Finney, Glenn E.	-	-	-	-	F	SOC	-	-
Fioravanti, Lennie A.	-	-	-	-	-	-	-	F
Fisher, A. Craig	-	-	-	-	-	-	F	-
Fitch, R. B.	-	-	-	-	F	F	-	-
Flack, Harold	SM	F	F	-	-	-	-	-
Flanagan, L. T.	-	-	-	-	NR	-	-	-

NAME	1920	'25	'30	'36	'50	'60	'75	'89
Flanagan, Leo J.	-	-	-	-	SM	-	-	-
Flanders, Deborah	-	-	-	-	-	-	-	AS
Flannery, Jerry	-	-	-	-	SM	-	-	-
Flannery, Robert W.	-	-	-	-	-	SOC	-	-
Fleming, D. Wayne	-	-	-	-	-	-	-	F
Fleming, Joel	-	-	-	-	-	SOC	-	-
Fleming, Robert J.	-	-	-	-	SM	-	-	-
Fletcher, R. H.	-	-	-	-	F	-	-	-
Flumerfelt, Ray R.	-	-	-	-	F	F	-	-
Flynn, Bernard	-	-	-	-	F	-	-	-
Foote, Charles	-	-	-	-	SM	-	-	-
Ford, Mabel	-	-	-	-	SL	-	-	-
Ford, W. R.	-	-	-	-	L	-	-	-
Forrester, William R.	-	-	-	-	-	-	HS	-
Forsyth, Mrs. W. L.	-	-	-	-	SL	-	-	-
Foster, Janet E.	-	-	-	-	JR	-	-	-
Foster, Jim R.	-	-	-	-	-	-	-	F
Foster, William J., Jr.	-	-	-	-	F	F	-	-
Foster, Mrs. William J., Jr.	-	-	-	-	-	-	HS	-
Frank, William W.	-	-	-	-	-	-	F	-
Freedman, Marvin	-	-	-	-	-	F	F	-
Fried, Jerome K.	F	F	F	L	-	-	-	-
Friedlander, William	-	-	-	-	-	-	-	F
Fry, George D.	-	-	-	-	F	F	-	-
Fry, Mrs. George D. (Louise T.)	-	-	-	-	-	-	S	R
Fuller, Howard	-	-	-	-	-	-	-	AS
Fulmer, Sterling J.	-	-	-	-	-	-	F	-
Fulton, C. W.	-	SM	-	-	-	-	-	-
Gage, Victor	-	-	-	-	SOC	-	-	-
Gallagher, Joseph D., Jr.	-	-	-	-	-	SOC	-	-
Gallagher, Richard H.	-	-	-	-	-	-	F	-
Gardner, Richard A.	-	-	-	-	-	-	AS	-
Garling, Mrs. Julia S.	-	-	-	-	SOC	-	-	-
Gates, Reeder D.	-	-	-	-	-	-	AS	F
Gauntlett, Mrs. J. C. (M.C.)	SL	SL	SL	-	-	-	-	-
Gay, Mrs. Marie	-	-	-	-	-	-	HS	-
Geer, William C.	-	-	F	F	F	SOC	-	-
Gelder, W. E.	-	-	-	F	-	-	-	-
Gentle, Avery D.	-	-	-	-	-	-	F	R
Georgia, Marianne	-	-	-	-	-	-	-	S
Gervan, R. B.	-	-	-	-	F	-	-	-
Getman, Roy A.	-	-	-	-	-	SOC	-	-
Gettig, William P.	-	-	-	-	-	-	-	F
Gibb, Arthur N.	F	-	-	-	-	-	-	-
Gibb, Mrs. Sally B.	-	-	-	-	-	-	F	-
Gibbs, Robert W.	-	-	-	-	-	SOC	-	-
Gibson, Frances E.	-	-	-	-	-	-	HS	-
Gibson, Michael J. W.	-	-	-	-	-	-	-	AS
Gill, A. Capen	F	-	F	-	-	-	-	-
Gill, W. R.	-	-	-	-	F	-	-	-
Gillespie, D. C.	F	F	F	-	-	-	-	-
Gillespie, Mrs. J. B.	-	-	-	L	-	-	-	-
Gillette, D. G.	-	-	F	F	F	SOC	-	-
Gillette, Mrs. D. G. (Maude)	-	SL	-	-	-	-	HS	-
Gilman, H. L.	-	-	-	F	-	-	-	-
Gilman, Mrs. H. L.	-	-	-	-	SL	-	-	-
Ginnetti, C. V. (Gus)	-	-	-	-	F	F	-	-
Giordano, Vincent	-	-	-	-	-	-	F	-
Giroux, J. T.	-	-	SM	L	-	-	-	-
Glover, Elson K.	-	-	-	-	-	SOC	-	-
Gober, A. T.	-	-	-	-	F	-	-	-
Goldberg, I. Stanley	-	-	-	-	-	-	F	-
Goldberg, Mrs. William J.	-	-	-	-	-	-	S	REC

NAME	1920	'25	'30	'36	'50	'60	'75	'89
Goldman, Richard L.	-	-	-	-	-	-	-	AS
Gomez, Gregory	-	-	-	-	-	-	JR	-
Gondek, Stephen	-	-	-	-	-	SOC	-	-
Goodhue, Everett A.	SM	-	-	-	-	-	-	-
Goodman, H. L.	-	-	F	F	-	-	-	-
Gorsky, John	-	-	-	-	-	-	-	REC
Gould, L. A.	-	F	F	-	-	-	-	-
Grade, Mrs. Arnold E.	-	-	-	-	-	-	HS	-
Grant, Frank W.	F	-	-	-	-	-	-	-
Grant, Mrs. Louis B.	F	-	-	-	-	-	-	-
Grant, Robert S.	-	-	-	-	F	F	F	R
Green, Douglas J.	-	-	-	-	-	-	-	CL
Greenfield, W. E.	-	-	-	NR	-	-	-	-
Gregg, James L.	-	-	-	-	-	SOC	-	-
Grossman, Peter G.	-	-	-	-	-	-	-	AS
Grover, Jeanne	-	-	-	-	-	SL	S	S
Guentert, Leo	-	-	-	-	-	-	HS	-
Guerlac, Henry	-	-	-	-	-	SOC	-	-
Guerlac, Mrs. Henry	-	-	-	SL	-	-	-	-
Guerlac, Othon G.	F	F	F	-	-	-	-	-
Guise, Cedric H.	-	SM	SM	SM	SM	SM	S	-
Guttery, Max	-	-	-	-	F	-	-	-
Hagan, W. A.	-	-	-	F	F	-	-	-
Hagin, Mrs. M. L.	-	-	SL	-	-	-	-	-
Haines, M. L.	-	SM	SM	-	-	-	-	-
Halbleib, William F.	-	-	-	-	-	F	-	-
Hall, Dennis	-	SM	-	-	-	-	-	-
Halleen, David H.	-	-	-	-	-	-	F	-
Halstead, Mrs. C. P.	-	-	-	-	-	SOC	-	-
Halverson, R. E.	-	-	SM	F	-	-	-	-
Hamlet, Mark J.	-	-	-	-	-	-	-	F
Hammond, A. K.	-	-	SM	-	-	-	-	-
Hammond, William A.	F	SM	SM	-	-	-	-	-
Hancock, Robert H.	-	-	-	-	-	F	F	-
Hanford, Nathan	F	F	F	-	-	-	-	-
Hanna, M. R.	-	-	-	-	F	-	-	-
Hanshaw, Frank	-	-	-	-	-	-	F	S
Hardin, Martin	F	F	F	-	-	-	-	-
Hardy, Ralph W. F.	-	-	-	-	-	-	-	HS
Hargett, Daniel T.	-	-	-	-	-	-	-	AS
Haring, Howard W.	-	-	-	-	-	SOC	-	-
Harman, John A., III	-	-	-	-	-	SOC	HS	HS
Hartnett, Joseph	-	-	-	-	-	-	HS	-
Hartnett, Mrs. Joseph M.	-	-	-	-	-	-	-	HS
Hartshorne, James M.	-	-	-	-	-	SOC	-	-
Hasbrouck, Kenneth W.	-	-	-	-	-	F	R	R
Hassan, Barbara T.	-	-	-	-	-	-	-	HS
Hassan, George	-	-	-	-	SOC	-	-	-
Hassan, Margaret	-	SL	SL	SL	SL	SL	-	-
Hauenstein, B. F.	-	-	F	-	-	-	-	-
Hauenstein, Mrs. B. F.	-	-	-	SL	-	-	-	-
Hause, Nancy E.	-	-	SL	-	-	-	-	-
Hawley, F. M.	-	-	-	-	NR	-	-	-
Hawley, Myron	-	-	-	-	F	-	-	-
Hawthorn, Jack	-	-	-	-	NR	-	-	-
Hazzard, James	-	-	-	-	-	-	-	S
Head, Clarence E.	F	F	F	F	-	-	-	-
Head, Laura A.	-	-	SL	-	-	-	-	-
Head, Ralph W.	-	-	-	-	SM	F	-	-
Head, Robert H.	-	-	-	-	-	-	HS	-
Head, Robert W.	-	SM	SM	F	-	-	-	-
Heasley, Walter C., Jr.	-	-	-	-	F	SOC	-	-
Heasley, Mrs. Walter C., Jr.	-	-	-	-	-	-	HS	HS

NAME	1920	'25	'30	'36	'50	'60	'75	'89
Heath, Riley	-	-	F	-	-	-	-	-
Hedlund, Glenn W.	-	-	-	-	SM	-	-	-
Heimlich, William T.	-	-	-	-	F	-	F	-
Hellewell, William	-	-	-	-	SM	-	-	-
Hemming, Miss Sandra	-	-	-	-	JR	-	-	-
Hemming, Raymond V.	-	-	-	-	F	F	R	R
Henderson, Michael D.	-	-	-	-	-	-	-	FD
Henderson, Ronald L.	-	-	-	-	-	-	-	F
Henshaw, Elmer G.	-	-	-	-	F	-	-	-
Herman, Mrs. Louis	-	-	-	-	-	-	S	-
Hermannson, H.	SM	-	SM	L	-	-	-	-
Herrick, Glenn W.	F	-	-	-	-	-	-	-
Herson, M. J.	-	-	-	-	F	F	-	-
Hessney, Michael	-	-	-	-	F	-	-	-
Hetherington, R. L.	-	-	-	-	-	F	-	-
Hewitt, Fay D.	-	-	-	-	-	SOC	HS	-
Hickok, Mrs. Gretchen H.	-	-	-	-	-	-	HS	-
Hildebrand, George H.	-	-	-	-	-	-	HS	-
Hill, Chester L.	-	-	-	-	-	-	F	S
Hill, Forrest F. (Frosty)	-	-	-	-	SM	-	-	-
Hill, G. A. (Nig)	-	-	-	-	F	SOC	HS	-
Hinckley, Henry N.	SM	SM	-	-	-	-	-	-
Hire, George	-	SM	-	-	-	-	-	-
Hirlemann, Richard C.	-	-	-	-	-	-	F	-
Hirschfeld, John W.	-	-	-	-	-	SOC	-	HS
Hodes, Philip	-	-	-	-	-	F	-	-
Hodge, Percy	F	F	F	-	-	-	-	-
Hodge, William	-	-	JR	-	-	-	-	-
Hodgkins, H. Follett	F	-	-	-	-	-	-	-
Hoff, Edward J.	-	-	-	-	SM	-	-	-
Hoffman, Lawrence	-	-	-	-	-	-	F	-
Hokkanen, Miss Aili	-	-	-	-	-	SL	-	-
Holcomb, Charles R.	-	-	-	-	-	-	F	-
Holland, A. G.	-	F	-	-	-	-	-	-
Holland, R. F.	-	-	-	-	SM	-	-	-
Hollister, Solomon Cady	-	-	-	-	SOC	-	-	-
Holmes, M. L.	-	-	-	SM	F	-	-	-
Holmes, R. W.	-	-	-	-	F	-	-	-
Holton, C. B.	-	F	F	-	-	-	-	-
Holton, Walter B.	F	F	-	-	-	-	-	-
Homa, John	-	-	-	-	-	SOC	-	-
Homan, P. T.	-	-	-	SM	-	-	-	-
Hoppenrath, Wesley N.	-	-	-	-	-	-	-	AS
Hoppenrath, William W.	-	-	-	-	-	-	F	F
Hornbrook, William R.	-	-	-	-	F	F	HS	-
Horton, Edith	-	SL	-	-	-	-	-	-
Horton, George William	F	-	-	-	-	-	-	-
Hospital, Ralph	F	-	-	-	-	SOC	-	-
Houck, Mrs. I. J.	-	SL	-	-	-	-	-	-
House, Miss Nancy E.	-	SL	-	-	-	-	-	-
Howard, Miss Clara	SL	-	-	-	-	-	-	-
Howayeck, Frederick A., Jr.	-	-	-	-	-	-	AS	-
Howe, Fred B.	F	F	-	-	-	-	-	-
Howe, John B.	F	-	-	-	-	-	-	-
Howe, Stewart	-	-	-	-	-	F	-	-
Howe, Mrs. Stewart	-	-	-	-	-	-	S	-
Howell, A. D.	-	-	SM	-	-	-	-	-
Howell, E. V.	-	-	-	-	F	F	R	-
Howell, George B.	F	F	-	-	-	-	-	-
Howison, Robert J.	-	-	-	-	-	F	-	-
Howland, Donald G.	-	-	-	-	-	-	CL	-
Howley, G. G.	-	-	F	-	-	-	-	-
Hoy, David F.	F	-	-	-	-	-	-	-

NAME	1920	'25	'30	'36	'50	'60	'75	'89
Hoy, Mrs. D. F.	-	SL	-	-	-	-	-	-
Hubbard, R. C.	-	-	F	-	-	-	-	-
Huckle, David G.	-	-	-	-	-	-	-	REC
Hudgins, H.	-	SM	-	-	-	-	-	-
Hughes, Richard E.	-	-	-	-	-	F	F	-
Hughes, Mrs. Richard E.	-	-	-	-	-	-	-	R
Hull, A. Lawrence	-	-	-	-	-	SM	-	-
Hull, Charles H.	F	F	F	-	-	-	-	-
Humphrey, Miss Ina W.	SL	-	-	-	-	-	-	-
Humphreys, John W.	-	-	-	-	F	F	-	-
Humphreys, Mrs. John W.	-	-	-	-	-	-	HS	-
Hunter, Miss Beatrice	SL	-	-	-	-	-	-	-
Hurley, J. S.	-	-	SM	-	-	-	-	-
Hutchinson, Robert A.	SM	SM	SM	F	F	-	-	-
Huttar, John C.	-	-	-	-	SM	-	-	-
Hyde, A. M.	-	-	-	NR	-	-	-	-
Hyde, Mrs. A. M.	-	-	-	NR	-	-	-	-
Hyers, Lewis C.	-	-	-	-	-	-	HS	-
Ideman, George W.	-	-	-	-	SM	-	-	-
Ierardi, Philip	-	-	-	-	-	-	F	-
Ingersoll, Barton R.	-	-	-	-	-	-	-	AS
Ingersoll, Miss Elizabeth S.	SL	-	-	-	-	-	-	-
Ingrasci, Paul C.	-	-	-	-	-	-	F	-
Iorio, Philip M.	-	-	-	-	-	-	F	-
Irvine, Mrs. Frank	F	-	-	-	-	-	-	-
Ivey, John S.	-	-	-	-	-	-	-	F
Jackson, Michael B.	-	-	-	-	-	-	-	F
Jackson, E. N.	-	-	F	F	-	-	-	-
Jackson, Mrs. E. N.	-	-	-	-	SOC	-	-	-
Jacobson, Mrs. Harry	-	-	-	-	-	SOC	-	-
Jacobson, Richard A., Sr.	-	-	-	-	-	-	F	F
Jacoby, Robert C.	-	-	-	-	-	-	AS	-
James, George K. (Lefty)	-	-	-	-	F	-	-	-
Janas, Frank S.	-	-	-	-	-	F	F	-
Jecen, Sandra B.	-	-	-	-	-	-	-	AS
Jenkins, J. G.	-	-	F	F	-	-	-	-
Jinks, Mrs. Rhonda	-	-	-	-	-	-	-	AS
Job, Leonard B.	-	-	-	SM	SM	-	-	-
Johndrew, Orvis F., Jr.	-	-	-	-	-	-	HS	-
Johns, Miss J. P.	SL	-	-	-	-	-	-	-
Johnson, Benjamin L., Jr.	SM	-	-	-	-	-	-	-
Johnson, Bob & Billie	-	-	-	-	-	-	-	F
Johnson, Clarence E.	-	-	-	-	-	-	F	-
Johnson, Clifford B.	-	F	-	-	-	-	-	-
Johnson, Don	-	-	F	-	-	-	-	-
Johnson, Dorothy L.	-	-	-	-	-	-	S	-
Johnson, Kenneth C., Jr.	-	-	-	-	-	SOC	F	-
Johnson, Miss Emma	SL	-	-	-	-	-	-	-
Johnson, Mrs. J. R.	-	-	SL	-	-	-	-	-
Johnson, Ray R.	-	-	-	-	NR	-	-	-
Johnston, Frances A.	-	-	-	-	-	-	HS	-
Johnston, Zelda	-	-	-	-	-	-	-	HON
Jones, R. F.	SM	F	-	-	-	-	-	-
Jones, William F.	-	-	-	-	-	-	F	-
Jordan, R. H.	-	F	F	-	-	-	-	-
Jordan, Robert	-	-	-	-	-	-	-	NR
Kahle, G. B.	F	-	-	-	-	-	-	-
Kahn, Nathaniel A.	-	-	-	-	-	SOC	-	-
Kalaf, Edward	-	-	-	-	-	-	F	-
Kalman, Miss Gladys E.	-	-	-	-	-	SOC	-	-
Kalman, Wilfred F.	-	-	-	-	SM	SM	-	-
Kane, Robert J.	-	-	-	-	F	SOC	-	HS
Kaplan, Barney	-	-	-	SM	-	-	-	-

NAME	1920	'25	'30	'36	'50	'60	'75	'89
Karapetoff, Vladimir	F	F	SM	SM	-	-	-	-
Karch, Mrs. H.	-	-	-	-	-	SL	-	-
Kassman, Leonard	-	-	-	-	-	F	F	-
Kassman, Noah J.	-	-	-	-	-	-	F	-
Kassman, Mrs. Noah	-	-	-	-	-	-	-	S
Kavanagh, Frank J.	-	-	-	-	-	-	HS	-
Kavanagh, Mrs. Frank	-	-	-	-	-	-	-	HON
Kaveny, Thomas, Jr.	-	-	-	-	-	-	HS	-
Kaveny, Mrs. Thomas, Jr.	-	-	-	-	-	-	-	HS
Keegan, L. Burr	F	F	-	-	-	-	-	-
Keep, Donald B.	-	-	-	-	F	F	-	-
Kelly, A. B.	-	-	NR	-	-	-	-	-
Kelly, Althea T.	-	-	-	-	-	-	-	HS
Kelly, G.	-	-	-	SM	-	-	-	-
Kelly, John H.	-	-	-	-	-	SOC	-	-
Kelly, John M.	-	-	-	-	F	-	-	-
Kelly, Miss C. A.	-	-	SL	-	-	-	-	-
Kelly, Miss S. M.	-	-	SL	-	-	-	-	-
Kelly, Thomas J.	-	-	-	-	-	-	AS	AS
Kelsey, Charles W.	-	-	-	-	F	F	R	NR
Kemple, Lucille S.	-	-	-	-	-	-	-	HS
Kenerson, C. H., Jr.	-	-	-	TN	-	-	-	-
Kenerson, C. J.	-	-	-	F	L	-	-	-
Kenerson, Donald	-	-	-	JR	-	-	-	-
Keniston, R. H.	F	-	-	-	-	-	-	-
Kent, R. S.	-	SM	SM	-	-	-	-	-
Kent, W. M.	-	F	-	-	-	-	-	-
Kiely, Jack	-	-	-	-	-	SM	-	-
Kiely, Joseph J.	-	-	F	L	F	-	-	-
Kiely, Mrs. Etta	-	-	-	-	-	SL	HS	-
Kiely, Paul J.	-	-	-	-	-	F	HS	-
Kimball, Dexter S.	-	-	F	-	-	-	-	-
Kimball, G. N.	-	-	SM	-	-	-	-	-
Kimball, Peg O.	-	-	-	-	-	SOC	-	-
King, D. R.	-	-	F	-	-	-	-	-
King, Edward C.	-	-	-	-	SOC	SOC	HS	-
Kingsley, R. R.	-	-	F	F	SOC	-	-	-
Kingsley, R. R., Jr.	-	-	-	-	SM	-	-	-
Kirkup, T. J., Jr.	-	-	-	-	F	-	-	-
Kittler, Alfred	-	F	F	F	-	-	-	-
Kittler, Mrs. Alfred	-	-	-	-	SOC	-	-	-
Klein, David	-	-	-	-	-	-	-	F
Klein, Julius P.	-	-	-	-	-	-	F	-
Klinger, Jeffrey A.	-	-	-	-	-	-	-	AS
Knapp, Miss Charlotte	-	-	-	-	-	SL	-	-
Knauer, Roy H.	-	-	-	-	-	-	-	S
Knight, William	-	-	SM	-	-	-	-	-
Knight, William, Jr.	-	-	JR	-	F	F	-	-
Knowles, Carleton	-	-	-	-	SM	-	-	-
Knudson, Giltner	-	-	-	JR	-	-	-	-
Knudson, Lewis	-	F	SM	SM	SM	-	-	-
Kohm, A. E.	-	-	-	SM	-	-	-	-
Kolar, Lawrence J.	-	-	-	-	-	-	-	HS
Kompf, Donald R., Jr.	-	-	-	-	-	-	-	REC
Koper, George D.	-	-	-	-	-	-	-	F
Kostrinsky, Doris	-	-	-	-	-	-	AS	S
Krebs, Philip J.	-	-	-	-	F	SOC	-	-
Krempa, Gertrude E.	-	-	-	-	-	-	-	S
Kulp, Claude L.	-	-	-	F	-	-	-	-
Kumpf, S. Scott	-	-	-	-	-	-	-	F
Kuppinger, John J.	-	-	-	-	-	-	HS	HS
Kyong, Oo Hyon	-	-	-	-	-	-	-	F
La Due, George U.	-	-	-	-	-	-	F	-

NAME	1920	'25	'30	'36	'50	'60	'75	'89
La Nasa, Robert C.	-	-	-	-	-	F	-	-
LaBonte, Harold	-	-	-	-	SM	-	-	-
LaBonte, Harold R.	-	-	-	F	F	F	F	-
LaBonte, Mary	-	-	-	-	SL	-	-	-
Ladd, Mrs. Carolyn	SL	-	-	-	-	-	-	-
Ladd, Tallman	SM	-	-	F	-	-	-	-
LaFrance, Eugene M.	-	-	-	-	-	SOC	-	-
Lalor, James	-	-	SM	-	-	-	-	-
Lama, Luciano L.	-	-	-	-	-	-	-	HS
Lambert, Frank	-	-	F	-	-	-	-	-
Lambert, John Y.	-	-	-	-	-	-	HS	REC
Langdon, Mrs. Jean	-	-	-	-	SL	SL	R	-
Larimer, Richard E.	-	-	-	-	-	SOC	-	-
Larkin, C. C.	-	SM	-	-	-	-	-	-
Larkin, Clarence C.	-	-	-	-	-	-	HS	-
Larkin, L. P.	-	F	F	L	F	-	-	-
Laux, J. D.	-	-	-	-	F	F	F	R
Lawrence, V. S.	-	-	-	F	-	-	-	-
Lawson, Edward	-	-	SM	-	-	-	-	-
Leach, Anthony J., Jr.	-	-	-	-	-	-	F	-
Leagans, William T.	-	-	-	-	-	-	F	-
Lee, C. P.	-	-	NR	-	-	-	-	-
Lee, Harold D., Jr.	-	-	-	-	-	-	F	-
Lee, W. F.	F	F	F	L	-	-	-	-
Lemak, Joseph J.	-	-	-	-	-	-	F	-
Lenowitz, Bernard	-	-	-	-	-	-	F	-
Leonard, A. K.	SM	F	F	L	-	-	-	-
Leonard, Nell B.	-	-	-	-	SL	SOC	-	-
Levin, Joanne	-	-	-	-	-	-	JR	-
Lewis, Carol P.	-	-	-	-	-	-	-	REC
Lewis, Murray F.	-	-	-	-	-	-	F	-
Lewis, Richard M.	-	-	-	-	-	-	HS	-
Lewis, Ronald M.	-	-	-	-	-	-	F	F
Lewis, Sydelle F.	-	-	-	-	-	-	HS	HS
Lewton, John W.	-	-	-	-	-	SOC	HS	-
Lieberman, Kenneth	-	-	-	-	-	-	F	-
Lieberman, Leonard B.	-	-	-	-	-	SM	-	-
Liebeskind, Arthur	-	-	-	-	-	SOC	-	-
Liguori, Daniel F.	-	-	-	-	-	-	-	REC
Lincoln, N. S.	-	-	-	-	SM	-	-	-
Lincoln, P. M.	-	F	SM	SM	-	-	-	-
Lindsay, J. R.	-	-	F	-	-	-	-	-
Lines, David C.	-	-	-	-	-	-	-	F
Lipinski, Stephen C.	-	-	-	-	-	-	AS	-
Listar, John	-	-	-	-	-	F	F	-
Litchard, Robert M.	-	-	-	-	-	-	F	-
Livermore, J. S.	-	-	SM	-	-	-	-	-
Livermore, Mrs. J. S.	-	-	SL	-	-	-	-	-
Livermore, Paul S.	F	F	-	-	SOC	-	-	-
Livermore, Mrs. Paul S.	-	-	-	SOC	-	-	-	-
Llewellyn, Mrs. Frank	-	-	-	-	-	SOC	-	-
Lonergan, Thomas J.	-	-	-	-	-	-	F	-
Long, Barry J.	-	-	-	-	-	-	-	HS
Long, Louis J.	-	-	-	-	-	-	HS	-
Long, Margaret R.	-	-	-	-	-	-	-	HS
Longo, Rocco	-	-	-	-	-	-	F	R
Lorbeer, James W.	-	-	-	-	-	-	F	HS
Lord, David H.	-	-	-	-	-	-	AS	-
Loveall, James	-	-	-	-	-	-	-	REC
Low, Ralph J.	-	-	-	-	F	-	-	-
Lowery, John C.	-	-	-	-	-	-	F	F
Luhr, Constance	-	-	-	JR	-	-	-	-
Luhr, J. Fred	-	SM	SM	SM	-	F	-	-

NAME	1920	'25	'30	'36	'50	'60	'75	'89
Lynah, James	-	-	-	F	-	-	-	-
Lynn, Emmet	-	-	-	F	-	-	-	-
Lyon, Mrs. T. L.	-	SL	-	-	-	-	-	-
Mac Adam, Sterling T.	-	-	-	-	-	-	F	HS
MacBain, James T.	-	-	-	-	-	F	-	-
MacDonald, John W.	-	-	-	F	F	F	HS	-
MacDonald, Rita	-	-	-	-	-	-	S	-
MacEachron, P. A.	-	-	-	-	L	-	-	-
Mack, George N.	-	-	SM	SM	-	-	-	-
Mackey, C. O.	-	-	F	F	-	-	-	-
MacMillan, J. W.	-	-	-	F	-	-	-	-
MacMillan, K. D.	-	-	-	SM	-	-	-	-
MacMurray, F. M.	-	-	SM	SM	-	-	-	-
MacNeil, Hugh S.	-	-	-	-	-	-	F	-
MacWethy, Albert	-	-	-	-	F	-	-	-
Maddren, William H.	-	-	-	-	-	-	-	REC
Mai, William F.	-	-	-	-	-	F	-	-
Maines, John G.	-	-	-	-	-	SOC	-	-
Mains, L. P.	-	SM	-	-	-	-	-	-
Malison, Michael J.	-	-	-	-	-	-	HS	-
Malison, Peter J. (Mike)	-	-	-	-	-	-	-	F
Malley, Reginald E.	-	-	-	-	-	-	-	AS
Maloney, John	-	-	-	-	SM	-	-	-
Maloney, John M.	-	-	-	-	F	F	R	-
Maloney, Mrs. John M.	-	-	-	-	-	-	-	HS
Maloney, John S.	-	-	-	-	-	-	CL	-
Maloney, William L.	-	SM	-	-	-	-	-	-
Malott, Deane W.	-	-	-	-	-	-	HS	HS
Mange, John I.	F	F	SM	-	-	-	-	-
Mange, John P.	-	-	SM	-	-	-	-	-
Manley, T. M.	-	-	-	-	F	-	-	-
Marcham, Frederick G.	-	SM	-	-	-	-	-	-
Markowitz, Burton S.	-	-	-	-	-	-	AS	F
Marshall, Fred S.	-	-	-	-	-	SOC	-	-
Marshall, Robert N.	-	-	-	-	F	SOC	-	-
Martin, Anselmo	F	-	-	-	-	-	-	-
Martin, Clarence A.	F	-	-	-	-	-	-	-
Martin, David J.	-	-	-	-	-	-	F	-
Martin, F.	-	F	F	-	-	-	-	-
Martin, Fred A., III	-	-	-	-	-	-	-	F
Masters, R. L.	-	-	SM	-	-	-	-	-
Mathewson, Joseph B.	-	-	-	-	-	SOC	HS	-
Mathewson, Mrs. Joseph B.	-	-	-	-	-	-	-	NR
Matthews, J. E.	-	-	-	L	-	-	-	-
Matthews, Robertson	SM	-	-	-	-	-	-	-
Mattice, Malcolm	-	-	-	-	SM	-	-	-
Maxfield, Thomas B.	-	-	F	-	-	-	-	-
May, Stacy	-	F	-	-	-	-	-	-
May, Wesley E.	-	-	-	-	-	F	-	-
Mayer, Harry F.	-	-	-	-	-	F	-	-
Mayers, Harry	-	F	-	-	-	-	-	-
Maynard, L. A.	-	-	-	-	SM	-	-	-
Maynard, Leonard A.	F	-	-	-	-	-	-	-
Mazza, Bruno A., Jr.	-	-	-	-	-	-	F	R
Mazza, Edward A.	-	-	-	-	-	-	-	AS
Mazza, Ralph J.	-	-	-	-	-	SOC	-	-
McAniff, Miss A. R.	-	SL	-	-	-	-	-	-
McArthur, E. G.	-	SM	-	-	-	-	-	-
McCann, Mrs. Ruth	-	-	-	-	SL	SL	-	-
McCargo, Stratton	-	-	-	-	L	-	-	-
McCarthy, Rollin H.	-	-	-	-	-	-	-	HS
McConnell, James A.	-	-	-	-	F	-	-	-
McConnell, Joseph A.	-	-	-	-	F	F	F	R

NAME	1920	'25	'30	'36	'50	'60	'75	'89
McCormick, Frank J.	F	F	F	F	-	-	-	-
McCormick, Mary	-	SL	-	-	-	-	-	-
McCune, Robert J.	-	-	-	-	-	-	CL	-
McDaniels, Minor	-	F	F	F	-	-	-	-
McDermott, Miss J.	-	-	-	SOC	-	-	-	-
McElwee, Mrs. Jean	-	-	-	-	-	-	-	HS
McElwee, Raymond F.	-	-	-	-	F	F	F	R
McFarlane, Ross A.	-	-	-	-	-	-	F	-
McGee, William J.	-	-	-	-	-	F	F	-
McGuire, Henry	-	-	-	-	-	-	-	F
McGuire, William	-	-	-	-	-	-	F	F
McHenry, Craig	-	-	-	-	F	-	F	R
McKay, Earle S.	-	-	-	-	-	F	-	-
McKeegan, Paul	-	-	-	-	F	F	F	-
McKeegan, Mrs. Paul L.	-	-	-	-	-	-	-	R
McKinney, James F.	-	-	F	F	F	SOC	-	-
McKinney, Mrs. Louise B.	-	-	-	-	-	-	HS	-
McKinney, Stuart	-	-	-	JR	-	-	-	-
McKinney, Susan	-	-	-	JR	-	-	-	-
McLaughlin, Donald C.	-	-	-	-	-	F	F	-
McLean, Marjorie	-	-	SL	-	-	-	-	-
McLean, Miss Lorna	-	-	-	-	SOC	-	-	-
McManus, John F.	-	-	-	-	-	SOC	HS	-
McMullen, Miss Eleanor C.	SL	-	-	-	-	-	-	-
McNamara, J. P.	-	-	SM	-	-	-	-	-
McPherson, Donald	-	-	SM	-	-	-	-	-
McPherson, Ellen	-	-	SL	-	-	-	-	-
McRobb, William Scott, Jr.	-	-	-	-	-	-	F	-
Mead, Robert	-	-	-	-	-	-	F	-
Mehrer, James D.	-	-	-	-	-	-	-	F
Mehringer, Vincent M.	-	-	-	-	-	-	-	FC
Meigs, Robert B.	-	-	-	-	SM	-	-	-
Meils, William D.	-	-	-	-	F	F	F	R
Meldrum, Miss Catherine	-	-	-	-	SL	-	-	-
Melotte, Miss Julia L.	SL	SL	-	-	SOC	-	-	-
Melrose, Grace	-	-	SL	SL	-	-	-	-
Mennen, Mrs. Mary E.	-	-	-	-	SL	-	-	-
Merrill, Miss Enid	SL	-	-	-	-	-	-	-
Merritt, E.	-	F	-	-	-	-	-	-
Meyn, A. W.	-	-	SM	F	-	-	-	-
Michael, James D.	-	-	-	-	-	F	F	R
Midgely, Thomas	-	-	-	F	-	-	-	-
Miles, Mrs. H. V.	-	SL	-	-	-	-	-	-
Miller, Donald H.	-	-	-	-	-	SOC	-	-
Miller, Erie J.	-	-	-	F	F	-	-	-
Miller, John H.	-	-	-	-	-	-	F	-
Miller, John S.	-	-	-	-	SOC	-	-	-
Miller, Josiah B.	-	-	-	-	-	-	-	HS
Miller, Robert S.	-	-	-	-	SM	F	-	-
Miller, William T.	-	-	-	-	-	-	-	HS
Milliman, Mrs. Thomas E.	-	-	-	-	-	-	HS	-
Mills, James F., Jr.	-	-	-	-	-	-	AS	-
Minty, Edgar S.	-	-	-	-	-	F	-	-
Mintz, L. M.	-	-	F	-	-	-	-	-
Mitchell, Don	-	-	-	-	-	-	F	-
Mitchell, Edward E.	-	-	-	-	-	SOC	-	-
Mitchell, Frederick M.	-	-	-	-	-	F	F	R
Mitchell, W. J.	-	SM	-	-	-	-	-	-
Moakley, John F.	F	SM	SM	-	-	-	-	-
Moeder, W. D.	-	-	-	F	-	-	-	-
Molleson, F. M.	F	-	-	-	-	-	-	-
Mone, F. M.	-	-	F	-	-	-	-	-
Mone, Frances	-	-	SL	-	-	-	-	-

NAME	1920	'25	'30	'36	'50	'60	'75	'89
Mone, Miss M.	-	-	SL	-	-	-	-	-
Mong, Miss Marjorie	-	-	-	-	SL	-	-	-
Monroe, B. S.	-	F	-	-	-	-	-	-
Monroe, Mrs. B. S.	-	-	-	SOC	-	-	-	-
Montgomery, A. M.	-	-	NR	-	-	-	-	-
Moore, Clyde B.	-	F	F	F	-	-	-	-
Moore, David S.	-	-	-	-	-	-	-	AS
Moore, Fred J.	-	-	-	-	-	-	-	AS
Moore, H. C., Jr.	-	-	F	-	-	-	-	-
Moore, Maxine	-	-	-	JR	-	-	-	-
Moore, Norman S.	-	-	SM	F	F	F	F	HS
Moore, Richard W.	-	-	-	-	-	-	F	F
Moore, V. A.	-	-	F	-	-	-	-	-
Moran, Hugh	-	F	F	-	-	-	-	-
Moran, Hugh, Jr.	-	-	JR	-	-	-	-	-
Morgan, C. L.	-	-	-	-	F	-	-	-
Morgan, Mrs. C. L. (Laura)	-	-	-	-	-	SL	R	-
Morgan, Mary E.	-	-	-	-	JR	-	-	-
Morgan, O. H.	-	-	-	SM	-	-	-	-
Morris, E. J.	-	-	SM	-	-	-	-	-
Morris, Robert J.	-	-	-	-	-	-	HS	-
Morrison, J. P.	-	SM	SM	-	-	-	-	-
Morrison, William H.	F	-	-	-	-	-	-	-
Morse, Anthony	-	-	JR	-	-	-	-	-
Morse, Clarence F.	F	F	F	L	-	-	-	-
Morse, Everett	-	-	-	L	-	-	-	-
Morse, Frank L.	F	F	F	-	-	-	-	-
Morse, Mrs. Frank L.	-	-	-	SL	SL	-	-	-
Morse, L. W.	-	-	-	TN	-	-	-	-
Morse, Mrs. Fleet	-	-	-	-	SL	-	-	-
Morse, Robert V.	F	-	-	-	-	-	-	-
Moses, Winifred	SL	-	-	-	-	-	-	-
Mosher, Thomas E.	-	-	-	-	-	SOC	HS	-
Mott, Daisy A.	-	SL	-	-	-	-	-	-
Moynes, John V.	-	-	-	-	-	F	-	-
Moynihan, J. R.	-	-	-	-	F	-	-	-
Moynihan, Miss Maureen	-	-	-	-	JR	-	-	-
Muchmore, G. B.	SM	-	-	-	-	-	-	-
Muchmore, Mrs. Fredericka	-	-	-	-	SOC	-	-	-
Mueller, Jeanne	-	-	-	-	-	-	-	REC
Mueller, John R.	-	-	-	-	-	SOC	-	-
Mueller, Robert M.	-	-	-	-	F	SOC	F	R
Mulholland, Mrs. M. H.	-	-	-	SL	-	-	-	-
Muller, Steven	-	-	-	-	-	SOC	-	-
Mulvey, Richard I.	-	-	-	-	-	-	HS	-
Mungle, Donald S.	-	-	-	-	-	-	-	F
Mungle, Ralph W.	-	-	F	F	-	-	-	-
Mungle, Mrs. R.	-	-	-	-	SL	-	-	-
Mura, David W.	-	-	-	-	-	-	CL	-
Murdock, Carlton C.	SM	F	F	-	-	-	-	-
Murphy, John F.	-	-	-	-	-	-	-	REC
Murphy, Royse P.	-	-	-	-	-	SOC	-	-
Murray, Harry	-	-	-	-	F	-	-	-
Murray, Miss Lois	-	-	-	-	SL	-	-	-
Myers, Kenneth	-	-	-	-	-	-	F	REC
Myers, Llewellyn	-	-	-	-	SM	-	-	-
Myers, W. I.	-	-	-	-	F	-	-	-
Nagle, Jack	-	-	-	-	F	F	F	-
Nardi, Michael T.	-	-	-	-	-	-	HS	-
Nardi, Michael T.	-	-	-	-	SM	-	-	-
Natoli, Philip C.	-	-	-	-	-	-	F	-
Needham, Mrs. Mabel A.	SL	SL	SL	-	-	-	-	-
Neil, L. D.	-	SM	-	-	-	-	-	-

NAME	1920	'25	'30	'36	'50	'60	'75	'89
Neish, Leroy D.	-	-	F	-	F	F	R	-
Neish, Mrs. Leroy D. (Blanche)	-	-	-	SL	-	-	-	HON
Neish, Walter Richard	-	-	-	JR	SM	F	F	-
Nelson, C. H.	-	-	-	SM	-	-	-	-
Neubig, Charles W.	-	-	-	-	NR	-	-	-
Neville, Mark A.	-	SM	-	-	-	-	-	-
Newhall, A. G.	-	-	SM	-	-	-	-	-
Newman, Charles H.	SM	SM	F	-	SM	SOC	-	-
Newman, Mrs. Charles H.	-	-	-	SL	-	-	-	-
Newman, George	-	-	-	-	-	SM	-	-
Newman, Jared T.	F	F	F	-	-	-	-	-
Newman, John M.	-	-	-	-	JR	-	-	-
Newman, William S.	-	-	-	-	SM	-	-	-
Nichols, H. W.	-	-	SM	-	-	-	-	-
Nichols, Melvin L.	SM	SM	-	F	F	-	-	-
Nichols, William John	-	-	-	-	-	-	F	F
Niefer, Ann	-	-	-	-	-	-	-	F
Niefer, James M.	-	-	-	-	-	-	F	-
Noble, Miss Margaret	SL	-	-	-	-	-	-	-
Nodder, Charles	-	-	NR	-	-	-	-	-
Noll, Mrs. A. Robert	-	-	-	-	-	-	-	HS
Norris, L. C.	-	-	-	-	SM	-	-	-
Norton, Thomas E.	-	-	-	-	-	F	-	-
Norton, William C.	-	-	-	-	-	F	F	-
Norton, William J.	-	-	F	-	-	-	-	-
Notestein, Wallace	SM	SM	-	-	-	-	-	-
Nulle, Mrs. Claire C.	-	-	-	-	-	SL	S	-
Nye, Miss Gertrude H.	SL	SL	SL	-	-	-	-	-
Nyman, Kenneth J.	-	-	-	-	-	-	-	HS
O'Connell, Mrs. Mary W.	F	-	-	-	-	-	-	-
O'Connell, T. J.	-	-	-	-	F	-	-	-
O'Connell, W. C.	-	F	F	-	-	-	-	-
O'Connor, James F.	-	-	-	-	-	SOC	-	-
O'Leary, Paul M.	-	-	-	-	F	F	R	R
O'Rourke, C.E.	-	-	F	-	-	-	-	-
Odell, L. L.	-	F	-	-	-	-	-	-
Oechler, W. F.	-	-	-	-	F	-	-	-
Ogden, Helen	-	-	-	JR	-	-	-	-
Ogden, Isabelle C.	-	SL	SL	-	-	-	-	-
Ogden, Mary	-	-	-	JR	-	-	-	-
Ogden, R. M.	-	F	F	F	-	-	-	-
Oldberg, Sidney	-	-	-	-	-	-	-	HS
Olsen, Alfred L.	-	-	SM	-	F	-	-	-
Olver, Neil R.	-	-	-	-	-	-	-	AS
Orndorff, Charlotte	-	-	-	SL	-	-	-	-
Orth, L. P.	F	-	-	-	-	-	-	-
Ortner, H. B.	-	-	F	L	-	-	-	-
Ott, Edward A.	-	F	-	-	-	-	-	-
Owens, F. W.	-	F	-	-	-	-	-	-
Owens, Helen B.	-	JR	-	-	-	-	-	-
Ozmun, Jack H.	-	-	-	-	-	-	F	-
Paige, John E.	-	-	-	-	-	SOC	-	-
Paine, Ernest T.	F	F	-	-	-	-	-	-
Paolangeli, Francis J.	-	-	-	-	-	-	-	F
Parise, Anthony F.	-	-	-	-	-	-	-	AS
Park, Barbara	-	-	-	-	-	-	S	S
Park, John W.	-	-	-	-	-	-	F	-
Park, Roy H.	-	-	-	-	-	F	F	HS
Park, Mrs. Roy H.	-	-	-	-	SL	-	-	-
Park, Roy H., Jr.	-	-	-	-	-	-	HS	-
Park, Warren S.	-	-	-	-	-	SOC	-	-
Parker, Esther	SL	-	-	-	-	-	-	-
Parmenter, Richard	-	-	-	-	SM	-	-	-

NAME	1920	'25	'30	'36	'50	'60	'75	'89
Parziale, Thomas J.	-	-	-	-	-	-	-	AS
Passman, Melvin L.	-	-	-	-	-	F	F	-
Passman, Mrs. Melvin L.	-	-	-	-	-	-	-	R
Patrick, H. J. Peter	-	-	-	-	-	-	F	-
Patten, Bert S.	-	-	-	F	F	-	-	-
Patten, Mrs. Bert S.	-	-	-	-	-	SOC	-	-
Patten, Miss Judy	-	-	-	-	-	SL	-	-
Patterson, Merle E.	-	-	-	-	-	-	F	-
Patterson, Woodford	SM	-	SM	SM	-	-	-	-
Pauli, Fern	-	-	-	-	-	-	-	AS
Paulison, Smith G.	-	-	-	-	-	SOC	-	-
Pawlowski, Anthony C.	-	-	-	-	-	-	F	-
Payne, Anna L.	-	SL	SL	-	-	-	-	-
Peer, Sherman S.	SM	-	-	-	-	-	-	-
Peiffer, V. R.	-	-	-	-	-	SOC	-	-
Penney, Norman	-	-	-	-	-	SOC	-	-
Perez, Mrs. P. E.	F	-	-	-	-	-	-	-
Perez, Stanley E.	-	-	-	-	-	-	F	-
Perialis, John	-	-	-	-	-	-	-	HS
Perine, Joseph B.	-	-	-	-	-	-	AS	-
Perkins, Stuart E.	-	-	-	-	-	-	AS	-
Perry, D. B.	F	F	F	F	F	-	-	-
Perry, D. S.	-	-	-	F	F	-	-	-
Perry, David	-	-	-	-	JR	-	-	-
Perry, Joseph H.	-	-	-	-	-	-	-	AS
Perry, Owen	-	-	-	-	JR	-	-	-
Perry, Richard A.	-	-	-	-	-	-	-	HS
Perry, Robert S.	-	-	-	-	-	-	F	F
Perry, Roger H.	-	-	-	-	-	-	F	F
Peter, Mitchell	-	-	-	-	-	-	F	-
Peter, Samuel	-	-	-	-	-	-	F	R
Peterson, Anne D.	-	-	-	-	-	-	-	AS
Peterson, Howard	-	JR	JR	-	-	-	-	-
Peterson, Howard C.	-	SM	F	NR	NR	-	-	-
Peterson, Mrs. Howard C.	-	SL	-	-	NR	-	-	-
Pettis, Charles R., Jr.	-	-	-	-	-	SOC	F	-
Pfann, George R.	-	-	-	-	F	F	-	-
Pfann, George R., Jr.	-	-	-	-	-	SOC	-	-
Phelps, A. C.	F	F	-	-	-	-	-	-
Phelps, Mrs. A. C.	-	-	SL	SL	-	-	-	-
Phelps, G. L.	-	SM	-	-	-	-	-	-
Philipson, Paul P.	-	-	-	-	-	-	F	S
Phillips, Karl L.	-	-	-	-	F	F	-	-
Phillips, R. M.	-	-	-	F	F	-	-	-
Piacentini, Pat	-	-	-	-	-	SM	S	-
Pickering, Louis S.	-	-	-	F	F	F	-	-
Pickering, Robert	-	-	-	-	SM	-	-	-
Piech, Peter	-	-	-	-	SM	F	-	-
Pierce, E. I.	-	-	-	SM	-	-	-	-
Pile, Robert F.	-	F	-	-	-	-	-	-
Pillsbury, Donald C.	-	-	-	-	-	SOC	-	-
Pirko, Mrs. Elizabeth	-	-	-	-	-	-	-	S
Pitcher, J. Osgood	-	SM	-	-	-	-	-	-
Pivirotto, Arthur M., Jr.	-	-	-	-	-	-	-	F
Pochily, Marnee E.	-	-	-	-	-	-	-	AS
Polk, Rollin S.	F	F	-	-	-	-	-	-
Poole, Arthur B.	-	-	SM	-	-	-	-	-
Poole, Barbara	-	-	JR	-	-	-	-	-
Poole, Bernard	-	-	JR	L	-	-	-	-
Poole, John	-	-	JR	-	-	-	-	-
Poole, Mrs. A. S. (Elizabeth)	-	-	SL	L	-	-	-	-
Pope, Ernst P.	-	-	SM	-	-	-	-	-
Pope, P. R.	-	F	-	-	-	-	-	-

NAME	1920	'25	'30	'36	'50	'60	'75	'89
Porter, Michael R.	-	-	-	-	-	-	-	F
Porter, William A.	-	-	-	-	-	SOC	-	-
Potter, Harry E., Sr.	-	-	-	-	SOC	-	-	-
Poucher, George E.	-	-	-	-	-	F	-	-
Powell, Whiton	-	-	-	-	SM	-	HS	-
Pratt, Mrs. Helen L.	SL	SL	-	-	-	-	-	-
Prescott, Frederick C.	F	F	F	F	-	-	-	-
Pribanic, Gerald J.	-	-	-	-	-	-	-	F
Price, Anna L.	-	SL	-	-	-	-	-	-
Price, Don	-	-	-	SM	-	-	-	-
Price, Stanley T.	-	-	-	-	-	F	-	-
Pritchard, Dale	-	-	-	-	-	-	F	-
Pritchard, Gordon L.	-	-	-	-	F	-	-	-
Pritchard, Leon C.	-	F	F	L	F	-	-	-
Pumpelly, Lawrence	SM	F	SM	-	-	-	-	-
Quarles, James T.	F	-	-	-	-	-	-	-
Quinlan, Pamela	-	-	-	-	-	-	-	HS
Quinlan, William R.	-	-	-	-	-	-	F	R
Quinn, M. P.	-	-	-	-	SOC	-	-	-
Rachun, Alexius	-	-	-	-	F	SOC	F	R
Raleigh, Edward	-	-	-	-	-	SM	-	-
Raleigh, William	-	-	-	-	JR	SM	-	-
Ramin, Richard	-	-	-	-	-	-	-	F
Ramstad, Paul E.	-	-	-	-	-	-	-	HS
Raney, Edward C.	-	-	-	-	-	SOC	HS	-
Rankin, Everett	-	-	-	-	NR	-	-	-
Ranney, Warren A.	-	-	-	-	-	SOC	-	-
Rantanen, John	-	-	-	-	-	-	-	F
Rappenecker, Casper	-	-	SM	SM	-	-	-	-
Ray, Margaret	-	-	SL	-	-	-	-	-
Read, N. G.	-	-	F	-	-	-	-	-
Recknagle, A. B.	F	F	SM	F	-	-	-	-
Rector, David D.	-	-	-	-	-	-	F	R
Reed, Harold L.	-	SM	F	F	SM	F	-	-
Reed, Hazel E.	-	-	-	-	-	-	-	HS
Reed, Kenneth	-	-	-	JR	-	-	-	-
Reed, Robert R.	F	-	-	-	-	-	-	-
Reed, Walter D.	-	-	-	-	F	-	-	-
Reese, J. P.	-	-	-	F	-	-	-	-
Reichert, C. J.	-	-	NR	-	-	-	-	-
Reid, William S.	SM	-	-	-	-	-	-	-
Reilly, Elizabeth	-	-	-	-	JR	-	-	-
Reilly, J. B.	-	-	-	-	F	-	-	-
Reinhardt, John R.	-	-	-	-	-	-	F	-
Renn, Peter E.	-	-	-	-	-	-	HS	-
Reulein, C. D.	-	-	-	L	-	-	-	-
Reycroft, Louis H., III	-	-	-	-	-	-	-	AS
Reynolds, Eben S.	-	-	-	-	-	F	-	-
Reynolds, Mrs. Eben S. (Ann)	-	-	-	-	-	-	F	-
Reynolds, Walter M.	-	-	-	-	NR	-	-	-
Rhode, Samuel	-	-	-	-	SM	-	-	-
Rhoode, F. G.	-	-	-	F	-	-	-	-
Rice, Frank E.	SM	-	-	-	-	-	-	-
Richards, Benjamin A.	-	-	-	-	-	-	-	F
Richards, Thomas E.	-	-	-	-	-	F	-	-
Ridley, Donald J.	-	-	-	-	-	-	F	F
Ridley, Douglas S.	-	-	-	-	-	-	AS	F
Ridley, Mrs. Marion	-	-	-	-	-	-	HS	-
Riley, H. M.	-	-	-	F	-	-	-	-
Ripley, Millard G.	-	-	-	-	-	F	-	-
Ritter, Alfred	-	-	-	-	-	F	-	-
Robb, Betty	-	-	-	JR	-	-	-	-
Robb, David	-	F	F	F	F	F	-	-

NAME	1920	'25	'30	'36	'50	'60	'75	'89
Robb, James	-	-	-	-	NR	-	-	-
Robbins, Richard S.	-	-	-	-	-	SOC	-	-
Roberts, E. R.	-	-	-	-	F	-	-	-
Roberts, J. H.	-	-	-	-	F	-	-	-
Roberts, Michael	-	-	-	-	-	-	-	AS
Robinson, Elmer D.	-	-	-	-	-	F	F	R
Rocker, B. L.	-	-	-	-	-	F	-	-
Rogalsky, George F.	F	F	F	-	-	-	-	-
Rogalsky, Mrs. F. A.	-	-	-	SL	-	-	-	-
Rogers, G. H.	SM	-	-	-	-	-	-	-
Rogers, Wallace B.	-	-	-	-	SM	SOC	F	R
Rokoski, Bernard C.	-	-	-	-	-	-	HS	-
Rothschild, Jacob	F	F	-	-	-	-	-	-
Rothschild, James N.	-	-	-	JR	F	F	F	R
Rothschild, Leon D.	F	F	F	F	F	SOC	-	-
Rowe, T. F.	-	-	SM	-	F	F	-	-
Royce, Edward	F	-	-	-	-	-	-	-
Ruane, James M.	-	-	-	-	-	-	-	F
Ruegsegger, Virgil	-	-	-	F	F	F	-	-
Rumph, Hugh B., Jr.	-	-	-	-	-	-	F	-
Rumsey, Hugh	-	-	-	-	SOC	-	-	-
Rumsey, L. S.	-	-	-	F	-	-	-	-
Russo, C. P.	-	-	-	-	F	-	-	-
Ruthig, Edgar J.	-	-	-	-	-	-	F	F
Ruzic, Ronald M.	-	-	-	-	-	-	-	F
Ryan, John F.	-	-	-	-	-	-	HS	-
Ryan, Neal	-	-	-	-	-	-	-	F
Ryan, Richard G.	-	-	-	-	-	-	-	AS
Sabroff, Alvin M.	-	-	-	-	-	-	F	-
Sadd, Arlene	-	-	-	-	-	-	-	HS
Safadi, David	-	-	-	-	-	-	HS	-
Sailor, R. W.	-	F	F	SM	-	-	-	-
Sainburg, P. C.	-	SM	F	-	-	-	-	-
Sale, Roger H.	-	-	-	-	JR	-	-	-
Sale, William M., Jr.	-	-	-	-	SM	-	-	-
Salter, Douglas C.	-	-	-	-	-	-	F	-
Saltonstall, Leverett	-	-	-	-	F	F	-	-
Saltonstall, Mrs. L. (Nancy)	-	-	-	-	-	-	F	R
Saltonstall, Peter & Tacie	-	-	-	-	-	-	-	AS
Sammons, Miss Ruth	-	-	-	-	SL	-	-	-
Sampson, Martin W.	F	F	F	-	-	-	-	-
Sanderson, James A.	-	-	-	-	-	-	F	F
Sanford, Benjamin E.	F	F	F	-	-	-	-	-
Sanford, R. H.	-	-	-	-	-	SOC	-	-
Saperstein, J.	-	-	F	-	-	-	-	-
Sarge, Elsie M.	-	-	SL	-	-	-	-	-
Sarkus, Peter J.	-	-	-	-	-	-	-	S
Saturn, Frank	-	-	-	-	-	F	-	-
Sauerborn, Eugene P.	-	-	-	-	-	F	-	-
Saunders, Byron W.	-	-	-	-	-	SOC	-	-
Schaufler, A. W.	-	-	-	-	-	-	F	-
Schaufler, Brenda C.	-	-	-	-	-	-	-	AS
Schindo, John J.	-	-	-	-	-	-	F	-
Schively, Mrs. F. C.	F	-	-	-	-	-	-	-
Schlaepfer, Walter W.	-	-	-	-	-	-	-	F
Schlotzhauer, W. R.	-	-	-	-	-	F	-	-
Schmidt, William F.	-	-	-	-	-	-	HS	-
Schoel, Loren W.	-	-	-	-	F	-	-	-
Schoenfeld, Otto B.	-	-	-	-	-	-	S	-
Scholl, Edgar H.	-	-	-	-	-	SOC	-	-
Schreiber, Gregory C.	-	-	-	-	-	-	-	AS
Schug, James F.	-	-	-	-	-	-	-	F
Schultz, Andrew S., Jr.	-	-	-	-	-	-	F	NR

NAME	1920	'25	'30	'36	'50	'60	'75	'89
Schurman, Catherine Forrest	SL	-	-	-	-	-	-	-
Schurman, Jacob Gould	F	-	-	-	-	-	-	-
Sciarabba, Andrew J.	-	-	-	-	-	-	AS	-
Scidmore, R. R.	-	-	-	F	-	-	-	-
Scofield, H. H.	-	-	SM	-	-	-	-	-
Scofield, Robert	-	-	JR	-	-	-	-	-
Scott, Milton L.	-	-	-	-	-	-	F	F
Scott, William S., III	-	-	-	-	-	-	F	-
Scott, William S., Jr.	-	-	-	-	-	-	F	HS
Scribner, Harry M.	-	-	-	-	SOC	-	-	-
Seaman, Thomas	-	-	-	-	-	-	F	-
Seamon, Max T., Jr.	-	-	-	-	F	-	-	-
Sebring, Edgar	-	-	-	-	-	-	HS	-
Seelye, Miss Grace	SL	SL	-	-	-	-	-	-
Serviss, George	-	-	-	-	F	-	-	-
Shackleton, Horace E.	-	-	-	-	SM	-	-	-
Sharp, Earl F.	-	-	-	-	-	F	HON	-
Sharp, L. W.	-	F	-	-	-	-	-	-
Sharp, Lauriston	-	-	-	-	-	-	HS	-
Sharpe, A. H.	-	SM	-	-	-	-	-	-
Shaw, Benjamin A., Jr.	-	-	-	-	-	SOC	-	-
Shayler, Howard	-	-	-	-	F	-	-	-
Shea, J. E.	-	SM	-	-	-	-	-	-
Shelley, Edward H.	-	-	-	-	-	SOC	-	-
Shephard, Edward J.	-	-	-	-	-	-	F	-
Sheppard, C. Stewart	-	-	-	-	-	F	-	-
Shew, Randall	-	-	-	-	-	-	F	-
Shipe, John A.	-	-	-	-	-	F	-	-
Shipos, Louis	-	-	-	-	JR	-	-	-
Shoemaker, Jesse C.	-	-	-	F	F	-	-	-
Short, Joseph	-	-	-	-	F	-	-	-
Shulman, Cecil B.	-	-	-	-	-	F	-	-
Shulman, Melvin	-	-	-	-	-	SM	-	-
Shulman, Michael D.	-	-	-	-	-	-	F	NR
Shulman, Morris M.	-	-	-	-	-	F	F	R
Shulman, Mrs. Lee	-	-	-	-	-	-	R	-
Shulman, Richard	-	-	-	-	-	-	F	F
Siany, Lawrence W.	-	-	-	-	-	-	-	F
Sidenberg, R. W.	-	-	-	-	F	F	-	-
Siegel, Benjamin M.	-	-	-	-	-	-	F	-
Sigmon, Steven H.	-	-	-	-	-	-	-	AS
Simmons, A. E.	-	-	-	-	-	SOC	-	-
Simmons, Donald M.	-	-	-	-	JR	-	-	-
Simmons, Mildred F.	-	-	-	-	-	-	HS	-
Simmons, Miss Helen P.	-	-	-	-	JR	-	-	-
Simmons, Mrs. Helen F.	-	-	-	-	SL	-	-	-
Simonds, Eleanor	-	-	SL	-	-	-	-	-
Simpson, Harold E.	-	SM	SM	L	F	F	-	-
Simpson, James R.	-	-	-	-	SM	-	-	-
Singley, David W.	-	-	-	-	-	-	F	R
Sinsabaugh, Howard	-	-	-	-	SM	F	-	-
Skoch, Dale F.	-	-	-	-	-	-	-	AS
Slights, J. R.	-	-	-	L	-	-	-	-
Smiley, D. F.	-	-	F	F	-	-	-	-
Smith, Albert W.	F	-	-	-	-	-	-	-
Smith, C. Wilson	-	F	-	-	-	-	-	-
Smith, Chris A.	-	-	-	-	-	-	-	F
Smith, Claude H.	-	F	-	F	-	-	-	-
Smith, Elliot G.	-	-	-	-	-	-	F	-
Smith, Elwood W.	-	-	SM	NR	-	-	-	-
Smith, Mrs. E. W.	-	-	-	NR	-	-	-	-
Smith, Harold G.	-	-	-	-	-	F	-	-
Smith, Harold H.	-	-	-	-	F	F	-	-

NAME	1920	'25	'30	'36	'50	'60	'75	'89
Smith, Joann	-	-	-	-	-	-	-	AS
Smith, John L.	-	-	-	-	-	-	CL	-
Smith, Julian C. (Ted)	-	-	-	-	-	F	F	R
Smith, L. P.	F	F	-	-	-	-	-	-
Smith, Mrs. F. O.	-	SL	SL	-	-	-	-	-
Smith, Ralph C.	-	-	-	F	-	-	-	-
Smith, Mrs. Ralph C.	-	-	-	-	SOC	-	-	-
Smith, Robert S.	-	-	-	-	-	-	-	HS
Smith, Ross H. (Jim)	-	-	-	-	F	F	-	-
Smith, Ruth A.	-	SL	-	-	-	-	-	-
Smith, Sheldon M.	-	-	-	-	-	F	-	-
Smock, David R.	-	-	-	-	JR	-	-	-
Snavely, C. G.	-	-	-	F	-	-	-	-
Snavely, Carl	-	-	-	JR	-	-	-	-
Soanes, David L.	-	-	-	-	-	-	AS	-
Sokol, Thomas A.	-	-	-	-	-	-	-	F
Spaeth, J. Nelson	-	F	-	-	-	-	-	-
Spaulding, A. K.	-	-	-	F	-	-	-	-
Spencer, Leland	-	-	-	-	-	-	HS	-
Speno, Anthony	-	-	-	-	JR	-	F	F
Speno, Frank	-	F	F	-	-	-	-	-
Speno, Frank, 2nd	-	-	-	-	JR	-	F	-
Speno, Leo	-	-	-	-	F	F	-	-
Speno, Martin (Dodie)	-	-	JR	SM	NR	-	-	-
Speno, Miss Miriam (Mimi)	-	-	-	-	JR	-	-	-
Speno, Thomas	-	-	JR	-	F	-	-	-
Spring, Gardiner	-	-	JR	-	-	-	-	-
Spring, Samuel N.	-	F	SM	-	-	-	-	-
Sprinkle, C. L.	-	-	-	-	-	F	F	R
Sprole, Robert R., II	-	-	-	-	-	-	-	F
Sprole, Zetta R.	-	-	-	-	-	-	-	S
St.John, Mrs. E. M. (Sheila)	SL	SL	SL	-	-	-	-	-
Stage, Everett M.	-	-	-	-	-	F	-	-
Stagg, C. Tracy	F	F	F	F	-	-	-	-
Stagg, Mrs. Madeleine G.	-	-	-	-	-	SOC	-	-
Stagg, Norman G.	-	-	F	F	-	-	-	-
Stainton, W. H. S.	-	F	-	-	-	-	-	-
Staley, Hanley W.	-	-	-	-	F	F	F	R
Staley, Roy E.	-	-	-	-	-	-	S	-
Stallman, Mrs. Arthur C.	-	-	-	-	-	-	HS	HS
Starner, E. C.	-	-	SM	F	SOC	-	-	-
Starner, Miss Frances A.	-	-	-	-	JR	-	-	-
Starner, W. S.	-	-	-	F	F	-	-	-
Steinmetz, R. G.	-	-	-	-	F	-	-	-
Stephans, Brent K.	-	-	-	-	-	-	-	AS
Stephens, Fitch H.	F	F	-	-	-	-	-	-
Stephens, Mrs. Lucy L.	-	-	-	-	-	SOC	HS	-
Stephenson, Carl	-	-	-	F	SOC	-	-	-
Stephenson, J. H.	-	-	-	JR	-	-	-	-
Stevens, Irvine R.	SM	-	-	-	-	-	-	-
Stevens, Jeremy J.	-	-	-	-	-	F	-	-
Stevens, Robert L.	-	-	-	-	-	-	F	-
Stevens, Robert S.	-	F	F	F	F	SOC	-	-
Stevens, Mrs. Robert S.	-	-	-	-	-	-	HS	-
Stevens, Shepherd	F	-	-	-	-	-	-	-
Stewart, Donald	F	F	-	-	SOC	-	-	-
Stewart, Edwin C.	F	-	-	-	-	-	-	-
Stocker, Miss Marion	-	-	-	-	SL	-	-	-
Stone, Albert G.	F	F	-	-	-	-	-	-
Stone, Charlotte	-	-	-	-	-	-	HS	-
Stone, Delia M.	SL	SL	SL	L	-	-	-	-
Stone, Joseph P.	-	-	-	-	-	-	AS	F
Stoneman, Peter	-	-	-	-	-	-	F	F

NAME	1920	'25	'30	'36	'50	'60	'75	'89
Storms, William H.	SM	SM	-	-	-	-	-	-
Stott, Mrs. Richard B.	-	-	-	-	-	-	CL	CL
Stout, Harold J.	-	-	-	-	-	-	-	F
Stoutenburg, Jane C.	-	-	-	-	-	-	S	-
Strong, O. F.	-	-	-	-	F	-	-	-
Strunk, W., Jr.	F	SM	-	-	-	-	-	-
Sturm, A. F.	-	-	-	F	-	-	-	-
Sturm, Mrs. A. F.	-	-	-	-	SOC	-	-	-
Sturm, Mrs. A. J.	-	-	-	-	SOC	-	-	-
Sturm, Paul	-	-	-	-	SOC	-	-	-
Sullivan, Louis W., Jr.	-	-	-	-	-	-	-	F
Sullivan, Thomas	-	-	-	-	-	-	AS	-
Summers, Robert S.	-	-	-	-	-	-	HS	-
Summerville, Joseph	-	-	-	-	F	-	-	-
Sumner, Miss H. B.	-	SL	SL	L	-	-	-	-
Sutton, Henry B.	-	-	F	F	-	-	-	-
Swerbenski, William C.	-	-	-	-	-	-	AS	F
Tallman, Carl C.	-	-	-	-	F	SOC	-	-
Tallman, Mrs. Claire	-	-	-	-	-	-	F	-
Tallman, Robert B.	-	-	-	-	F	F	-	-
Tanner, John Henry	F	F	-	-	-	-	-	-
Tarallo, Dominic	-	-	-	-	-	-	F	-
Tarbell, Carlon	-	-	-	-	-	SOC	-	-
Tarbell, George S.	F	F	F	-	-	-	-	-
Tarbell, S. C.	-	-	-	-	F	-	-	-
Tarr, Curtis W.	-	-	-	-	-	-	-	HS
Tarr, Mrs. Ralph S. (Kate)	SL	SL	SL	SOC	-	-	-	-
Taylert, Carl V.	-	-	-	-	-	SOC	-	-
Taylor, Charles L.	F	-	-	-	-	-	-	-
Taylor, Lucy	-	SL	-	-	-	-	-	-
Taylor, W. W.	NR	-	-	-	-	-	-	-
Teeter, Ruth M.	-	-	SL	-	-	-	-	-
Telford, Mrs. Bess B.	-	-	-	NR	NR	-	-	-
Ten Broeck, Delphine L.	-	-	SL	-	-	-	-	-
Terrill, E. S.	-	-	SM	L	-	-	-	-
Thaler, Manley H.	-	-	-	-	-	-	HS	-
Thatcher, J. S.	-	-	-	SM	-	-	-	-
Thilly, Frank	F	F	-	-	-	-	-	-
Thilly, Mrs. Frank	-	-	SL	-	-	-	-	-
Thilly, Gertrude	-	-	SL	-	-	-	-	-
Thilly, Margaret	-	-	SL	-	-	-	-	-
Thomas, B. D.	-	SM	-	-	-	-	-	-
Thomas, Fred H.	-	-	-	-	-	-	F	HS
Thomas, Howard A.	-	-	-	-	F	SOC	-	-
Thomas, Oliver W.	SM	-	-	-	-	-	-	-
Thomas, William T.	F	F	F	NR	-	-	-	-
Thomas, Mrs. W. T.	-	-	-	NR	-	-	-	-
Thompson, Janet	-	-	-	-	-	-	-	HS
Thompson, Mrs. George J.	-	-	-	-	-	-	HS	-
Thoren, Ted	-	-	-	-	-	-	-	HS
Thorne, W. J.	-	SM	-	-	-	-	-	-
Thoron, Gray	-	-	-	-	-	F	HS	HS
Thorsland, Edgar	-	-	-	-	F	-	-	-
Thuesen, Mrs. Ralph	-	-	-	-	-	-	-	HS
Tilley, Mary E.	-	-	-	-	-	-	HS	HS
Tilton, J. N.	-	-	-	SM	-	-	-	-
Timber, Charles	-	-	-	-	-	-	F	-
Tinker, Charles D.	-	-	F	SM	-	-	-	-
Tinker, Mrs. M. B.	-	-	SL	-	-	-	-	-
Tisdale, Eben D.	-	-	-	-	-	-	F	F
Todd, C. L.	-	F	-	-	-	-	-	-
Tompkins, S. W.	-	-	F	-	-	-	-	-
Tompkins, W. R.	-	-	F	-	-	-	-	-

NAME	1920	'25	'30	'36	'50	'60	'75	'89
Torbert, J. Guy	-	SM	SM	-	F	F	R	-
Torbert, Miss June	-	-	-	-	JR	-	-	-
Tottey, Robert L.	-	-	-	-	-	-	AS	-
Townley, Lucy	-	-	SL	-	-	-	-	-
Townsend, L. B.	-	-	F	F	F	-	-	-
Tracy, W. M.	-	-	-	-	F	-	-	-
Trainor, D. W., Jr	-	-	F	-	-	-	-	-
Treadwell, Anthony C.	-	-	-	-	-	-	-	F
Treman, Allan H.	-	SM	F	L	F	SOC	-	-
Treman, Mrs. Allan H. (Pauline)	-	-	-	-	-	-	HS	HS
Treman, Arthur B.	-	S	F	F	-	-	-	-
Treman, Charles E.	F	F	F	-	-	-	-	-
Treman, Charles E., Jr.	-	-	SM	F	F	F	F	R
Treman, Robert E.	F	SM	SM	-	-	-	-	-
Treman, Robert H.	F	F	F	L	-	-	-	-
Trevor, Mrs. Joseph E. (Margaret)	SL	-	-	-	-	-	-	-
Trigger, Miss June E.	-	-	-	-	-	SOC	-	-
Tucker, James W.	-	-	-	-	-	-	F	-
Turcotte, Donald L.	-	-	-	-	-	-	F	F
Turnbull, John M.	-	-	-	-	-	F	-	-
Turner, Roger R.	-	-	-	-	-	-	F	-
Turton, Gary J.	-	-	-	-	-	-	-	F
Tuttle, Viola	-	SL	-	-	-	-	-	-
Tyler, Wilbur S.	-	-	-	F	-	-	-	-
Udall, D. H.	-	-	SM	-	-	-	-	-
Udall, Mary C.	-	-	SL	-	-	-	-	-
Udall, Richard P.	-	-	-	-	-	SOC	-	-
Underwood, E. Victor	-	-	-	-	-	SOC	-	-
Unger, Mrs. I. M.	SL	SL	SL	-	-	-	-	-
Upchurch, Frederic	-	-	-	-	F	F	-	-
Urquhart, Donald T.	-	-	-	-	-	-	F	-
Urquhart, L. C.	F	F	F	SM	-	-	-	-
Usher, A. P.	SM	-	-	-	-	-	-	-
Usher, F. R.	-	SM	SM	-	-	-	-	-
Van Alstine, Daniel P.	-	-	-	-	-	-	-	F
Van Arsdale, E. Redner	-	-	-	-	F	F	-	-
Van Cleef, Miss Eugenia	-	-	-	SL	-	-	-	-
Van Cleef, Mynderse	F	F	F	-	-	-	-	-
Van Dyk, Orrin J.	-	-	-	-	-	-	-	F
Van Epps, George	-	-	-	-	-	-	HS	-
Van Geluwe, John	-	-	-	-	SM	SOC	-	-
Van Gordon, W. Rex	-	-	-	-	-	-	-	REC
Van Houtte, Raymond	-	-	-	-	-	-	HS	HS
Van Lent, Leonard	-	-	-	-	-	F	HS	R
Van Natta, Doris	-	-	-	JR	-	-	-	-
Van Natta, J. E.	-	F	F	F	F	-	-	-
Van Natta, Mrs. J. E. (Edna)	-	-	-	-	SL	SL	-	-
Van Orman, Ray	-	NR	NR	-	-	-	-	-
Van Pelt, H. L.	-	-	F	F	-	-	-	-
Van Pelt, Mrs. Abbie	-	-	-	-	SOC	-	-	-
Van Pelt, Miss Helen J.	-	-	-	-	SL	-	-	-
Van Valkenburg, Harold	-	-	-	-	-	SOC	-	-
Van Wagenen, R. D.	-	SM	-	-	-	-	-	-
Vasse, John J.	-	-	-	-	-	-	F	R
Vaughn, F. L.	-	-	-	-	F	F	-	-
Vedder, Earl C.	F	-	-	-	-	-	-	-
Vogel, Cynthia V.	-	-	-	-	-	-	-	AS
von Engeln, O. D.	-	-	-	-	SOC	-	-	-
von Engeln, Mrs. O. D.	-	SL	-	SL	-	-	-	-
Voss, Miss Ruth	-	-	-	-	SL	-	-	-
Wafler, Harold	-	-	-	-	F	-	-	-
Wagner, E. C.	-	-	-	-	F	F	F	-
Wagner, Lynn M.	-	-	-	-	F	-	-	-

NAME	1920	'25	'30	'36	'50	'60	'75	'89
Wakeman, Seth	SM	SM	-	-	-	-	-	-
Waldo, Lucius A.	-	F	F	F	-	-	-	-
Walford, Richard O.	-	-	-	-	SM	F	-	-
Walker, Joanne M.	-	-	-	-	-	-	AS	-
Wallace, C. Stewart	-	-	-	-	F	F	-	-
Wallace, Mrs. C. Stewart	-	-	-	-	-	-	HS	-
Wallace, C. Stewart, Jr. (Skip)	-	-	-	-	-	F	-	-
Wallace, David C.	-	-	-	-	-	-	-	F
Wallace, Harold	-	-	-	-	-	F	F	NR
Wallace, Maury	-	-	-	-	-	F	F	-
Wallace, Neil	-	-	-	-	-	-	-	AS
Walsh, James E.	-	-	-	-	F	F	-	-
Walter, George S.	SM	SM	F	F	-	-	-	-
Waltz, Orman H.	F	F	-	-	-	-	-	-
Ward, A. A.	-	-	SM	-	-	-	-	-
Ware, Raymond	F	F	F	-	-	-	-	-
Waring, Gordon E.	-	-	-	-	-	SOC	-	-
Warner, John	-	-	-	-	F	-	-	-
Warren, Calvin R.	-	-	-	-	-	-	AS	-
Warren, Charles V.	-	-	-	-	-	-	AS	-
Warren, E. W.	-	-	-	-	SOC	-	-	-
Warren, J. F.	-	F	SM	-	-	-	-	-
Warren, James H.	-	-	-	-	-	-	AS	F
Warren, Mrs. Maud R.	SL	-	-	-	-	-	-	-
Warren, Victor C.	-	-	-	-	-	F	HS	F
Wasilchak, Myron	-	-	-	-	-	F	F	R
Waterfield, Mrs. Adelaide L.	-	-	-	-	-	SOC	-	-
Waters, Martin J.	-	-	-	-	-	-	-	NR
Waters, William J.	-	-	SM	SM	-	-	HS	HS
Watson, Ellen	-	-	-	-	SOC	-	-	-
Watt, E. R.	-	-	-	-	SM	-	-	-
Watt, Mildred	-	SL	-	-	-	-	-	-
Weatherby, David C.	-	-	-	-	-	SOC	F	-
Weatherby, E. M.	-	-	-	-	-	F	HS	-
Weatherby, Norma J.	-	-	-	-	-	-	-	HS
Weaver, John	-	-	-	JR	-	-	-	-
Weaver, Paul J.	-	-	F	F	-	-	-	-
Webster, C. H.	-	SM	-	-	-	-	-	-
Webster, Edwin R.	-	-	JR	-	-	-	-	-
Webster, Robert L.	-	-	SM	-	-	-	-	-
Weeks, G. M.	-	-	F	-	-	-	-	-
Weeks, Mrs. G. M. (Ann)	-	-	-	SL	-	-	-	-
Weeman, Frederick G.	-	-	-	-	-	-	-	F
Wegner, F. R.	-	-	SM	-	-	-	-	-
Weinhold, Julius F.	-	-	-	-	-	SOC	-	-
Weinsheimer, Oliver	-	-	-	-	-	-	HS	-
Weld, H. P.	F	F	F	-	-	-	-	-
Wells, A. J.	-	-	-	-	F	-	-	-
Wells, Aaron	-	F	-	-	-	-	-	-
Wells, Gerald E.	-	-	-	-	-	-	HS	-
Wells, Mrs. Emily R.	-	-	-	-	-	SOC	-	-
Wertheimer, Albert	-	-	-	-	-	F	-	-
Westermann, U. L.	F	-	-	-	-	-	-	-
Westinghouse, Henry H.	F	F	-	-	-	-	-	-
Whalen, James J.	-	-	-	-	-	-	HS	HS
Wheater, Arthur S.	-	-	-	-	-	-	F	R
Wheeler, Daisy	-	-	JR	-	-	-	-	-
Wheeler, J. K.	-	F	F	-	-	-	-	-
Wheeler, Levi J.	-	SM	SM	-	-	-	-	-
Wheeler, Mrs. D.	-	-	SL	-	-	-	-	-
Wheeler, W. D.	-	SM	SM	NR	NR	-	-	-
Whitaker, Clair L.	-	-	-	-	-	-	F	-
Whitaker, Mrs. Clair L.	-	-	-	-	-	-	-	HS

NAME	1920	'25	'30	'36	'50	'60	'75	'89
Whitcomb, Mrs. A. G.	-	-	SL	SOC	-	-	-	-
White, C. H.	-	-	SM	-	-	-	-	-
White, Joan A.	-	-	-	-	-	-	F	-
White, Marc A.	-	-	-	-	-	-	F	F
White, Miss Francis C.	SL	-	-	-	-	-	-	-
White, Miss Georgia L.	SL	SL	-	-	-	-	-	-
White, Mrs. Andrew D.	SL	-	-	-	-	-	-	-
White, Philip M.	-	-	-	-	-	-	HS	-
White, Wester A.	-	-	-	-	-	SM	-	-
Whitehead, Harry	-	-	-	-	NR	-	-	-
Whiteside, Horace E.	-	F	F	F	SM	-	-	-
Whiting, Miss Nancy	-	-	-	-	-	SL	-	-
Wickens, Miss Betty	-	-	-	-	JR	-	-	-
Wickens, Robert	-	-	-	-	F	-	-	-
Widman, K. Peter	-	-	-	-	-	-	-	F
Wiggans, R. G.	-	-	-	SM	-	-	-	-
Wightman, H. B.	-	-	-	-	F	F	S	-
Wilcox, M. E.	-	-	-	-	F	-	-	-
Wilcox, Mrs. Maurice E.	-	-	-	-	-	-	HS	-
Wilcox, William R.	-	-	-	F	-	SOC	-	-
Wilcox, William R., Jr.	-	-	-	-	-	-	F	F
Wilcynski, Paul	-	-	-	-	-	-	F	-
Wilkerson, Miss M. D.	-	-	SL	-	-	-	-	-
Willcox, Walter F.	F	SM	F	L	-	-	-	-
Williams, C. W.	F	F	-	-	-	-	-	-
Williams, Emmons L.	F	-	-	-	-	-	-	-
Williams, Mrs. E. L. (Grace)	-	SL	SL	-	-	-	-	-
Williams, G. C.	-	-	F	F	F	-	-	-
Williams, Gordon	-	-	-	-	JR	-	-	-
Williams, Howard L.	-	-	-	-	F	F	R	-
Williams, Lawrence K.	-	-	-	-	-	-	HS	HS
Williams, Miss Deborah	-	-	-	-	JR	-	-	-
Williams, Miss L.	-	SL	-	-	-	-	-	-
Williams, Miss M. C.	-	SL	-	-	-	-	-	-
Williams, Roger B.	F	SM	SM	-	-	-	-	-
Williamson, Robert	-	-	-	-	-	SM	HS	F
Willis, Miss Marjorie	SL	-	-	-	-	-	-	-
Wilson, B. D.	-	SM	-	-	-	-	-	-
Wilson, C. R.	-	-	-	-	F	-	-	-
Wilson, E. B.	-	-	-	-	F	-	-	-
Wilson, Wilford M.	F	SM	SM	-	-	-	-	-
Wiltberger, John F.	-	-	-	-	-	SOC	-	-
Winans, James A.	SM	-	-	-	-	-	-	-
Winter, Stephen	-	-	-	-	-	-	-	C
Winterroth, T. J.	-	-	-	NR	-	-	-	-
Wittling, George	-	-	-	-	-	-	F	F
Wood, Judith R.	-	-	-	-	-	-	-	AS
Wood, Merritt L.	SM	-	-	-	-	-	-	-
Wood, Miss Mary C.	SL	-	-	-	-	-	-	-
Wood, Percy O.	-	F	F	L	-	-	-	-
Wood, R. D.	-	-	SM	-	-	-	-	-
Woodrow, Constance B.	-	-	-	-	-	-	-	S
Woodward, Julian L.	SM	-	-	-	-	-	-	-
Wooster, Mrs. John B.	-	-	-	-	-	-	-	HS
Wooster, R. O.	-	-	-	-	F	-	-	-
Wray, A. B.	-	-	F	SM	-	-	-	-
Wray, Hanna	-	-	JR	-	-	-	-	-
Wray, Mrs. Hazel F.	-	-	-	-	SL	-	-	-
Wray, W. D.	-	-	JR	-	-	-	-	-
Wright, John D.	-	-	-	-	-	-	F	-
Wright, Theodore P.	-	-	-	-	F	-	-	-
Wuori, Leo A.	-	-	-	-	-	-	F	-
Wyckoff, Clare C.	-	-	-	-	NR	F	-	-

NAME	1920	'25	'30	'36	'50	'60	'75	'89
Wyckoff, Mrs. C. C.	-	-	-	-	NR	-	-	-
Wyckoff, Clarence F.	F	F	F	-	-	-	-	-
Wyckoff, Mrs. Edward G.	SL	SL	-	-	-	-	-	-
Wyckoff, W. O.	-	-	SM	-	-	-	-	-
Wyllie, Robert O.	-	-	-	-	-	F	F	-
Yager, Donald W.	-	-	-	-	NR	-	-	-
Yarussi, Eugene	-	-	-	-	-	-	AS	F
Yengo, Carl J.	-	-	-	-	-	F	F	-
York, W. H.	-	-	SM	SM	-	-	-	-
Young, Allyn A.	F	-	-	-	-	-	-	-
Young, Benjamin P.	-	SM	SM	SM	SM	-	-	-
Young, Charles V. P.	F	F	-	F	-	-	-	-
Young, J. P.	-	F	F	F	-	-	-	-
Young, Miss Gertrude P.	SL	-	-	-	-	-	-	-
Young, Mrs. Dorothy P.	-	-	-	-	SL	-	-	-
Young, William F.	-	-	-	-	-	SM	-	-
Young, William J.	-	-	-	-	-	F	-	-
Younger, Irving	-	-	-	-	-	-	F	-
Zader, Paul	-	-	-	-	F	-	-	-
Zeissig, Edith	-	-	-	-	-	-	HS	-
Zikakis, William	-	-	-	-	-	-	F	HS
Zimmer, Edward A.	-	-	-	-	-	CL	-	-

APPENDIX E-1

Number of Members

YEAR	F	SM	SL	NR	Total
1900	52	30	15		97
1902	65	26	19		110
1903	62	24	13		99
1904	64	25	14		103
1905	58	18	16		92
1906	58	14	15		87
1907	65	17	19		101
1908	69	16	17		102
1909	69	21	22		112
1910	78	21	18		117
1911	89	20	18		127
1912	126	23	18		167
1913	127	34	25		186
1914	132	43	28		203
1915	119	40	24		183
1916	107	45	28		180
1917	101	31	25		157
1918	87	29	19		135
1919	102	32	37	1	172

YEAR	F	SM	SL	NR	JR	AS	TN	SOC	LV	Total
1920	132	42	48	1						223
1921	130	48	47	3						238
1922	142	50	44	11						257
1923	145	89	50	12						296
1924	154	56	50	10						270
1925	131	52	53	19	19					274
1926	158	68	58	26	20	32				362
1927	167	55	39	22	29	37				349
1928	177	57	37	23	30	36				360
1929	168	72	44	30	26	40				380
1930	163	83	50	21	31	40				388
1931	166	92	37	20	45	52				412
1932	156	81	29	17	31	37		5		356
1933	117	49	30	17	22			5		240
1934	104	43	24	13	20			4		208
1935	113	44	24	14	24			6	29	229
1936	117	47	26	18	20		4	6	29	238
1937	121	52	25	20	21		3	5	17	247
1938	111	46	27	22	19		5	7	15	238
1939	128	47	24	16	22		6		8	243

F = Family   SM = Single Man   SL = Single Lady   NR = Nonresident
JR = Junior   AS = Associate   TN = Tennis   SOC = Social   LV = Leave

APPENDIX E-2

YEAR	F	SM	SL	NR	JR	SRV	SOC	LV	Total
1940	126	60	27	22	21		6	21	262
1941	139	50	27	21	27		4	28	264
1942	109	39	18	11	20		9	40	206
1943	93	37	21	7	15	12	25	48	210
1944	103	45	27	15	14	31	31	39	266
1945	114	38	21	15	19	25	48	41	280
1946	160	49	22	17	18	2	46	11	314
1947	183	46	25	23	22		49	14	348
1948	199	64	24	23	26		50	4	386
1949	203	60	28	22	25		46	7	384
1950	211	63	35	27	35		44	13	415
1951	169	68	35	21	32		38	32	395
1952	152	69	27	26	33		37	37	344
1953	158	70	25	19	41		26	12	339
1954	143	68	28	13	50		24	12	326
1955	129	58	24	12	53		19	2	295
1956	99	54	22	8	31		21	8	235
1957	91	42	20	8	22		21	4	204

YEAR	F	SM	SL	AS	CL	JR	SOC	SRV	LV	Total	EFM
1958	153	8	12	8	3	4	61		5	249	208.3
1959	165	8	12	8	3	4	95			295	220.4
1960	177	25		9	2	6	136		1	355	287.3
1961	193	27		8	5	16	120	1	12	369	289.4
1962	197	31		5	5	12	120	1	6	370	293.3

YEAR	SR	JR	CL	SRV	LV	Total	EFM
1963	318	3	5	1	9	326	311.1
1964	300	3	5		7	308	293.5
1965	308	2	4		4	314	300.7
1966	306	1	4		3	311	298.6
1967	293	0	7			300	286.3
1968	279	0	6			285	272.4
1969	285	0	5			290	278.0

F = Family
NR = Nonresident
SOC = Social
SRV = Service Leave

SM = Single Man
SR = Senior
CL = Clergy
LV = Leave

SL = Single Lady
JR = Junior
AS = Associate
EFM = Equivalent Full Membership

APPENDIX E-3

YEAR	F	R	S	AS	JR	CL	HS				Total	EFM
1970	235		32	14	0	5	36				322	280.6
1971	227		34	14	0	8	51				334	279.7
1972	231		36	15	0	8	60				350	288.9
1973	237	11	31	23	2	8	70				382	308.0
1974	224	13	29	26	3	8	89				392	303.8
1975	225	16	26	35	3	8	100				413	314.8
1976	231	17	26	33	1	11	109				428	323.3
1977	208	23	23	29	1	12	116				412	301.9

YEAR	F	R	S	AS	JR	CL	HS	REC	NR	LV	Total	EFM
1978	182	26	20	19	1	12	122	6			388	281.2
1979	189	24	22	21	0	13	127	21	6		423	305.7
1980	170	24	22	18	0	8	101	24	11		384	276.0
1981	171	23	32	24	0	8	109	32	15		414	291.5
1982	152	24	33	18	0	7	102	25	10	2	371	262.2
1983	120	28	26	11	0	6	87	19	8		305	213.4

YEAR	F	B	C	D	JR	CL	HS	REC	NR	HN*	Total	EFM
1984	110	61	1	0	0	6	75	17	8	6	278	193.8
1985	95	82	2	0	0	4	74	17	7	5	284	193.6
1986	96	87	3	0	0	4	77	17	7	5	291	199.9
1987	102	101	4	0	0	5	84	20	9	5	325	221.5
1988	96	111	2	1	0	4	77	17	13	6	321	220.0
1989	109	122	2	1	0	4	77	17	11	5	343	240.5

*Complete information on honorary
memberships before 1984 is not available.

F = Family	R = Retired	S = Single
AS = Associate	HS = House	NR = Nonresident
CL = Clergy	JR = Junior	B = (AS + S + R)
C = Under 30	D = Under 25	REC = Recreation
HN = Honorary	LV = Leave	EFM = Equivalent
		Full Membership

APPENDIX F
LAND TRANSACTIONS

LAND PURCHASES BY CCI

From	Liber	Page	Date	Refs.
John H. and Clara W. Tanner	155	377	1/01/02	L156, p.350
Cornell Heights Land Co.	171	337	8/01/10	
Arthur W. Kline, et al.	186	276	6/05/16	
William McKinney (Exec'x Maggie Heggie)	187	117	9/30/16	L166, p.223
Jared T. Newman	205	49	6/12/23	
Cornell University	196	544	8/30/24	
Matsujiro and Kame Asai	226	71	6/06/31	
Stella Hanford	226	73	6/06/31	94.393 acres
Frank L. and Florence Tyler	251	42	8/29/39	
Samuel L. Boothroyd	303	119	10/01/47	2.34 acres
Cornell University	402	130	11/27/57	2 acres
Samuel L. Boothroyd	402	407	12/13/57	
Ethel and Robert Krisek	459	45	9/16/65	3 small plots on Hanshaw Rd.
Earl F. Sharp	479	923	2/07/69	Recording 1957 purchase. Map Book F7, p. 27

LAND SALES BY CCI

To	Liber	Page	Date	Refs.
Cornell Heights Land Co.	159	113	1/26/03	
Ernest G. Merritt	187	21	6/01/16	
Village of Cayuga Heights	190	274	3/25/18	
Ernest G. Merritt	190	498	10/08/18	
Franklin C. Cornell, Jr.	209	169	12/16/24	
Earl A. Flansburgh	209	176	12/17/24	
Acacia Fraternity	209	178	12/18/24	
Albert H. White and Charles McCormack (trustees, Eleusis Fraternity, Inc.)	209	308	12/19/25	L209, p.18
J. Lakin Baldridge	211	9	7/19/26	
Paul M. Lincoln	211	15	7/26/26	
Stanley W. Warren	237	432	8/21/35	40 acres
Robert and Ethel Krisek	252	41	9/19/39	
(Cornell University)	396	409	5/06/57	(Agreement re sale to C. U. of 63.7 acres)
Cornell University	402	490	12/20/57	63.7 acres
Frank J. Gilmore, Jr.	465	766	10/11/66	Asai house
(Offer Asai house to Cornell University)	466	84	11/01/66	For first refusal
(NYSEG)	483	873	9/18/69	Easement for erecting a pole
(Merle E. Patterson)	567	1088	11/02/78	Amendment and modification of restrictions on rear lot

APPENDIX G

Presidents of the
Country Club of Ithaca

1900–1905	Wilder D. Bancroft
1906–1912	William A. Hammond
1913–1920	Charles E. Treman, Sr.
1921–1924	Frank L. Morse
1925–1926	Charles E. Treman, Sr.
1927–1928	Tracy Stagg
1929–1930	Wilder D. Bancroft
1931–1932	Minor McDaniels
1933–1934	Cedric H. Guise
1935–1936	David B. Robb
1937–1938	Horace E. Whiteside
1939–1940	Ralph Mungle
1941	Lewis Knudson
1942	Lewis Knudson; Carl Snavely
1943–1944	Carl Snavely
1945	Robert A. Hutchinson
1946–1947	Robert L. Causer
1948	T. Fred Rowe
1949–1950	Robert A. Hutchinson
1951	Malcolm O. Mattice; Charles F. Fagin; David E. Cynoske
1952–1953	M. E. Campbell
1954	Harold E. Reed
1955	Alfred Blomquist; Charles Benjamin
1956–1960	W. Robert Farnsworth
1961–1962	Clifford E. Brew
1963–1964	Karl L. Phillips
1965	George D. Fry
1966–1968	W. Robert Farnsworth
1969–1972	James J. Clynes, Jr.
1973–1975	Wallace B. Rogers
1976–1977	Charles W. Bell
1978	Melvin L. Passman
1979	W. Scott McRobb
1980–1982	Eben D. Tisdale
1983	Eben D. Tisdale; Charles W. Bell
1984–1986	Reeder D. Gates
1987–1989	Francis E. Benedict

APPENDIX H

GOLF CHAMPIONS

Men

Year	Champion	Runner-up
1921	Ralph Jones	Clarence Elmer
1922	John Quine	Cedric H. Guise
1923	John Quine	Ralph Jones
1924	Ralph Jones	George Bancroft
1925	Clarence Elmer	Robert Hutchinson
1926	Charles Treman, Jr.	Robert Hutchinson
1927	Charles Treman, Jr.	Robert Hutchinson
1928	A. K. Hammond	Robert Hutchinson
1929	A. K. Hammond	Charles Treman, Jr.
1930	Robert Causer	George Howley
1931	Norman Stagg	Robert Causer
1932	Robert Hutchinson	Richard Chase
1933	Robert Hutchinson	Charles Treman, Jr.
1934	Robert Hutchinson	David Durham
1935	Robert Hutchinson	John Carver
1936	Martin Speno	John Carver
1937	Martin Speno	William Carver
1938	Charles Treman, Jr.	Martin Speno
1939	Charles Treman, Jr.	John Carver
1940	Martin Speno	Robert Hutchinson
1941	Robert Hutchinson	Charles Treman, Jr.
1942	Louis Barnard	Bernard Clarey
1943	Louis Barnard	Robert Causer
1944	Carl Snavely	Bernard Clarey
1945	Louis Barnard	Robert Causer
1946	Barney Pelotte	Robert Hutchinson
1947	Louis Barnard	John Carver
1948	James Clark	Adam Bucci
1949	Louis Barnard	Robert Hutchinson
1950	Louis Barnard	Fargo Balliett
1951	John Carver	W. Richard Neish
1952	Louis Barnard	Ross H. Smith

Year	Champion	Runner-up
1953	Louis Barnard	John Carver
1954	Louis Barnard	John Carver
1955	John Carver	Fargo Balliett
1956	Skip Wallace	Louis Barnard
1957	Skip Wallace	Louis Barnard
1958	William Raleigh	Warner Berry
1959	Skip Wallace	W. Richard Neish
1960	Skip Wallace	Herbert Broadwell
1961	Warner (Butch) Berry	Skip Wallace
1962	Skip Wallace	Gordon Light
1963	Skip Wallace	Robert Dean
1964	Louis Barnard	Robert Dean
1965	Herbert Broadwell	Louis Barnard
1966	Richard Shulman	Robert Dean
1967	Greg Abbott	Donald Turcotte
1968	Neil Wallace	Paul Wilcynski
1969	Steve Torrant	Herbert Broadwell
1970	Steve Torrant	Robert Mazza
1971	W. Richard Neish	Louis Barnard
1972	Paul Leurgans	Anthony Treadwell
1973	Paul Leurgans	Francis Benedict
1974	W. Richard Neish	Robert Caryl
1975	Richard Shulman	John Schindo
1976	Tony Treadwell	David Soanes
1977	Chad Jacobson	Charles Bell
1978	Francis Benedict	Robert Caryl
1979	Chad Jacobson	Randall Knight
1980	Robert Caryl	W. Richard Neish
1981	Edward Mazza	Joseph Bugliari
1982	Edward Mazza	Bernard (Bud) Addis
1983	Edward Mazza	Ted Coviello
1984	Dom Cafferillo	Tony Treadwell
1985	Tony Treadwell	Dom Cafferillo
1986	Tony Treadwell	Dom Cafferillo
1987	Tony Treadwell	Robert Caryl
1988	Tony Treadwell	Dom Cafferillo
1989	Robert Caryl	Edward Mazza

Women

Year(s)	Champion
1928–30	Ann Weeks
1931	Beulah Robb
1932	Alice Baldridge
1933–34	Beulah Robb
1935	Doris Van Natta
1936	Beulah Robb
1937–38	Doris Van Natta
1939	Betty Robb
1940–43	Doris Van Natta
1944	Betty Robb
1945–46	Doris Van Natta
1947	Jeanette Brown
1948–49	Flo Rowe

Year	Champion
1950	Jean Langdon
1951	Lois Murray
1952	Flo Rowe
1953	Lois Murray
1954	Marion May
1955	Jean Langdon
1956	Flo Rowe
1957	Dorothy McKeegan
1958	Isabelle Speno

Year	Champion	Runner-up
1959	Flo Rowe	Millie Rocker
1960	Isabelle Speno	Jean Langdom
1961	Isabelle Speno	Ting Thomas
1962	Millie Rocker	Jeanne Grover
1963	Jeanne Grover	Dorothy Hemming
1964	Jeanne Grover	Jean Langdon
1965	Ting Thomas	Jeanne Grover
1966	Lorraine Mazza	Dorothy Hemming
1967	Jeanne Grover	Lorraine Mazza
1968	Isabelle Speno	Dorothy Hemming
1969	Doris Wright	Helen Seamon
1970	Doris Wright	Blanche Neish
1971	Doris Wright	Martha Hanshaw
1972	Doris Wright	Louise Heimlich

1973	Isabelle Speno	Lise Addis
1974	Doris Kostrinsky	Kathy Tobin
1975	Doris Kostrinsky	Dawn Treadwell
1976	Sharyn Heliseva	—
1977	Barbara Durland	Pat Mead
1978	Doris Kostrinsky	Sharyn Heliseva
1979	Nancy Salter	Lise Addis
1980	Sandy Speno	Lise Addis
1981	Lise Addis	Barbara Durland
1982	Bev Wyatt	Karen Hartman
1983	Bev Wyatt	Ann Niefer
1984	Lise Addis	Karen Hartman
1985	Lise Addis	Judy Dunning
1986	Judy Dunning	Lise Addis
1987	Barbara Collyer	Lise Addis
1988	Lise Addis	Judy Dunning
1989	Doris Kostrinsky	Barbara Collyer

Juniors

Year(s)	Champion
1959	Scott Poucher
1960	Bill Mai
1961	James Buyoucos
1962	Neil Wallace
1963–64	Bill Farnsworth
1965	Al Smith
1966	Rob Mazza
1967	Steve Torrant
1968–69	J. Bebbington III
1970	Wes Hoppenrath
1971–72	John Clifford
1973–76	Chad Jacobson
1977	Steve Turcotte
1979–81	John Hulbert
1982	Michael Longo
1983	Dan Hartman
1984	Nick Cafferillo
1985	Greg Shulman
1986–89	Mark Pribanic

APPENDIX I
Country Club Employees
1989

Mark H. Davies	General Manager
Elizabeth B. Ford Linda S. Beebe	Office
Todd Slauson Russ Johnson	Bartenders
Sue Battaglini Don Downing	Restaurant
Pat Gillespie Noah Leavitt JoAnne Miller Cathy Mosely Kris Musser Phyllis Parish Frankie Van Ostrand	Wait Staff
Shawn E. Monroe Eric S. Seliga Randy M. Trask John Weber Anna L. Welser	Kitchen Staff
Calvin L. Whirley	House Maintenance
John C. Belcher, Sr.	Locker Room
Gordon B. Richardson	Golf Professional
C. J. Parry	Assistant Pro
Don Haringa Grant Richardson	Pro's Shop
Peter M. Wittko	Greens Superintendent
Dale E. Slocum Galen L. Truesdail	Greens crew

APPENDIX J

Reciprocal Clubs—1989

Binghamton CC	Binghamton, N.Y.
Brook Lea CC	Rochester, N.Y.
Clifton Springs CC	Clifton Springs, N.Y.
Corning CC	Corning, N.Y.
Cortland CC	Cortland, N.Y.
Elgin Golf Club	Elgin, Scotland
Elmira CC	Elmira, N.Y.
Irondequoit CC	Pittsford, N.Y.
Lakeshore Yacht & Country Club	Clay, N.Y.
Owasco CC	Auburn, N.Y.
Ridgemont CC	Rochester, N.Y.
Seneca Falls CC	Seneca Falls, N.Y.
Shepard Hills CC	Waverly, N.Y.
Yahnundasis GC	New Hartford, N.Y.

BIBLIOGRAPHY

Bishop, Morris. *A History of Cornell.* Ithaca, N.Y.: Cornell University Press, 1962.

Directory of Living Alumni, Cornell University. Ithaca, N.Y.: Cornell University, 1967.

Fussell, Paul. *Class.* New York: Ballantine Books, 1983.

Gibson, Nevin H. *Encyclopedia of Golf,* pp. 14-15. New York: A.S. Barnes & Co., 1958.

Gibson, Nevin H. *Pictorial History of Golf.* South Brunswick, N. J.: A. S. Barnes & Co., 1968.

Hannigan, Frank. "Golf's Forgotten Genius," *The Golf Journal,* May 1974, pp. 14-28.

Hewett, W(aterman) T(homas). *Cornell University - A History,* vol. 3, p.383. New York: The University Publishing Society, New York, 1905.

Manning's Ithaca City Directory (title varies). Schenectady, N.Y.: H.A. Manning & Co., 1899-

The Register, Cornell University. Ithaca, N.Y.: Cornell University, 1899-1900.

Sisler, Carol U. *Enterprising Families.* Ithaca, N.Y.: Enterprise Publishing, 1986.

Sisler, Carol U., Margaret Hobbie and Jane Marsh Dieckmann, eds. *Ithaca's Neighborhoods.* Ithaca, N. Y.: DeWitt Historical Society of Tompkins County, 1988.

U.S. Bureau of the Census. *Statistical Abstract of the United States,* 109th ed., Table 387. U.S. Government Printing Office, Washington, D.C., 1989.

Wind, Herbert Warren. *The Story of American Golf,* 3rd ed. New York: Knopf, 1975.

Ithaca Journal (various titles), Ithaca, N. Y.

Mar 2, 1900	-	Organization of Country Club
May 7, 1900	-	Ad for golf goods, p.6
Jun 1, 1900	-	Course opening
Nov 16, 1901	-	Sale of land
Mar 28, 1903	-	Moving clubhouse
Feb 24, 1906	-	Election of officers
May 4, 1907	-	Huffcut suicide
Feb 23, 1912	-	Elections, club improvements
Feb 22, 1913	-	Elections
Feb 19, 1915	-	Women's golf fashions, p.5
Feb 25, 1916	-	Elections, clubhouse, renovations, p.7
May 10, 1920	-	New course opening
May 4, 1923	-	CCI opening tournament, p.8
Jun 23, 1923	-	Christopher Conner, hole-in-one, p.8
Jul 30, 1923	-	Finger Lakes Tournament, CCI yardages
Aug 11,13, 1923	-	Sarazen exhibition, yardages, p.6, p.8
Jun 23, 1925	-	Clarence Elmer's course record, p.11
May 15, 1926	-	Club to add nine new holes, p.5.
Jul 2, 1926	-	Ad for golf rainwear, p.13
Jan 13, 1930	-	Clubhouse fire
Apr 10, 1931	-	Walter Bells' death
Jul 20,26, 1933	-	Sarazen-Kirkwood exhibition
Aug 19, 1935	-	Parks-Newlove exhibition
Dec 10, 1936	-	L. M. Dennis' obituary
Jun 2,10, 20, 1939	-	Wood-Kirkwood exhibition
Aug 12,14, 1940	-	Sarazen-Oliver exhibition, p.9, p.8
Aug 13,16,19, 1940	-	NYS Left Handers Tournament
Jun 2, 1942	-	Snavely replaces Knudson as pres., p.3.
May 25, 1943	-	Exhibit of Chandler's drawings, p.3
May 26, 1943	-	Injured caddy, Clarence Newhart, p.3
Oct 2, 1945	-	Chandler retirement, p.3
Aug 29, 1946	-	Kirkwood exhibition, p.17
Jun 15, 17, 1949	-	Chandler died
Jun 30, 1949	-	Middlecoff exhibition
Aug 15,26, 1949	-	Chandler League, p.11 both issues
Jul 28, 1950	-	Sarazen exhibition, p.11
Jul 14, 1956	-	Albert Collins interview, p.9
Jun 24, 1966	-	Dick Shulman course record
Sep 5, 1983	-	Ed Mazza course record, p.14

PICTURE CREDITS

Abbreviations:

BWB	Betty Wyckoff Balderston
CA	Department of Manuscripts and Archives, Cornell University.
CCM	Country Club minutes
CCS	Country Club scrapbook
CET	Charles E. Treman, Jr.
CUChem	Chemistry Department, Cornell University.
CUMMN	Department of Maps, Microtexts and Newspapers, Cornell University
DHS	DeWitt Historical Society of Tompkins County
GBR	Gordon B. Richardson
JCS	Julian C. Smith
JL	John Listar
JNR	James N. Rothschild
MHD	Mark H. Davies
PB	Patrick Bucci
PM	Paul McGraw
RTJ	Robert Trent Jones, Inc.
SM	Sterling Mac Adam
TCDA	Tompkins County Division of Assessment
TCTC	Tompkins County Trust Company
USGA	United States Golf Association Museum
WAW	Wester A. White
WRF	W. Robert Farnsworth

Chapter 1. 1-1(a), 1-1(b), CUChem. 1-1(c), 1-1(d), 1-3, 1-7, 1-8, CA. 1-1(e), 1-6, DHS. 1-1(f), BWB. 1-4, CUMMN. 1-5, JCS.

Chapter 2. 2-1, 2-9, JCS. 2-2, 2-3, 2-7, DHS. 2-4, 2-5, 2-6, 2-8, 2-11, CA.

Chapter 3. 3-1, JCS. 3-2, USGA. 3-3, PB. 3-4, CET. 3-5, CUMMN.

Chapter 4. 4-1, 4-5, JCS. 4-2, 4-3, 4-9, 4-11, PB. 4-4, 4-6, CA. 4-7, TCDA. 4-8, RTJ. 4-9, JNR.

Chapter 5. 5-1, JCS. 5-2, 5-3, 5-5, 5-6, 5-8, 5-9, PB. 5-4, TCTC. 5-7, WAW.

Chapter 6. 6-1, JL. 6-2, CCM. 6-3, 6-4, 6-8, 6-9, 6-10, PB. 6-5, 6-6, 6-7, 6-11, JCS.

Chapter 7. 7-1, WRF. 7-2, 7-3, 7-5, 7-10, WAW. 7-4, 7-6, 7-7, 7-8, PB.

Chapter 8. 8-1, 8-2, 8-6, 8-7, 8-8, 8-9, PB. 8-3, PM. 8-5, JCS.

Chapter 9. 9-1, 9-2, 9-6, 9-7, 9-10, 9-12, JCS. 9-3, 9-4, CCS. 9-5, MHD. 9-8, SM. 9-9, TCDA. 9-11, GBR.

INDEX

Page numbers in italics indicate illustrations;
an *n* following a page number indicates a footnote.